Inside Counselling

Inside Counselling

*Becoming and Being a
Professional Counsellor*

Anthony Crouch

SAGE Publications
London • Thousand Oaks • New Delhi

SAGE Publications Ltd
6 Bonhill Street
London EC2A 4PU

SAGE Publications Inc.
2455 Teller Road
Thousand Oaks, California 91320

SAGE Publications India Pvt Ltd
32, M-Block Market
Greater Kailash – I
New Delhi 110 048

British Library Cataloguing in Publication data

A catalogue record for this book is available from the British Library.

ISBN 0 8039 7528 7
ISBN 0 8039 7529 5 (pbk)

Library of Congress catalog record available

Typeset by Mayhew Typesetting, Rhayader, Powys
Printed in Great Britain by Biddles Ltd, Guildford, Surrey

I'd like to dedicate this book to my clients, my students, my supervisees, my psychotherapist Nigel, my consultant David and my counselling supervisors Robert and Peter. I'd also like to dedicate it to Margaret, Barry and Guna for their love and support and Gita, Jacinta and Miro – because I know they'll love to see their names in print. I also need to thank the Counselling and Psychotherapy Central Awarding Body (CPCAB) and Counselling South West for their support throughout the extended writing process, together with Sandera for struggling with my handwriting and typing the book.

Contents

Important Notes

This book has been written as a complete fiction. There are numerous descriptions of clients, counsellors and students but they are all made up – the product of my imagination. The only crumbs of truth in the book come from my life, and even these have been substantially reworked – being used as springboards to help me enter into certain feelings or perspectives and not as real-life examples. My hope, however, is that you, the reader, will become emotionally involved in the subjective lives of these fictional people and that the various characters, and their perspectives on the world, will thus feel very real.

Through that emotional involvement the book may help to unveil aspects of the sometimes bewildering therapeutic process. It aims to help the developing student and practitioner understand a little more of the complexity of counselling relationships and the ways in which clients *can* move forward. In my view, it isn't enough for the professional counsellor to simply know the theory and be able to intellectually identify the client's problem or pattern. The practitioner only begins to work effectively when she is able to work intimately with the client's subjectivity in a catalytic process of facilitating therapeutic change, growth and development.

The book also includes personal development exercises that can help you to open the door to intense feelings that you may have forgotten – the exercises can therefore be experienced as very personally challenging. Always make sure that you have plenty of time to recover emotionally from an exercise – for example by exploring your experience in your counselling journal. The book, and the exercises, are written for practising and trainee counsellors – it is not recommended that you follow any of the exercises without the normal support systems in place (training group, supervision and personal counselling).

Preface

'Pay no attention to that man behind the curtain.' (The Wizard to Dorothy, *The Wizard of Oz*)

This book isn't written in the 'normal' way – it's not a book about the theory of counselling. Instead it's written in a fashion designed to give you a sense of what becoming and being a counsellor is really like – from the inside out. There aren't that many references to theory in the book – not because I don't advocate studying the various theories of counselling, but because there are plenty of counselling theory books and very few 'subjective' books. I'm trying to balance that.

When I began work as a practising counsellor I found that there was a huge difference between a theoretical concept and the actual counselling experience. For a theory to have any real meaning for me I had to make it my own – both personally and in my practice. In the process of making it my own it came alive – it became a part of my art as a counsellor. This, for me, is the true test of a theory – can I make it come alive, can I make it a part of my personal, and then my practitioner 'bones'? Can I use it to paint a richer picture? Does it grow?

I've tried to pitch the book at a certain level of work – most of the writing is about working with fairly explicit psychological problems with people who have a fairly solid sense of self. The book isn't directly aimed at people *starting* a training in counselling, although such readers may find it very interesting. Neither is it mainly about working with really 'deep stuff' (implicit psychological problems) – although I have included quite a few examples of working at this kind of level. Finally it's not concerned with working with clients who have special psychological needs – people who have a fairly fragile sense of self.

Empathy

In a way, I've written the book a bit like a novel – there are various fictional characters describing various fictional experiences. I've tried to imagine a whole series of other people's points of view and write from their perspectives – clients, counsellors, supervisors, students and tutors. I've imagined myself inside their hearts (and heads) and I've imagined various dialogues between these characters. This is mainly what the book consists of – a collage of various fictional people, their feelings, their thoughts and their talk. I don't feel it's right to write about my actual clients or my actual students – somehow that would feel like a betrayal of them and I'm not prepared to do that. What I have tried to do is give you, the reader, a kind of pointer – a glimpse of what the counselling process, in my experience, is really about. And it is only my experience.

This is also, therefore, a rather biased book – it's based upon my particular view of counselling. There are lots of characters in the book, but they've all come out of my imagination – so, in some sense, they all contain something of me. They are also a bit too good at being clients, students, supervisors, or counsellors – they are, for example, a bit condensed, a bit too skilled, a bit too articulate. The main point of writing the book in this way, however, is not to show the world how bad I am at seeing the world from other people's points of view, but rather to enliven and enrich the reader's sense of the counselling process, to sprinkle a little water on all those old dry theories.

Acceptance

There are, however, other flaws in the book. Quite a number of the characters, for example, are preoccupied with relationship and sexual issues. I've chosen to focus on relationship issues because I believe they are the primary source of people's problems and difficulties – we are, in essence, social beings. Sexual issues are chosen because they are the classic taboo area and therefore, for example, the classic area for the development of internal conflicts. I also have a special interest in the nature of intimate relationships – in particular the relationship between love (and hate) and sex, the differing attitudes of men and women to these experiences and how our attitudes to them change and develop as we grow older. Overall, however, this means there's an imbalance in the book – with too much on relationship and sexual issues – and that says more about *my* special interests than it says about the range of problems that clients bring to counselling. On the other hand, the book is not about working with particular presenting issues but rather with the therapeutic process of working with patterns – patterns in self, personal history and interpersonal relating. My interest has been to help the reader gain a little more insight into this process – the presenting issues aren't, therefore, so important.

As I've reworked the book, I've discovered more and more flaws – 'Oh no, I can't write that', 'Oh God, that's terrible.' Looking at it now, I'd like to have written from a greater diversity of counselling styles and interventions. I'd also like to have included much more diversity in the characters – more people from a wider range of ethnic cultures, for example. But then, maybe I was a bit frightened of doing that – am I really that good at seeing things from the perspective of other cultures? In the end I came to accept that if you are ever going to read this book it will have to be warts and all. The book is about my experience and it inevitably reflects the fact that I'm a rather flawed counsellor, and a rather flawed person too.

It's actually been quite a therapeutic experience for me to write this book. I've come to understand and accept a great deal about myself – including some of my more flawed motivations for wanting to write a book in the first place. Right now, for example, after admitting to you that both this book and its author are fundamentally flawed I've been feeling quite . . . good.

'Is this it? Have I finally come to accept that I'm a flawed person *and* that's OK!'

I'm actually feeling *wow* – and I could just get up, step out of the front door and . . . be me. It really feels, deep down, quite liberating.

I know that I've always tried to be the person 'I should be' or 'who other people will like' or the 'good little (now big) boy'. I know all that, and have known it for quite a long time, but right this minute I actually *feel* differently – deep down in my bones. This is who I am: flawed, imperfect, disapproved of (in some people's eyes) and I really do sense, in the far-off corners of myself, OK about that. Well, nearly.

Genuineness

The fact that I've found writing therapeutic mirrors my experience of being a counsellor and a tutor. I've always learnt something about myself, I've always 'moved forward' when working with my clients and my students. Counselling and tutoring has been a developmental process for me. Sometimes I've wondered whether counselling would actually work quite so well if it stopped being a developmental experience for me. Would clients really move forward if I stopped moving? Would students learn and develop so much if I stopped developing with them? Unlike most books on counselling I've written about this process too – about my personal experience as the author. That has felt quite a risky thing to do, a very frightening thing to do – the book may well be disliked, rejected and even vilified by some readers.

Counselling involves intimate personal exploration and exposure. I haven't written about my experience as the author because I'm a really interesting person, but because I believe that at heart counselling, and becoming a counsellor, is a process of exploring and exposing oneself in the presence of another.

When we do expose ourselves in the 'world out there' we are often, however, rejected and even attacked for not being good enough, for being flawed people. Unless we do expose ourselves, however, it isn't possible to 'move forward' – the counselling process can't work. You can't fix a leak in the plumbing without first exposing the pipe. At a deeper level, however, if we never really expose ourselves in the world, if we hide behind our images of ourselves, or hide behind our defences against being rejected and attacked, then we're not really in the world. We're not living in it, we're hiding from it.

This feels really important. Honest and open communication – being genuine.

I only feel fully alive when I'm not hiding from the world, when I'm out here in it – with the important people in my life out here too.

Perhaps you can now understand why accepting that I'm basically flawed feels so liberating – no great need to defend that fact any more, no great need to try and appear not flawed, no great need to hide my warts, my ugliness. No great need to hide. Thank you, oh unknown reader, for whom I have bothered to go on this writing journey. Thank you.

The book is what it is and I am what I am. Some people may find it interesting and useful, others may find it boring. Some people may 'get it', others may not. A few may love it, a few may hate it.

Like me, and Melanie Klein, the book is both 'good' and 'bad' – at the same time.

Truly mixed up!

A first exercise: hiding from you

Try and identify some of the ways in which you hide from other people. Start this exploration by focusing on the following kinds of interpersonal experiences:

- being uncomfortable with someone who is important to you, but hiding that uncomfortable feeling;
- a recent time – with your partner or a close friend – where you kept your feelings to yourself (for example, feelings of disapproval or being disapproved of);
- feeling you 'had to be with' a friend or relative, when you wanted to do something, or be somewhere, else;
- being the person your mother expects you to be;
- being the person your father expects you to be

Now try and examine your process of hiding in more detail – by re-enacting one of the situations you have just explored. The objectives here are firstly to make your implicit hiding processes more explicit (and thus widen your choices) and secondly to experiment with appearing – what gets in the way of your appearing, and what is triggered in you when you do try and appear?

Finally consider:

- What are you afraid of?
- What are your common patterns of hiding?
- What happens to you if you do appear?
- How does (might) the other person respond?

Follow-on questions/tasks

1 Consider the implications of this exploration for your work with your clients.
2 Try to imagine being a 'fly on the wall' with your various clients and observe any patterns of 'hiding and appearing'.
3 Spend a day examining your personal experience of 'hiding and appearing'.
4 Develop the habit, in your client notes, of devoting a section specifically to this.
5 Explore 'hiding and appearing' in relation to gender.

1

Introduction – the Subjective World of Client and Counsellor

At such moments there is a voice inside which speaks and says: 'This is the real me!' (William James, Letter to his wife, 1878)

Something about how counselling 'works'

If this book is not about finding answers then what is it about?

I feel very stuck again with the writing. I want to give up.

I have found it very difficult to try and write such a long work as a book. I was reasonably OK at writing shorter pieces – articles, essays, and so on, but a book is so big. Most of all I have found it difficult to write to a plan. I have been great at coming up with the plans but useless at writing to them. Over the past few months I have been sitting at my writing table and 'squeezing out' the odd few hundred words – in a morning. Useless. And today, once again, I feel completely stuck – so I have decided to give up. There – 'The End.' Fuck it!

I have become quite good at what I do. People, clients, who come to me in a state of crisis or confusion, generally go away 'better'. Yet this does not mean that I can avoid the everyday pains of living or the pains of growing old.

Today I feel quite down and hopeless. Right at this particular moment I don't really believe in what I am doing as a professional – as a counsellor and tutor – and I *don't* want to write this book.

In fact I don't want my working life to be the way it is. I want to be a film director or a travel writer (no, scrub that one – forget about writing). I want to be younger. I want to be a young Anthony at university travelling around Europe in the summer. Most of all I want to be excited by life!

Today I'm not so sure about my personal life either. Are we really right for each other – or do we argue too much? Do we have enough common interests? Does she really love *me* – rather than her image of me or what she would like me to be? Do I really love her for her? Does she really want to be with me, and I her – for the rest of our lives?

I feel I am growing old and life is not quite what I would have wished for. I feel a failure. I do.

There is sometimes an abounding optimism in the field of counselling – that somehow counselling can sort it out. That counselling is *the* answer. Things get tough – send in the counsellors.

It has been good for me – my own counselling – and I believe it has been good for most of my clients. But I'm not a 'sorted out' person with all, or even a few of, 'the answers' to the problems of my life. I still feel down – like today. I still feel stuck, bored, hopeless, frustrated. I still have bad arguments with my partner. I'm still quite capable of being very selfish and insensitive. I'm still 'human'.

What really bugs me about some people is that they expect a counsellor to be 'sorted out' and 'good'. Inherently sensitive, kind, caring, always willing to listen, etc. etc. Sure we are . . . NOT!

I'm nice, and nasty too.

What is good is that I can sit here and write that I don't want to write this book, that I am giving up, that I feel down and hopeless, that I don't have the answers, that my life is still very difficult and that I'm still very unsure about things. What is good is that I am no longer denying my thoughts and feelings and then pretending to be 'the writer', the 'teacher', the person who 'knows'. Today I don't know anything, today I'm quite unsure of everything.

And, at the same time, the fact that I have just written the above, and decided to make it the introduction to the book, now begins to make me feel as though I have achieved something . . .

In fact I almost feel quite hopeful.

Perhaps it is the most difficult thing of all – to be who I am, whatever that is. To live my life in a way in which my subjectivity is not denied. To know myself and be true to myself. This is also one of the key things I am seeking to help my clients to achieve – to accept their personal experience, to be true to themselves.

I have found this to be enormously liberating – to become more and more able to live my life in touch with my personal experience. Today it has been liberating for me to write exactly how I was feeling about writing this book.

And perhaps there is something here about how counselling 'works', or at least an aspect of how it works. I was sitting here trying to 'be an author'. In the same way the client sits there trying to be the person they think they are supposed to be. I was feeling hopeless about the whole enterprise of writing; the client might be feeling that life is hopeless, that the counselling is hopeless. If I, as the counsellor, can help the client to accept and express how he or she is feeling then the client will, in my experience, begin to feel better, become 'unstuck' or whatever. Most of all they begin to accept themselves more.

This is not, however, always easy – especially if the client's feelings concern the counselling process or me, the counsellor. What would it be like for you, as a client, to be free to express your thoughts, feelings, fantasies and desires – including those directed towards the other person sitting there with you? What would it be like to be helped to do so by your counsellor, and for your counsellor to accept your words without rejecting you, or defending him/herself, or counter-attacking, or avoiding your thoughts or feelings, or pretending to be 'tough'? What would it be like to be helped to explore them, whatever they were? What would it be like to be free to be whoever you are during your counselling session, including being free to express your personal experience of this other person – your counsellor?

Client: 'I am feeling quite frightened – of you'
or   'I am in love with you'
or   'I feel very hurt by you'
or   'I feel angry with you'
or   'I feel disappointed by you'
or   'I feel rejected by you'
or   'I feel sexually attracted to you'

And what would it be like for you – as the counsellor – to help the client to express her experience – including her disappointment in the counselling, in you, or her anger, attraction, rejection, hurt, or fear, in relation to you? How would it be for you to hear and feel this from your client? How would you automatically want to react? How might you respond differently – in a way that enabled you both to explore your client's experience? How would you deal with your client's attraction to you – in a way that maintainted the boundaries of the counselling relationship but didn't make the client feel that it was not OK to have these feelings and desires? How would you keep the boundaries and yet maintain the counselling as a space to explore – free to feel and express and work through, but not to act out?

Valuing the subjective

The Western world view all too often subtly excludes personal experience from its picture of what is 'real': 'That's very subjective!' is the kind of statement that is often made – meaning that the subjective is not important, not real, not to be valued. In some situations it may be important to try to put a person's subjective experience to one side and try to see the world in an 'objective way'. This is perhaps particularly true when we realize how easily the subjective can be coloured by the past, or by strong emotions in the present. But this is no reason to deny its reality – that's like throwing the baby out with the bath water.

Because the subjective can be 'distorted' we, in the West, tend to undervalue it – yet it is the essence of our lives because we subjectively experience everything. Even an objective event such as a bump on the head only has meaning because we experience and respond to the pain subjectively. One person experiences and responds to a bump on the head in a certain way – shouting out and hitting the low branch. Another person, however, experiences and responds to it very differently – perhaps saying to herself that next time she will look before she leaps.

We are the subjective

Counselling is all about the subjective – the subjective world of the client and the subjective world of the counsellor. Most of what makes a good counsellor is her ability to empathize with the personal experience of her client, her ability to notice her own personal experience and her ability to work with these two interwoven subjective perspectives. The former we call empathy, the latter self-awareness. Self and other awareness. Awareness of thoughts, desires, feelings, sensations, intuitions – all that makes up the subjective world of direct personal reality.

This all sounds very simple – valuing and focusing on the subjective – but I have worked with many students and one of the most difficult aspects of the training, for so many of them, was just this. This is why I haven't written this book in the normal way. I do talk about this or that theory, this or that technique, but much of the writing isn't like that. The book is mainly written from the subjective point of view – of imagined clients, counsellors and students. Two subjective worlds – experiencing and responding to each other – that is the essence of counselling and I have tried to take you inside that world.

But what you need to do is to explore this for yourself. If I was your tutor I would ask you to write a piece for me, a piece that took me into your subjective world – the world of your experiences and responses to being in your training group, to the course and to being with your clients. In my experience, most students don't find this very easy – it takes practice and is significantly helped by your own personal counselling.

I've been in my own personal counselling for many years now. I always tell my students this in the hope that they will all, over time, come to value and take up their own personal counselling. I don't believe it's right to *require* novice trainees to have counselling because being forced to have counselling isn't the right motivation for such a potentially important and intimate relationship. There's no way, however, that I could have got to where I have without my own personal counselling. It has been really important to me – both professionally and personally. I often think that it's been the best bit of being in this profession – through it I've learnt from the 'inside out' all about what it is to be a client and, most of all, I've learnt about *being myself*. In many ways I have actually *become myself* – where, for example, there were fragile areas in myself I feel there are now firm foundations. Foundations that hold me in the world in a much more . . . I was lost for words for a few moments then . . . it's very difficult to describe exactly what it is . . . 'I feel much more at home in my subjective reality' is about as close as I can get. Then, because I feel more at home in myself I'm much better able to invite clients into my 'home' – to be open-hearted.

Inviting someone to come for counselling is like inviting them into your world. Although most of the time your attention is on your client's world, they are actually sitting in your world. If you are at home in your world, they will feel that; if you are not at home, they will feel that too. One of the problems is that you may not even quite realize that you are not that at home in yourself. I certainly didn't: I thought I was fine, not perfect, but certainly OK. Looking back I can hardly believe that now. I was, in comparison to today, a psychological wreck full of gaping holes and driven by fears and desires that I had very little awareness of. That's what it looks like now – some 13 years on from really starting my personal development process.

I am feeling tired now so I shall stop writing in a minute.

Feeling at home in your subjective world; empathizing with what is going on subjectively for your client and checking out your empathic understanding with her; knowing what is going on for you subjectively when you are with her – these are all vital aspects of the everyday process of counselling. I suggest that you learn to value your subjective world and the subjective world of your client – make it the focus, the centre, the heart of your attention and thus the counselling process. In my view this is of the utmost importance.

Honest and open communication

Jamie: So what's the procedure with this counselling lark?

Robert [thinks/feels: '*Off to a good start here – this guy really has a lot of faith in counselling. I wonder if he's been forced to come here by somebody or other – wife, or girlfriend, perhaps? Not the easiest of clients.*' Robert remembers various clients he has had in the past who could be described as '*reluctant*' to be sitting there in the client's chair. The worst was a drug addict referred by the court. For much of the time with Linda he thought they would have been better off not bothering to talk. '*No, each of us could have got on with something else – me with the case study I was writing for my diploma and she with planning her next robbery. Yes, well perhaps it wasn't as bad as that – just almost as bad. No, I definitely have a bit of a block nowadays with reluctant clients.*'] Well there are certain things we have to get clear about, certain rules of the game if you like. The number one rule is that if you turn up under the influence we cancel the session, OK? [Jamie's eyes turn a little wary, but he nods.] There are various other things we need to agree on too – things to do with confidentiality, when we'll meet up and for how long, initially; what we're going to aim to achieve in that time and a couple of other basic rules of the counselling centre here. We can take a look at all of that before the end of today's session but to answer your question I guess I'll say a little bit about what counselling is and what it *can* achieve. How's that sound, Jamie?

Jamie [thinks/feels: *'Sounds bloody stupid if you ask me but then I wouldn't be here if it was up to me. Anyway, since I am here I might as well give the guy a chance. Not that bad a sort, really – I was expecting a puny old woman with a snooty nose, Mrs Bloody Goody Good. He actually looks like an ordinary kind of a bloke.'*] Fine with me.

Robert [thinks/feels: *'Let's give it a go then – can't say I'm any more enthusiastic about this than you, mate. Maybe I should get out of this agency and start working privately. Not so much for the money – though it would be nice to be paid a decent amount for my time – but because you don't get many reluctant clients in private practice. Not easy, though – setting up in private practice. I guess I could start things while I'm still working here – a couple of evenings perhaps. How to go about it though, that's the question. Guess I just haven't had the confidence. Maybe I do now, though. Anyway I'm not doing very well here – mind off all over the place. Hardly the attentive, accepting, warm, empathic listener today.'* At that moment something Robert's first supervisor Sue had once said springs to his mind. 'You need to develop the habit of looking for reflections between your responses and those of your client – they can often be the doorway to what you're looking for. (Robert always felt that half of what Sue said made as much sense as a raincoat on a sunny day but today it did make sense – he could see that both he and Jamie were caught up in a similar mood of lack of enthusiasm as if neither of them really wanted to be sitting there.] I don't know, Jamie but before I go into what counselling is all about I'm just wondering if you need to say something about why you're sitting here. I wouldn't normally bring it up but, I don't know, it feels like you're less than enthusiastic about coming to counselling and perhaps you need to get that off your chest first? [Thinks/feels: *I wouldn't normally have said that – hope I haven't gone too far?*]

Jamie [thinks/feels: *Well there's giving it to me straight! You don't pull any punches do you, Robert? I like that. I'm impressed.*] [Robert closes the pages of his case study.]

> Robert: So as a result of noticing that I was tuning into Jamie's feelings I was able to almost lift myself out of the bad mood and try out a challenging intervention that actually initiated a relationship with Jamie.
>
> Clara (Robert's current supervisor): I agree with you. If you hadn't remembered your first supervisor's little recommendation and if

you hadn't noticed the fact that you were getting caught up with Jamie's mood of negative expectation, then you might well have gone with it and lived out that expectation – that the counselling was a bad idea with nothing to offer him. It all boils down to the way we respond to each other and whether or not a meaningful relationship can be initiated and developed – I believe that without the sense of interpersonal contact there really can't be any counselling. Counselling is first and foremost two people entering a relationship in which one person will share his or her deepest intimacies and the other person will respond to that intimate exposure. I really don't believe there ever was a 'blank screen' – the early psychodynamic approach used to advocate that the therapist take up the position of a blank screen on to which the patient could project his or her transference. I don't believe it was ever like that because even studiously *not* responding, is actually *experienced as a response*, and a rather rejecting response at that. Nowadays, the modern psychodynamic field has left the whole idea of the blank screen far behind and the therapist's intimate involvement in the relationship is seen to be the critical element of the therapeutic process. My secret view is that the whole blank screen theory was a defensive reaction to Breuer's early experience with his patient Anna O. Anna fell in love with Breuer and, from the description of Breuer's involvement with Anna, I wouldn't think it was too far fetched to say that Breuer secretly fell in love with Anna. Anyway, when Breuer finally decided to terminate the relationship with poor Anna, Anna developed a fantasized pregnancy in which Breuer was the father. That completely freaked this fine upstanding Viennese doctor and he quit the whole infant psychotherapy enterprise. Freud was left to carry on the work having 'learnt' something from Breuer's experience with Anna. Thus was born the blank screen – as an attempt to make sure that the Breuer/Anna fiasco didn't repeat itself. Well, that's enough of my mumblings.

    Not that you made a full response to Jamie's lack of enthusiasm – but you have acknowledged your response and intervened on the basis of that awareness.

Robert: And a fuller response would have been to say what? Express something of what I was feeling when initially faced with Jamie's lack of enthusiasm – something like 'You come across as pretty reluctant to be sitting here and I have to confess that seeing you like this doesn't exactly fill me with enthusiasm for this session.'

Clara: Yes, although I'd say that it was much too early on in the relationship for that level of honesty. Certainly, once some kind of real contact has been developed, but not on the first, or even the first few, sessions.

Robert: This is really what Rogers calls being genuine, isn't it?

Clara: Indeed it is, my dear little supervisee. A small but important example of the concept. Of course you've actually got to have reached a certain point of self-acceptance and self-awareness before you can be genuine. You could also begin to question what your genuine response actually was – a subtle but important shift for you, I think. Were you feeling unenthusiastic because that was your genuine response or unenthusiastic because you were caught up with Jamie's feelings and perceptions? You plumped for the latter, which leaves open the question of what was your genuine response?

Robert: Hmmm . . . Right now I really don't know.

Inside the counselling process

Throughout most of this book I have tried to take you, the reader, *into* the therapeutic process:

- What does it really mean to be working with psychological patterns – patterns in self, personal history and interpersonal relating, patterns of internal and interpersonal conflict, patterns of avoidance and confusion, patterns of unresolved issues and unmet needs?
- How can you, the counsellor, help these patterns to become more explicit for your client?
- How can you help the client to change, or move on from, those patterns that are clearly getting in the way of her life?
- What does all the theory really mean – in terms of actual work with clients?
- What does it mean in terms of yourself?

By focusing on *taking you inside* the therapeutic process, rather than simply *talking about it* from the outside, I hope that you will learn about the practice of counselling in a direct and living way. As already mentioned, I believe that much of what it means to become a counsellor is precisely this process of *moving inside* and learning to *work from within*. Most of our education, however, is all about being 'outside' – thinking objectively, rationally, at a distance from the intense feelings that arise in living and working with people. Pick up most books – even on counselling or psychology – and they will nearly always be written from the 'outside': they will be written from the objective perspective. Written in the way that I have been writing in this and the preceding paragraph – whereas the first section of this introduction is written from my inside, from my subjective perspective.

From the 'outside', for example, I can talk to you about how psychological patterns are formed during our development and how they then tend to repeat themselves in our life and our relationships. I can talk about how a particular trauma in late childhood might leave a child feeling very hurt and vulnerable and that, as a result of an inadequate environment for the expression of the feelings associated with that trauma, the child represses that hurt and vulnerability. In so doing she sets up the basis for a conflict within herself that will repeatedly emerge in her adult relationships. She may choose, for example, a partner who is also out of touch with the hurt side of himself and they will live their lives together in a way that repeatedly avoids the acknowledgement of their hurt. As you continue with the book, however, you will be offered opportunities to engage with various inside descriptions of this kind of theory.

Talking to you on the outside in this way can be very useful and interesting – and developing theoretical understanding of this kind is an important part of the process of becoming a counsellor. A problem emerges, however, when theories are approached *primarily* from this outside perspective. Not only is it more difficult to apply them in practice, it also actively encourages this kind of outside-way-of-thinking about client-work – rather than the inside-way-of-feeling-and-thinking about clients. If a person develops a strong habit of looking at things from the outside, it makes it *more* difficult to develop the capacity to look at things thoroughly from the inside. So, yes, every counsellor needs a coherent understanding of what and why they are doing what they do but it mustn't be at the expense of 'the inside view'. Such an 'inside' theory is rooted in the ground of personal and interpersonal reality, whereas the 'talking about', objective way of thinking, is at a distance from subjective experience. The counsellor needs to develop a subjectively understood theory – achieved through an emphasis on learning from within, rather than learning at a distance.

A counselling training group begins

The large room feels quite informal – comfortable chairs in an attractive combination of pine and emerald fabric are arranged around the room. In the corner there is a pile of multicoloured cushions. The floor is covered in a thick woolly sand-coloured carpet. A large patio window looks out onto a well-kept garden area with bushes and a lawn. On the far wall there is a huge framed poster of Picasso's *Guernica* – the picture lends a very sombre note to an otherwise tranquil setting. Off to the left there is a door leading into two smaller rooms containing three or four of the emerald chairs, and behind them a simple kitchen, laid out in pine once again. Except for a single small table at the side of the main room and a coffee table in each room, there is a noticeable lack of desks. The only clue to the nature of this space is a flip chart by the wall opposite the *Guernica* picture. In other respects it feels as far removed from the traditional classroom setting as one could get. Most noticeable is the quiet.

A quiet broken by the arrival of two people – a man and a woman. They enter the main room together chatting in a relaxed kind of way. The observant eye, however, would notice a certain edge to their voices – they are not as relaxed as they first appear. Together they arrange the chairs in a loose circle. As they do this they continue their conversation, which seems to have become more serious.

The man is in his late thirties and noticeably younger than the women, who is in her early sixties. He is thin, she rounder. He is dressed in smart-casual cotton trousers and a colourful Scandinavian style jumper, she is dressed even more informally. There is a certain intensity to the man – particularly in his eyes, which occasionally focus very intently on the woman's face. She seems much less intense, her eyes softer and warmer. She seems to be enjoying herself, whereas he seems to be working hard – checking this and that in the various rooms and writing on the flip chart. The woman exudes a quiet welcoming. Whereas she feels happy to meet you, he doesn't feel like that, no, he feels as though he is examining you quite intently and you are not at all sure whether he is thinking something good or bad about you. Or so Amanda felt when she came into the large room with the *Guernica* picture and the emerald chairs. Yes she felt very welcomed by Marjorie's bright smile and happy eyes and not at all welcomed by Anthony's 'stony glare' – as she put it to her husband later that evening.

'Yes, he did smile, but it was his eyes – they sort of looked right at me and I couldn't tell what he was thinking. I like Marjorie but I'm not sure about Anthony, he unnerves me.'

By 9.25 a.m. all but one of the chairs had been taken up. The assembled group was a bit of a motley crew – one or two very smart indeed with hair that looked as though it had come straight from the hairdresser's, one or two quite sloppy in comparison, with old jeans and T-shirts. Once again an observer would have noted a similar, more pronounced edge to all the voices – a sense of high expectation mixed with anxiety. Most were chatting away, but some were sitting back in their chairs looking tense. Only one member of the group appeared relaxed – but even he seemed a little *too* mellow, a little *too* laid back.

But even the most casual of observers would have noticed one thing – there were more women than men. One man in particular looked as though he felt out of place, uncomfortable with all these women chatting away together. Our observer might have felt a little sorry for him.

At 9.30, precisely, Anthony interrupted the various conversations:

'It's 9.30 and I'd like to start our first session by welcoming you to the first day of this intermediate training in therapeutic counselling.'

The voices quickly subsided.

Anthony continued: 'We are still waiting for one member of the group but I would like us to start as we plan to go on – that is, at the scheduled time for the session. Today is an induction day which means that by the end of it you will all, hopefully, have a reasonably clear idea of the course, the role of the tutors and your responsibilities as a student together with the course requirements and the schedule of assessments. We will also be spending some time developing and agreeing upon a contract for the group – in which issues of confidentiality, for example, will be addressed. Perhaps we could begin, however, with a little exercise designed to help us to start to get to know each other. My name is Anthony and I'll be joining in with this exercise – so you'll find out more about me in a little while. Marjorie, my fellow tutor, will be taking you through the exercise. OK, Marjorie?'

Marjorie: Normally we will begin each course day with half an hour for the group – each of you will have the opportunity to say something about how you are feeling as you start the day. It's a way for each of us to leave behind the world out there and enter into the course here. It also helps us to keep track of how each of us is feeling – both in terms of our personal and professional life and in relation to the course and what it may have been stimulating for us. We'll have a similar sort of half an hour at the end of each day where we have the opportunity to share any thoughts or feelings that have been important for us during the day. Just as we use the first half-hour to leave behind our lives outside we can use the time at the end of the day to leave behind the course.

These open half-hours are important time, although sometimes we might not feel they are. It's easy, for example, to want to leave early or arrive late because that first and last half-hour aren't quite so structured as the rest of the course. From the beginning, therefore, I want to ask you to make the effort to really use these times.

This first half-hour of the first day, however, I have a little exercise which is also designed to help us start the slow process of getting to know each other – an important part of any counselling training programme. It's quite a simple exercise – I want you to pair off with the person on your right or left, firstly spending a few minutes introducing yourself to your partner and then turning to these two questions [Marjorie unveils two questions written up on the flip chart]. Then we'll come back into the group, at which point I want each of you to introduce *not* yourselves but your partner. OK? [Various mumbles from the group]

Amanda: How long do we have?

Marjorie: If you spend five minutes on introductions then five minutes on each of the questions we'll come back in 15 minutes – I'll keep time and tell you when time is nearly up.

The group split off into pairs, both tutors joining in with the exercise and some pairs wandering into the nearby rooms. What had previously been idle chatting now took on a more focused atmosphere – everyone knew that they really had to listen if they were going to introduce their partner to the group. Knowing that gave the exercise a kind of intensity and a touch of anxiety. This wasn't a basic counselling skills course – everyone was supposed to be a good listener by now.

After 15 minutes Marjorie recalled the students into the large room and the group set about briefly introducing each other. Anthony went first and introduced Sarah – a former nurse with three children (now at school) who wants to return to work as a counsellor and has already begun voluntary work for an agency focused on chemical dependency. In turn, Sarah introduced Anthony – married with children, he is a practising counsellor and enjoys the movies. The rest of the group introduced each other and then Belinda arrived, about 35 minutes late, apologizing and explaining that she'd had child-care problems. She introduced herself as a housewife, although she also works part-time for a careers advisory centre. Finally Marjorie was introduced as a practising counsellor with a husband and three grown children – two boys and a girl.

Exercise: becoming more aware of your subjective experience

Ask yourself the following question:

'What has been happening – subjectively?'

Note: to answer this question look at what has been going on for you, subjectively – your emotions and feelings, your images, your thoughts, your intuitions, your bodily experience, your motivations and desires.
  Next ask yourself the following question:

'What is happening – subjectively – right now?'

Note: to answer this question look at what is going on for you, subjectively – your emotions and feelings, your images, your thoughts, your intuitions, your bodily experience, your motivations and desires. If I were here with you what might be going on between you and me? What might be going on for me – in relation to you?

Journal work

In your journal explore your experience of this exercise together with your response to the following paragraph:

Beyond the mechanical fact of sexual reproduction human beings experience the subjective dimensions of desire and jealousy, love and hatred, happiness and rejection. Beyond the material fact of death we experience the personal dimensions of yearning and tragedy, anger and guilt, terror and suicide. At the very centre of our lived reality we experience a very precious, very special 'heart'. There we find the very essence of what it is to be a human being – the experience of a

subjective psychological life. To label and think of our lived experience of the world as an interior life is often to devalue it – an inside,
immaterial world in contrast to an outside reality. As counsellors we
need to develop the habit of noticing and valuing the subjective – for
counselling is primarily concerned with subjective reality.

2

So What Is This Thing Called Self?

Know thyself. (Inscription in the Temple of Delphi)

Ronnie develops his self-confidence

The man sitting in front of Jane was not very physically attractive. In fact he could be described as quite ugly. In his early forties, he came over as quite a passive person – sitting in front of her as if waiting for the 'doctor' to say something. Her initial response to Ronnie was *not* one of immediate liking or interest. This was all worth noting since first impressions and first responses, although often quite wrong (in terms of the actual person), are also quite often of later interest and value. Her first response to this man was also likely to be similar to the first response of many other people with whom Ronnie came into contact. It was important since it said something about how Ronnie might fit into his social world and how his social world might respond to him. She also found herself sitting at a greater distance from Ronnie than usual, not just physically but, at a more important level, psychologically. It was as if Ronnie was over *there* and she was very much over *here*. Again she notes this as both an unusual feeling and possibly one that might be worth looking at in her review of the session later. Yes, it was almost as if there was a divide between her and this man – him on one side and her on the other. Although this feeling might be hers alone and thus 'her stuff', it didn't feel that way. No, it felt both unusual for her and usual for Ronnie.

Jane: Please carry on, Ronnie, I'd like to hear more about your panic attacks. Perhaps you could describe one or two examples of them for me.

Ronnie: [thinks/feels: *'Jane seems like a nice woman. I hope she can help me. It was a pity about my first counsellor Sandra – I quite liked her but I could see why she felt the way she did. A bit awkward but nevertheless you have to get the right person for the right job. No sense in having the wrong person. She seemed to think that Jane would be the right person – which is good enough for me. No, it was honest of Sandra – I respect her for that.'*] Err, right, well mmm. The last time was last Thursday, I think. Yes, I was out doing a little shopping for the wife and well I got into a right tizz, had to sit down in the supermarket and calm down. Took five minutes or so. The time before that . . . that must have been on the Monday. Not quite such a bad one that one. Happened in the market – down by the car park – the open market, that is. I thought I lost the keys to the car. Anyway I hadn't, as it turned out. Gave me a real turn though, at the time.

Jane: [thinks/feels: *'Once again, after responding to my question he seems to stop and sit there as if waiting for the "doctor" to speak.' It was almost as if her questions pressed a button that made Ronnie move for a short time then stop still – waiting for her to press the button again. She wondered what was going on in Ronnie's mind during these still periods. She also noticed a slight irritation on her part and again noted that at the back of her mind for future reference.*] So your panic attacks are relatively frequent? Perhaps you could describe what one feels like – do you think you could, for example, take me through the feelings last Thursday? What was happening before the panic began, what was it like when you were in the panic and how did you recover?

Ronnie [thinks/feels: *'Yes, she does seem to know what's she's doing, which is good. It would be good to be rid of these things – they are a bit of a nuisance, to say the least. Time to get them sorted – as the wife said.'*] Certainly, Jane. Well I was waiting in the line at the checkout desk when I suddenly thought I hadn't got enough money to pay for all the shopping in my basket. I'd picked up a few extras as I went round, you see. As soon as I thought that I began to get in a bit of a tizz. I quickly counted up how much I had in my wallet and I was halfway through counting up the cost of all the items when it was my turn. I'd already been getting worse as I stood in the line thinking that all these people were looking at me counting everything up but when I hadn't finished and it was my turn I really started to get shaky. Yes, I really got into a panic. As it turned out I did have enough money but my hand was shaking as I handed it to the girl. She must have noticed, which made it even worse. Anyway when I was through I went straight to one of the seats and sat there, as I say, for about five minutes or so – to calm down, as it were.

Jane [thinks/feels: *'There is definitely something important here in the way Ronnie just stops and sits there. He actually reminds me of a tortoise – sticking his head out from his shell when I ask him a question then "whoop" – pulling it straight back in after answering me. I really do wonder what is going on in the shell? Feeling safe I guess, feeling safe. If only he could stay in his shell all the time – then there would no panics? There's a little assessment of Ronnie for you – might be a bunch of worthless wheat-flakes – but it's a first session assessment and a good enough one to begin with.' Jane's mind turns to her youth and her pet tortoise. She remembers how, if she tickled the opening of his shell he would put out his head, then if she tickled him under his chin he would stretch out his neck as far as it would reach.*] That sounds extremely uncomfortable, Ronnie, and it's also giving me a much more detailed picture of your particular experience of panic attacks. Perhaps you could go on and describe a few more of these attacks to me – in much the same way as you've just done – so that I can build up a broader picture of your problem. Hopefully we can then go on to look at whether there might be commonalities in these attacks that can point us to how they might be coped with a bit better.

Ronnie [thinks/feels: *'Yes, Jane definitely does know what she's doing – the wife will be pleased. I think they get on her nerves as much as mine. Now let's think, there was the one at the car park. Before that . . . no wait a minute, perhaps I should tell her about the bad ones first. Better ask her about that.'*] I just had a thought Jane. Well, a question actually – shall I describe any ones that I can think of or should I focus on the bad ones, the ones that really knocked me for six, as you might say? I could certainly think about some of the worst – would that suit you?

Jane's client notes

Ronnie S.: Age 43. Married with one child now left home.
Referral: Marjorie T. (referred on by one of Marjorie's supervisees).
Presenting issue: Panic attacks.
Doctor: H. McDermott Tel.: 731562

Brief description of the session: Ronnie began by explaining why he had come for counselling and briefly mentioned that he had been referred on by another counsellor who had too much other work on at the moment. He came over as a pleasant enough man, somewhat lacking in spontaneity, and throughout the session I felt I had to provoke him to talk. Under my prompting Ronnie detailed a number of descriptions of his panic attacks. Towards the end of the session we considered whether there might be any patterns to them and tentatively concluded that, in all of his descriptions, there was an anxiety about appearing foolish in front of others. We agreed on an initial 12 sessions with the focus very much on exploring how Ronnie might deal with these kind of situations differently.

Initial assessment: Ronnie struck me as quite an introverted man who keeps his real feelings to himself. During the session I had an image of Ronnie's self as like a tortoise – it felt like, inside, Ronnie feels quite vulnerable and has learnt to cope by hiding inside a shell. I certainly felt 'at a distance' and held at bay by a divide. I believe that therapeutic work at this level (working on his deep-seated vulnerability and distancing tendencies) would *not* be appropriate. Such work would be long term, I'm not at all sure Ronnie would take to it and I further doubt it would be that successful. I have therefore decided to follow a much more problem-focused approach drawing on cognitive-behavioural techniques with the aim of enabling Ronnie to cope more effectively in situations where panic tends to overwhelm him. I may also try some fairly active techniques – such as exaggeration of the worst scenario.

Things to remember: I must ask Ronnie for his telephone number again. I noted it on a scrap of paper when he first called me but have since lost it. I must also remember to ask Ronnie if he has always suffered from these panic attacks or whether he can identify the specific date of their onset. Oh, I also need to warn him that I will be away for the week of the 17th of next month and won't be able to see him that week.

One third of the way through session 8

Ronnie [thinks/feels: *'I've never thought of myself as a very imaginative person, that's the problem with this kind of thing. It's quite hard to be somewhere else and feel the feelings that I would be feeling. Just doesn't seem to work for me. Leave all that imagining stuff up to painters and people like that – that's what I've always thought.'*] No, I'm sorry Jane I find it quite hard to imagine such a situation and feel the kinds of feelings I would be feeling. Not much good, am I?

Jane [thinks/feels: *'Well let's focus for a moment on what we have achieved. It's become quite clear that the panics occur in situations where Ronnie feels put in the spotlight. The thought-stopping worked to some extent and you are using that now. I keep coming back to the main issue, however – being in the spotlight and that being a terrible thing to happen to you. If only we could shift your sense of that equation "spotlight = terrible event". Clearly there must be something in your past that leads you to that kind of conclusion but I hesitate to start rummaging around in your personal history. We could unsettle things even more and then we would be into long-term work. I know – perhaps we could simulate a situation here in this room, rather than imagine one elsewhere.'*] As I said to you before we tried any of these more imaginative techniques, they don't work for everyone, Ronnie. If imagining things isn't your strong point then that's OK. We've certainly got somewhere with some of the other techniques. I'm wondering whether we could try something else – something that doesn't rely so much on the imagination but might prove to be just as useful.

Ronnie [thinks/feels: *'She's trying, that's for sure. Pity I'm not the best of clients. I hope I get on OK with this new technique. Still, it's true that some of the things we've been doing have started to have an effect.'*] Certainly Jane, fire away.

Jane [thinks/feels: *'Fire away indeed. Sometimes I feel as if I'm doing the work and you're doing the listening. I could confront you on this but, I don't know, that just doesn't feel right. If we're going to work at this level, then we've got to stay at this level, and confronting you about who is or who isn't doing the work feels like moving to another level.'* Jane thought for a moment *about how to introduce this new technique. She disliked the feeling of being the expert authority figure – which was clearly who she was for Ronnie. Jane had always been more comfortable with a humanistic approach, although she felt quite capable of working with the cognitive mode too. It felt a bit of a strain, sometimes, though.*] What I'm wondering is whether we could practise in here certain situations that you find difficult out there. We can then see what goes on in your mind and see if we can use some technique to help you to cope better. For example, we could pretend you were at the checkout – you remember that situation? [Ronnie nods.] Instead of trying to imagine it in your head we could act it out together. I could be the checkout person. There, you're getting in a tizz about the possibility that you haven't got enough money. What happens now?

Ronnie [thinks/feels: *'Checking my money, that's what I'd be doing.' Ronnie fumbles for his wallet and as he does so he feels under Jane's spotlight – will he get it right or will he fail and get it wrong? His anxiety rises.*]

Jane notices that Ronnie seems to have touched into some anxiety as he takes out his wallet and glances at the contents.

Jane: So what's happening to you, Ronnie? Can you describe the kinds of thoughts going on in your mind as we practise this scenario?

Ronnie [thinks/feels: *'I've only got £8.50 – that's how much I had, I remember the amount. So what's in the wallet – how much does it add up to?*] I'm looking in the basket now. I've only got £8.50. What am I thinking? I'm thinking 'God I haven't got enough money for all of this – what am I going to do?'

Jane [thinks/feels: *'We seem to be getting somewhere here – at last.'*] Carry on, Ronnie.

Ronnie: I'm going to have to say I haven't got enough money and everyone is going to be looking at me and thinking, 'Silly old man – can't add up' and then I'm going to be shaking in front of all of them and they'll be thinking, 'Stupid old fool – look he's shaking, how embarrassing he is.' Then everyone will look away, pretend that they don't see me and I'll be, I'll be . . . I don't know, shut off or something like that and feeling like some stupid fool and that will be just awful.

Jane [thinks/feels: *'Yes, it does feel as if we are getting somewhere – shut off – much like in the "shell"? That makes sense – at the heart of the panic is the fear of being shut off from other people. Which in a certain respect he already is – hidden away in his shell.'*] This feels very important – well done, Ronnie. What I'd like you to also try is this – when you've checked your wallet and you're worried about whether you've got enough money to pay for all the items, just tell me your worry. Try again from the beginning, OK? [Ronnie nods somewhat hesitantly.]

Ronnie [thinks/feels: *'I'll give it a go. I'm in the line and I suddenly think "Have I got enough money?"'* He takes out his wallet and fumbles with it, checking how much he has got.] Oh dear, I don't think I've got enough money to pay for all of this. [Ronnie's voice is visibly shaking.]

Jane [thinks/feels: *'Good, very good, let's continue.'*] Very good. Try again but this time see if you can make light of it, even make a little joke. I know that's probably very difficult, but we can try a few times to see if you can get the hang of it.

Ronnie [thinks/feels: *'You know, that felt a lot better – just saying it out loud to Jane, the checkout girl. Don't know that I could make a joke of it though.'* Ronnie goes through the scene again. On the fifth-run through his tone has changed – he almost sounds as if he's enjoying saying the words.] Oh dear, not much in the old wallet – I hope there's enough to pay for all of this. Sorry if there isn't – I wasn't really working it out on the way round the store. Silly old me!

Jane [thinks/feels: *'This time. I'll respond and see how he reacts to that.'*] Don't worry sir, done it myself actually. I'm sure we can work something out if you haven't got enough. [Ronnie smiles.]

Ronnie [thinks/feels: *'Well, well, well. I never thought of that – it probably has happened to most people. Nice girl, I mean nice Jane.'* Ronnie feels very pleased with himself – perhaps most of all because he can see that Jane is very pleased with him.] How did I do?

Jane: [thinks/feels: *'Well I never, that really seemed to work very well.'* She smiles at the beaming Ronnie and then thinks, *'The real test, however, is how he does out there – in the frightening world.'*]

Ronnie's learning to share himself a little – but how is he doing that?

What is the reason for Ronnie's growing self-confidence – is it the techniques Jane uses, or the growing relationship? Ronnie is clearly getting a lot out of the techniques, but the fact that he's able to articulate his anxiety is surely the result of the relationship he is building up with Jane – a relationship in which she is much like the good teacher/parent and he is the cared-for child. Ronnie is learning a particular kind of skill, but he is also learning how to be a 'good boy' in Jane's eyes – and he is certainly basking in her praise. I also wonder how effective Jane would be without her background thoughts/feelings about the deeper issues that she has decided to steer clear of working on directly with Ronnie. Although not voiced directly, these are, nevertheless, being worked on at some level. Just a couple of thoughts for you to consider – in counselling, things are seldom as simple as they may seem at first sight, and that may well be the case with Jane and Ronnie.

Question 1 – how do we know anything about a self?

The problem: We can't see, hear, touch, taste or smell a 'self'.

When I think about the people in my world I have a sense of who each of them is – I have a sense of their identities, their personalities, that which makes them who they are. I have a sense of each person in my life and what is striking is how different they are – how each of them has his or her own unique self. Whether it is my friend Pedro or my colleague Peter or my cousin Katherine or my mother Rose, I have a sense of them as particular persons, as very individual selves about whom I have very different thoughts and feelings.

If I ask myself the question 'Who is Pedro?' I don't answer it by pointing out to myself what Pedro looks like, or what work he does, or what he wears, or the kind of life he leads. Instead I answer the question by thinking about the person that is Pedro – the 'self' that is Pedro. I have a strong sense of who Pedro is and he is very different from my sister Sophia, my gay friend Paul or my partner Josephine. They each have a very different self and although I can use my five senses to see, to touch, to listen to, to smell or even to taste them, they – the selves that are these people – remain a step beyond my senses.

The self is something that we can't touch, or point to, or observe in any direct way at all. In this sense the self is actually invisible – and yet the self that is Pedro or Sophia or Josephine is certainly there and it is also, as far as I or they are concerned, the most important aspect of each of them.

Exercise

Try this out for yourself. Think about five important people in your life and ask yourself 'Who are you, Janet? Who are you, John?' Compare your senses of each of these people and see if you can describe each of their selves. Take some time out from reading to complete this exercise.

How easy did you find it to describe the important people in your life? How much have your words managed to describe them? Did you actually take time out to do the exercise? Naughty! My guess is that if you have done it you will have found that you do have quite an in-depth sense of each of their unique, invisible selves – although describing your sense of each person's self was quite difficult. It's a bit like trying to describe your response to a novel, or painting or piece of music. The words can give a partial flavour of what the creative work means to you but they don't capture all that much. In comparison to your overall sense of a creative work, or an important person in your life, your verbal description may well feel small, limiting and inadequate.

Now take a completely different tack – choose one or two of these important people and ask yourself the following questions:

- What kinds of *animal* is he or she like?
- What kinds of *texture* does he or she feel like to be with?
- What kinds of *colour* does this person remind you of?
- What kinds of *rhythm* does this person feel like?

Did you manage to come up with *a number of* rhythms, animals or textures – perhaps representing the different moods or sides of his or her self?

Now choose just one person and try one of the following:

- Write a poem or a song about this person.
- Write a short scene in a play or a novel in which this person is a key character.
- Paint this person – preferably using a non-figurative style of painting or collage.
- Make a video about this person.

Perhaps this is why we reach for other forms of expression – be they painting or music or dance or theatre or poetry – to enable us to express aspects of ourselves and our experiences of other selves that are otherwise very difficult to articulate.

So what is the self? It can't be seen, it can't be touched, it can't be heard and yet we all believe we have one. What do *you* mean – when you refer to your 'self'?

When we think about each of the important people in our lives we are thinking about their unique 'selves' but it's difficult to say what exactly this unique self is – what he or she is made up of, or how we develop our particular picture of him or her. It's certainly much easier to talk about what people look like, or what they do, or the kind of life they lead. In fact, when we first meet someone else, *these* are the kinds of things we tend to ask and talk about.

Question 2 – what if there are lots of answers?

The problem: To what extent is my picture of each of the important people in my life *really* who he or she is and to what extent is my picture 'coloured' by *my own self* – by my own way of seeing the world?

The counsellor needs to develop a habit of questioning perceptions and their associated responses – both her perceptions and the perceptions of her client. Seeing may be believing but it is not 'what is'. In fact it is very difficult to say that anything really 'is' – because of the colourful nature of our perceptions. We perceive through our own 'glasses' – some are grey, some are rose-tinted but all help create 'what is'. To say that our perceptions distort the world is to miss an important point. If no one is looking at 'the beautiful sunset' then there is no 'beautiful sunset'. There is something, surely, but to someone else it is a sad sunset or to some other being, like a night owl, it is time to come out to find something to eat. What we normally consider to be an outside 'reality' is, in actuality, a co-created 'reality' – a joint creation of world and perceptions, of self and other, inside and outside.

Some questions to consider

1   How do your perceptions shape your responses?
2   In what sense are your perceptions 'true'? To what extent do you (and other people) universally assume them to be true and to what extent are they actually very particular to each particular self?
3   To what extent do you assume that other people see the world in the same way as yourself? When you do, is this a safe assumption to make?
4   'I look at you and perceive you from my subjectivity. Your presence with me. You are warm or cold, exciting or dull, open or closed, someone I enjoy laughing with or someone I would rather not be with at all. And when I am with you I feel how you are, what "shape" you are, whether I can "touch" you, whether you are dangerous, whether you are someone I can share with.' How do you respond to that passage?
5   Ask yourself whether counselling should be seeking the kind of perception (objectivity) that science aims for. To what extent does the counsellor need to value the reality of human perception – a perception essentially, and importantly, coloured by feeling, emotion, intuition and desire?

Question 3 – which pair of spectacles?

The problem: We create theory from our very colourful perceptions. Viewing the world through a theory, therefore, is a bit like putting on a pair of someone else's spectacles.

There are many theories of the self – theories that often try, for example, to describe the 'shape' of this invisible aspect of a person. These theories underlie the different approaches that make up the field of counselling and each of these 'approaches' is a bit like one of the different 'schools' that make up the field of music or art. Like music, there are more 'classical' schools (for example Freudian) and more 'contemporary' schools (for example Transpersonal) and like art there are more figurative/literal schools (for example Behavioural) and more abstract schools (for example Gestalt). Each school, however, is founded on its own particular view of the self – its own particular pair of spectacles.

The most important factor in a theory, however, is not its academic clarity or academic neatness but its usefulness in the difficult process of working with this invisible 'thing' we call self. In many ways that usefulness is dependent as much on the person using it as on the actual theory itself – so it is very important that the student of counselling *makes the theory her own*, makes it as personally and professionally meaningful as possible. A theory, any theory, needs to become an integrated part of the counsellor's way of seeing his or her world and this is much more difficult than 'parroting' a theory.

The following extract, from a student's journal, is an example of one student's struggle to make one particular theory of self meaningful to her.

Extract from Belinda's journal

We've been looking at the self for a number of weeks now and I'm trying to develop a practical understanding of the various theories. I'm not too sure what I'm supposed to do with some of them. I don't quite see how to relate, for example, 'id, ego and super-ego' to myself or my work with clients. My tutor, Marjorie, says that we have to develop our own understanding of self – through relating it both to ourselves and to our client-work. I feel I'm a long way off from that.

Part of the point of this journal is, again according to Marjorie, to provide us with the time and space to explore, assimilate and clarify our understanding – an understanding that's got to be related to both the personal and the professional. Well that's what I'm trying to do right now. Hmmm ... I don't know, I'm not sure I see a great deal of point in some of these theories. They don't seem to relate much to me or to my work. What am I supposed to do with them? It's a bit frustrating.

In the Freudian theory of the self, for example, the id is supposed to be that part of ourselves that is, more or less, uncontrolled instinctual desire. What does that mean? Freud mainly seemed to mean uncontrolled sexual desire. A bit like some men I know, I guess, but I don't think that's the same for women at all. I've never felt an inkling of uncontrolled sexual desire for every man I meet – which is, as I understand it, what the id is supposed to feel. I've certainly felt very strong sexual attraction for particular men – but not in an uncontrolled way. A lot of men do seem to be less picky about who they'd have sex with. Perhaps this is a man's theory about men – but it's not true of all men. What about the controlling ego? Marjorie said that this part of the self was the more adult part – the part we tend to identify with, our conscious part, the part that we refer to when we use the words 'I' or 'me'. Again I don't feel I have to control my uncontrolled desires in order to live a normal adult life.

I do have to control my eating, it's true – because I don't want to get too fat. You know that's something I noticed the other day over lunch with some of the other women in the group – we're always talking about eating, or rather how not to eat so much, or what to eat to keep thin and what not to eat to keep from getting fat. Then I was in the local newsagent's and I noticed it again – every single woman's magazine in there had something on the cover about slimming or eating or food and diets in general. Perhaps the female id is this gobbling creature inside every woman that would gorge itself on cream cakes, chocolate and every fattening food it could lay its hands on, if it was let out. Perhaps the job of the female ego is to imprison this gobbler in some psychological dungeon and only feed her dry biscuits and fat-free milk.

Or perhaps it's simply that most men are such selfish pigs when it comes to sex that most women prefer food to sex, yes – what was that word Marjorie used? – sublimate – yes, perhaps women sublimate their sexual desires into a longing for food and then have to control them. The only problem with that theory is that the only reason we're so obsessed with being thin is so that we will look attractive – in the eyes of men! Or is it, maybe in the eyes of women? Most of the women (and there are only women) at my aerobics class, for example, spend a great deal of time and effort to look really nice at the aerobics class – with their make-up and hairdos and their fancy aerobic costumes. It used to be the same when I went to pick up the children from school: many of the mothers would obviously spend ages on themselves before they ventured up to the school. But there was hardly ever a man there. Men like fat bums anyway.

Anyway I've wandered off. Mmmm ... Certainly both men and women would seem to have certain desires – sex and food being two of them but I can probably think of others – which they try to control. That's a bit of a theory, isn't it – that within the self there are both desires and the attempt to control desires. Yes, that's quite good – that makes sense to me – I can see how it relates to myself and my women friends and to men. It's also quite frustrating – controlling my desires; in fact sometimes it's very frustrating. So in this theory ('which is mine and belongs to me' – I remember that phrase from an old Monty Python sketch about Ann Elk who had a theory about dinosaurs being thin at one end, much, much thicker in the middle and thin again at the far end) ... Yes, the Belinda Theory of Self is that the self both desires and controls its desires, which leads to frustration, and dissatisfaction.

And the controlling part of the self feels more like the 'super-ego', not the ego, the 'strict parent' part of the self, as someone put it in the seminar. The part that says, 'You shouldn't be looking at that bar of chocolate' or, 'You ought to be doing your exercise now.'

So we have the mad gobbling cream cake eater (the id) the strict parent with her oughts and shoulds (the super-ego) and the ego ... stuck in-between the two? I remember Marjorie talking about this part of the self as the more rational part, the part that has a bit of common sense.

I feel as though I've got a clearer sense of what id and super-ego mean but I'm not sure about the ego ... Maybe the ego is simply 'Belinda'. Belinda is ... I don't know, this is pretty hard. Belinda is ... feeling frustrated trying to understand what this means. Belinda is ... trying to do this because she wants to be a better counsellor. Belinda is ... struggling with how to get what she wants in a difficult situation. 'Gobbler' would like to lounge in front of the TV, eat a take-away pizza and an ice-cream and just enjoy the evening. 'Strict parent' just loves to boss Gobbler (and Belinda) about – 'Do this, don't do that'. Belinda is ... trying to sort things out so her life is better in the longer run. Belinda is, what was the phrase Marjorie used, 'reality orientated'. Belinda is aware of the social situation she lives in, Gobbler isn't very concerned about that and 'Strict parent' isn't very much more than a bunch of rules that she shouts out like some demented parrot. Desire, the frustration of desire and the negotiator – id, super-ego and ego. Yes, it's actually starting to make a little sense to me – at least in terms of my self – 'I am applying the theory personally,' as Marjorie would put it.

But what would I do with this theory when I'm working with my clients? What good would 'Belinda's Theory of the Self' be? Hmmm ... Has it done me any good? It's certainly quite an interesting way of looking at myself – a part that desires without much thought for the social situation I live in, a part that is telling me off and a part whose main concern is the social situation I live in. How does this, or might this, picture of myself help me as a counsellor? I can't think of an answer to that at the moment but I have thought of one client who might benefit from this theory. I'll call him John.

I think John has always been a bit spoilt – spoilt by his mother, his girlfriends and now his wife. John has come to see me because he's been feeling down. He says that he started to feel down a few months before his 40th birthday and has been feeling down most of his 40th year. He says that he is very old now – since reaching 40 – and as a result feels he's never going to have the life that he wants. On occasions I've been a bit annoyed with John because I sometimes think he is simply wanting me to say 'It's OK John if you have had affairs' – because that's what it's also about. I noticed that I was getting annoyed with him and feeling sorry for his wife 'Mary' – I'll call her that. So I took John along to my supervisor.

We explored his 'case' and my supervisor referred me to a book on 'the mid-life crisis' and suggested that I examine my prejudices towards men in my own personal counselling. Which is fine for him to say and I wish I could be in personal counselling at the moment but I can't afford it right now – I did have a series of 12 sessions earlier in the year. I got annoyed with my *male* supervisor, George, that session – although I didn't tell him. Sometimes I wonder how useful he is – whether he's really that good a supervisor and maybe someone else would be a lot better. A woman, perhaps! I ought to talk to Marjorie about that.

Anyway what I'm thinking is that John has a rather spoilt 'id'. John hasn't really learnt how to cope with being frustrated, he hasn't really learnt how to frustrate himself. If he could he might be able to get what he says he really wants – a happy life with his wife and children. He says he loves his wife Mary, but I would say that he's primarily very emotionally dependent on her. He married late, in his mid-thirties, but continued to have relationships with other women. When his young secretary came on to him one day, for example, he went with it – he let his id go off on full swing without a thought for his wife and what she might feel.

Only he now realizes that his life with his wife has become one huge deceit and that deceitfulness has got in between him and his wife. He feels distant from her, he has to watch himself when he's with her, he worries that she'll find out. Basically he has 'ruined' his relationship with her, as he puts it, and he can't see how he'll ever get it back to what he feels it was when he first met her. Plus he's worried that he'll have other affairs and he just won't be able to stop and his life will get worse and worse. In fact he seemed to turn to the most recent woman because he was feeling so distant from his wife, and emotionally distressed, that he wanted comfort as much as sex (and also continuing proof of being young and attractive).

No, John doesn't seem that able to either frustrate himself or to organize his life – manage himself in his social situation – in the way that his 'ego' ought to. John is dominated by the 'id' with a weak 'ego' and ... And what? Actually his super-ego is quite a nasty one. He spends quite a lot of his day 'beating himself up' about what he's done and how bad and 'rotten' he is and how he has ruined everything and so on. I did wonder one session about whether John was suicidal. Something he said – I think his use of the word 'rotten' to refer to himself and I particularly noticed the way he said it. George was actually quite good when I took that to supervision. We explored that issue very closely and looked at what kinds of indications there might be with a suicidal client, together with how I would deal with the issue with John. In the end we decided that he wasn't suicidal because, although he had this strong guilt and 'beating up' of himself, it wasn't the main aspect of his 'interior life' – that's what George calls people's thoughts and feelings. We also decided that he hadn't actually said or done anything that would indicate suicidal thoughts. I agreed with George that I was probably being somewhat over-sensitive to this issue because of my own fear that a client would commit suicide and that it would then be 'my fault' – or at least I would see it that way.

So John has a too-strong id, a super-ego that doesn't seem to work very well and a weak ego. If he could 'weaken' his id, make his super-ego more effective and strengthen his ego he'd be a lot better off. How he, we, would go about doing that is a different question. One that can wait too – I'm getting somewhat tired – my ego is keeping me up too late writing this journal. (I almost wrote 'blasted' journal but I have actually enjoyed this 'time and space to assimilate and apply my learnings of the course'.) My id is getting rather tired of waiting around for a bit of pleasure and my super-ego is starting to go on about being a good wife and spending at least half an hour with my husband before we fall asleep – who knows, perhaps even satisfying his uncontrolled sexual desires. Oh, if only that was the case – James having uncontrolled sexual desires – hmmm ... yummy yummy, fill my tummy ... what a thought. That reminds me of a time years ago ... and, well that's not for this journal.

Marjorie's comments You've certainly been trying very hard to apply the theory to yourself and your client-work and are really starting to make the theory personally and professionally meaningful. You've come a long way over the year – I remember my earlier feedback on your journal being about regurgitating the seminars. The section of your journal that I've highlighted, in which you struggle to make sense of Freud's theory of the self, is really quite fun. I've never seen it interpreted in quite the way that you've done. You've clearly made a real effort to make the theory mean something to yourself and your work. I particularly like the way you use the theory to develop a clear aim for your therapeutic work with John. Hopefully the recent course sessions on working with conflict within the self have helped to address your final question regarding what you might do with such a conflict, once identified. Finally I love your humorous down-to-earth approach to it all and I hope that your humour is carried through in your work with clients – humour can be exceedingly therapeutic. *Note*: Please take a look at the course guide sheets on emergencies and suicidal clients.

Question 4 – do I even know who I am and what I want?

The problem: 'I don't always know who I really am and, associated with that, I don't always know what I'm really thinking, feeling or wanting in this or that situation.'

We are continually faced with choices with regard to our desires and our associated sense of who we are. Unfortunately we can be so unaware, or unclear about, what we need and what we want that some of us tend to get by through a process of swinging from over-indulgence to self-retribution. Not all of us have developed the kind of 'good enough' ego explored above. In contrast we live a life of inner conflict in which, in Freudian terms, the id, ego and super-ego are in some form of continual unhealthy battle.

Some of us develop, for example, selfish or self-sacrificing personalities – in the former we live a life denying the reality of the importance
of others, in the latter denying the reality of the importance of our own
wants and needs. Finding a way through to some sense of balance –
between self and other, between meeting desires and the reality-based
frustration of having those same desires not met, isn't an easy task.
Added to this we have often 'forgotten' what we want and need – as a
way of coping, for example, with the pain of the frustration of those
wants and needs not being met. In fact we often come to want many
things in the place of what we really and truly want. (Think about this
in relation to John.) Finally, many of us have never really learnt how to
go about asking for what we really need and want – in ways that others
can accept and that will enable them to co-operate with us.

I believe that the ability to know and ask for what we want – our
capacity for open and honest communication – is central to our sense of
self:

> I want to do that, I can do this, I am going to do this, I will be doing
> that.

This capacity for open and honest communication is founded on the
sense that 'I am the agent of my own affairs, I act from a place that I
know to be myself, I act within a social world but I do so as my own
agent.' Equally, much of what we experience as internal conflict – the
subject of the next chapter – is essentially a confusion about our sense of
agency:

> I'm not sure whether I want to do this or that; part of me wants this,
> part of me wants that; I don't know whether I want to do this or that.

Intimately tied up with our sense of self, therefore, is our sense of
personal agency – who am I and what do I want?

Some questions to consider

What can you do?
What can't you do?
What do you most want?
What do you least want?
What do you have to do?
What don't you have to do?

*David begins the process of finding out about who he is and what he
wants*

In the following extract from a client's diary, David isn't sure about who
he is or what he wants – he seems to have lost his sense of personal

agency – and he is finding that very distressing. In counselling any client, a great deal of what we can do concerns helping the client clarify their sense of agency – helping him or her to get clearer about what he or she can or can't do, wants and doesn't want, can and can't get. In the process we will have to work with the client in uncovering and working through internal conflict.

Extract from David's diary

28 February

I realized during today's session that I don't really know who I am or what I want. I'm just kind of sitting here in my life. I've done all this work over these past few years and I don't really know why. Yes, I've achieved something in terms of career and all of that but, at the same time, I feel empty – as if in the process I have also missed out on so much.

It's quite strange to realize that I don't really know what I want – that I do things because ... well because I'm supposed to do them. I felt quite blank when I left the session with Jane. Since then I've been feeling depressed. Sometimes I sit here at my desk and discover that I've stopped. That I'm just sitting here and, well, wanting to stop it all. I never thought counselling would be like this. I'm worse off than I was before. Perhaps I should give it up.

7 March

Jane asked me how I was feeling. I lied – 'Great,' I said. *Wanker – you couldn't even tell her*. This made me feel even worse. Anyway, we carried on looking at what I want from my life but it felt hollow. There was a moment at the end when she said 'I hope we can clarify this more next time' and she looked at me with a really 'nice' smile. I wanted to say 'fuck off'. I don't know if I'm going to go back next week.

14 March

I went back – although, as I approached the door to the centre, it felt like I was dragging my feet along the pavement. I guess it was bleaker to give up the hope I have in counselling than to give up the counselling. The receptionist gave me a really nice smile too which depressed me even more – just as I went into Jane's room. Jane smiled at me again – from her multicoloured chair. I don't like her chairs – they are too brash. Anyway, to my surprise, Jane seemed different this week

– more on my wavelength. I quite got on with her this time.

Most of the session concerned what I want out of my life (again!) but this time, I don't know, I was able to talk about how it felt not to know what I want. She said something that helped: 'I was imagining what it was like for you to feel so unsure about your life and I felt quite sad, I've been wondering if you've been feeling sad too?' I said 'no', perhaps as a bit of a put-down, but then I told her about how I'd been feeling really blank and empty. I described one of the occasions when I was sitting at my desk at the office and had looked out of the window at the streets with all the bustle and the traffic. I went on about the traffic – 'I hate traffic,' I said. 'If there was one thing I'd do as prime minister it would be to get rid of as many trucks and cars as possible.'

'That feels important' she said. I asked her why. 'Well we've been looking at your life and how you don't really know what you want and then when you were speaking about being prime minister and getting rid of the traffic and I had a sense that for a moment you knew what you wanted.' I thought: That's not much use – I'm not going to be prime minister am I? I didn't say that though.

But I did get on with her more this week, in fact I felt more relaxed in the session this time and it was good to feel that she had been thinking about me in between our sessions. It made me feel as though she cared – which I wasn't so sure about before. In fact I haven't been feeling quite so empty, quite so often, since.

Some questions to consider

1 How do you respond to the phrase (in the 28 February passage) 'wanting to stop it all'? Are you aware of the sorts of signs that can indicate that someone is feeling suicidal? What would you do if you felt a client was exhibiting those signs?
2 What would you identify as the key therapeutic elements of this client's experience?
3 How might you go on to work with this client?
4 What would you take to supervision?
5 Is there anything you might take to your personal therapy?
6 What would your focus be in the next session with this client, and in the next 12 sessions?

Two exercises to explore the public and private aspects of your self

Your 'real' self and your 'false' self

Note down expressions that are used to describe our subjective experiences of ourselves to others. For example we might say to a friend or colleague: 'I wasn't feeling myself yesterday', 'I'm feeling like my old self again', 'I don't know *what* came over me.' When you have a list of expressions spend some time examining them together with examples of actual situations with others in which you have used them or they have been used with you.

Take some time to explore experiences where you feel you were interacting with others in a 'real' way. Continue with an exploration of examples of when you feel split – part 'real' and part 'pretending' or 'false'. Allow yourself a minute or two to exaggerate your 'false self' – this is how I really fake it!

- Are there times when you lose your sense of who you really are? If so, explore an example of that.
- What would it be like to be more 'real' more of the time?
- What prevents you and what might help you?

Review this exercise in your journal.

Two faces

You will require a mirror for this exercise.

Take a few minutes to reflect upon your 'public' aspect – the face you put on for people in general. You can draw this face if you like.

With your mirror:

1 Imagine that the face in the mirror is your public face and speak for five minutes about that face. Speak to the face directly.
2 Now imagine that your face in the mirror is your private face and spend five minutes speaking about your 'private' face – your hidden aspect. When your five minutes are up, stop and consider whether this is a more vulnerable and perhaps a more precious part of your self.

Review this exercise in your journal.

3

A Creative Way of Working with Internal Conflicts

What's in a name? That which we call a rose
By any other name would smell as sweet
(William Shakespeare, *Romeo and Juliet*, II, ii, 43–4 c. 1597)

The Freudian theory of the self, described by Belinda in the last chapter, is only one of many theories that try to understand and work with different aspects of the self in conflict with each other. In this chapter we will be exploring a creative approach to internal conflict.

Freud believed that sexual desire was the classic taboo area and therefore the classic area for the development of internal conflicts and, at the beginning of the century that may have been fairly true of certain sections of Western society. In our post-1960s society, however, taboos around sex have lessened and they are no longer 'the' source of internal conflict. In the modern world various forms of desire can be a source of internal conflict – we've all had experiences of internal conflicts between a broad range of our desires and their internal frustration and repression.

Here we continue to explore this theme but do so by focusing on a technique for working with internal conflict that has been developed by the counselling approach, called Gestalt. In Gestalt the emphasis is on enabling the client to identify his or her own theory of the different sides of his or herself. The Gestalt technique we will be exploring here works, very creatively, with whatever emerges within the client and does so in terms of the different aspects of the self and the associated internal conflicts.

What is internal conflict?

Although we've all had experiences of internal conflict we might not always be aware of it as 'internal conflict'. Sometimes we experience such conflict as a mental argument when, for example, we can't seem to make a decision, or are feeling pulled in different directions:

A: I love this dress.
B: It's far too expensive.
A: I could get it on credit – it wouldn't be that much each month.

B: Where would you wear it? It's a lot of money to pay for something that's hardly ever going to be used.

A: It would encourage me to go out more – that would be good for me.

B: You said something like that about those shoes you bought – they've hardly been out of the cupboard.

Most of us have had this type of mental argument in our heads at some time. Perhaps they weren't quite as clear-cut as this argument about the dress but, nevertheless, the example gives the flavour of this sort of relatively healthy internal conflict. On other occasions, however, internal conflict is more at the feeling level – different and opposing feelings that each take over for a period of time and then swing the other way (optimism: 'Yes I can do it, it is possible' followed by despair: 'It won't work. I'll never make it, I'm wasting my time'). Sometimes we can experience both feelings at the same time – a thoroughgoing mixed-up-ness.

Internal conflict will usually involve feelings at some level and can also take place between the thinking and feeling aspects of ourselves – between our head and our heart. This is another 'classic' area for internal conflict and is explored in many love stories.

In the example of the mental argument over the desire for the dress we could, for example, ask the person whether there were deeper, more hidden feelings that were symbolized by, or in some way associated with, the dress.

Romeo: I'm wondering what else the dress might mean to you?

Juliet: If I had bought the dress I would have felt beautiful . . . younger, perhaps . . . yes I would have felt young and beautiful – like I did before the divorce. Now I feel old and ugly, a waste of space, a broken bottle on the back shelf of life.

Romeo: That sounds really quite important.

Juliet: Yes, it feels it. I wish I'd bought it now.

Romeo: It also sounds as if the dress isn't as important as what it symbolizes – that to buy the dress is to buy back your sense of youth and beauty.

Juliet: Hmmm . . . of course – it's not the dress. I wouldn't have felt like that if I'd bought it. I didn't really want the dress, I wanted, want, to feel . . . alive again, young, attractive! But I don't, I feel quite old and ugly.

Thus, in this seemingly benign example of an argument in the head over whether to buy a dress or not, a deeper level of feeling and conflict is uncovered. The deeper conflict concerns a much deeper desire – to feel young and beautiful. Notice also that two aspects of the self are emerging – on the one side is the sense of the self as an 'old and ugly' woman and on the other a lost 'young and beautiful' woman. Two very different self-images and self-experiences – one desired (perhaps loved – as was the dress) and the other unwanted (perhaps unloved):

> 'I love this dress' – joyful, warm, sparkly, fun-loving part of the self. 'It's far too expensive' – disapproving, cold, strict, not fun-loving part.

The feelings might then be explored further, the conflict made more explicit and, in the process, worked on and worked through. This opposition between two different aspects of the self, two different experiences of self – lies just below the surface of this internal argument. In therapeutic counselling it's possible to work more directly with this kind of opposition – to work with the different 'sides' of the self. If you are going to do this, however, you do need to approach the work very responsibly – checking with the client, for example, whether or not it feels right to them, that it's making sense and that they feel they can stop the process if it gets too uncomfortable. Most importantly you really need to know yourself in this kind of way – you need to have done a lot of work on the different aspects of yourself and have worked through your internal conflicts. This is the first and most important step in being able to utilize this technique of working. Further, although some clients find this direct and creative way of working very easy and very valuable, others find it quite difficult and anxiety provoking. You therefore need to work with the technique both carefully and sensitively.

Important note: The following assumes that Romeo and Juliet have been working together for a sufficient period of time to develop a good working relationship.

Romeo: If you like we could try a therapeutic technique that you may find quite valuable. It involves taking up the different parts of yourself and giving them a voice. Not everyone finds it that easy, however, so it's important that you feel you can say stop if that's what you want – at any time during the process.

Juliet: I'm not sure what you mean – giving different parts of my self a voice?

Romeo: Yes, you might for example give voice to the 'young and beautiful' woman that the dress seemed to symbolize and also to the 'old and ugly' woman – the divorced woman. Or you might give more of a voice to the part of yourself that loved the dress together with the part that disapproved of the purchase.

Juliet: Why?

Romeo: Well clearly there is some kind of conflict between the latter two and there is a kind of conflict between the former – in that you like being the young and beautiful woman and don't like being the old and ugly one. By giving voice to these different aspects of yourself we may be able to make the conflict more explicit and then work to resolve it in some way, or at least make it more bearable.

Juliet: I still don't really know what you mean, but I'm willing to give
it a go, if you think it might help.

Romeo: OK. Before we start, however, I want to emphasize to you
again that not everyone finds it that easy and so it's important that
you understand that you can say stop at any time.

Further warning: The counsellor's use of this kind of direct and creative
technique for working with the self needs to be set within the context of
a well established client–counsellor relationship. It also has to be set
within the relationship in a more subtle way. Using a technique such as
this does imply a more directive approach on the part of the counsellor
and that may not sit well with other aspects of a particular counsellor's
approach. Well managed, well introduced and well integrated into the
relationship and the counsellor's approach as a whole, however, the
technique can prove very useful and valuable to a variety of clients. I
want to stress, once again, that for any counsellor to use this technique
with clients they must first have used it extensively on themselves – in
their own counselling and on training workshops on this specific
technique.

The essence of the technique is to enable the client to give value, voice
and attention to different aspects, or sides of themselves. How you help
to facilitate the client in gaining a sense of the different 'shapes' her self
takes up, and the associated conflicts that go on between the different
parts of themselves, is a key to the process. Two, usually opposing, parts
can often be identified by the client and the counsellor can help to move
the process forward by encouraging the two parts to 'dialogue'. Sometimes this can lead to a powerful sense of conflict reduction.

It must be said that just as certain clients find the technique difficult or
uncomfortable the same is true of counsellors. For those counsellors who
find themselves in this category I would suggest that it is worth sticking
with it a little – even if you decide not to use it in your work. Not only
can it provide a very clear sense of the self in conflict but it is also a
valuable method for developing your capacity for empathy.

Another problem many students can find at first is the difficulty in
'seeing' the opposing parts of the self within their client. I think the main
answer to this is to keep trying it out on yourself but you might also
find the metaphor of painting a picture useful. The artist starts with a
broad sketch in which the whole picture is mapped out in skeletal form.
In a similar way the counsellor, when using this technique, needs to be
able to sketch out, or help the client sketch out, a picture of the 'shape'
of the client's self. With that initial sketch the counsellor can help the
client to explore and test it out – to see if it is 'right' or 'wrong' at a
feeling level. You might also think of it as a special kind of listening – a
listening to the shape of the self – and then reflecting that back to the
client. Most of all you must remember that it should always be the client
who decides whether, and to what extent, the sketch feels right or not.

In our imaginary piece of client-work we have already seen this sketching process happening – two sketches in fact. The first is of the young beautiful woman and the old and ugly woman and the second is of the fun-loving and the disapproving sides of the client's self. Romeo might now seek to move the work forward by helping Juliet to explore and test out these sketches – how real do they feel to her and how can the two aspects of the self be brought together into some kind of dialogue?

Exercise

The next section will give you a greater feel for this technique. After reading it, try continuing this Romeo and Juliet client-work in role-play with a partner and observer.

Working with different aspects of the self

A client, Tim, has been mentally arguing with himself, over the past few days, about whether to continue a relationship with a friend. Part of him has found the friendship very valuable indeed and would like it to continue. Another part of him doesn't trust his friend, feels his friend may be gay, and attracted to him, and he doesn't want to see him again because of that.

Note: The client–counsellor relationship is already well advanced and the client has been helped, in the earlier part of the session, to identify two opposing sides to his self – one saying 'yes', the other 'no'. I, as the counsellor in the following passage, seek to help the client give voice to both of these parts of himself – allowing each part a fuller expression and space. Often it's good to give each part a name – I always ask the client for his or her suggestion. Tim named these two parts of himself 'Silly' (the yes part) and 'Strict' (the no part). It's also important to note that these names can, and perhaps should, change as the session progresses. I began by asking the client to give voice to the first of these parts of himself:

> Silly: Well I don't like being called silly at all. I have found the friendship with Peter very valuable. I don't care if he is gay and he is attracted to me – he's been very helpful. I like him a lot, too, and I trust him. I feel very frustrated by this whole argument and especially by the way Strict has taken over and is making the decisions. I don't see anything wrong with it at all. The best thing would be to go round and talk to him about it.

Note: When there is a natural conclusion to the voice – a rest, perhaps – it is then possible to facilitate the client in switching over and giving voice to the other part of their self – usually by actually moving to another chair. As the counsellor, I will usually ask the client whether now is a good time to switch.

> Strict: I don't want to see him at all. I don't trust him and I don't like him touching me – when we met up last time he gave me a head massage. I feel quite put off. I was OK about him before, but this last time I felt quite revolted by his touch. I definitely felt he was enjoying touching me in a sexual way and I didn't like it at all. I'm not going to see him again and that's that.

Note: There are two very strong and opposing views of this relationship. Two parts of the client's self are quite clearly in conflict with each other. As a counsellor there are two main ways I might seek to move the work forward. One is to explore these differing positions more closely and deeply, the other to help the client to develop a dialogue between the two parts of himself.

It doesn't always have to be a two-part dialogue – sometimes three (or even more) aspects of the self can be in the picture. A third aspect often needs to be facilitated to find a space and a voice – sometimes emerging during the dialoguing between two opposing parts (often as a very neglected and un-listened-to-part). Working with three voices can be very valuable. With this client a third voice did emerge – a voice for his 'body':

> Body: I loved the head massage – it felt very good, very caring, very relaxing. I want to go back to see him. I need to be cared for and he sees that. I feel very neglected, very uncared-for, very un-nurtured. I enjoyed his touch, it didn't feel 'abusive'. I felt very good afterwards – more alive, more open, more real.

Note: Finding this third voice – a voice for his body – felt crucial. It obviously gave a lot more weight to the 'yes' side of himself, but it's very important to value all parts of the self and not to allow two of them to gang up on the third, in this case the 'no' voice. That's essentially what unhealthy internal conflict is all about – different parts of the self ganging up on each other. We're not interested here in coming to a democratic decision. No, the aim is to develop a sense of clarity about what is going on inside the self and, ultimately, co-operation within the self. Co-operation in relation to this particular relationship but, much more importantly, in relation to the client's life in general – in other words a therapeutic rather than a problem-centred outcome.

Various thoughts and feelings came up for Tim after this dialoguing exercise and, as the counsellor, I will usually check out with my client how he or she is feeling. This is especially relevant towards the end of a session – making sure the client has plenty of time to come out of the exercise and explore any thoughts, feelings or insights that may have emerged.

Anthony: There seems to be quite a lot going on for you in the silence at the moment and I'm wondering if you'd like to talk about that – perhaps back in your 'normal' sense of self as Tim.

Tim: Yes, there is a lot. I've realized three things about myself – when I tried to give voice to a third part of myself I could feel there was something there but it was really difficult to hear that part of me. When I spoke as Tim's 'Body' the voice felt very faint at first but then grew a little stronger. It made me realize how much I neglect my body – how little value I give that part of myself. I already knew that, in my head as an idea, but giving voice to my body, and the difficulty in doing so, really brought it home to me. I also found it difficult to become my body, to speak from my body's view of the world – it was almost as if I couldn't find it. Overall, it feels like I'm really out of contact with my body.

Note: Perhaps it's worth focusing, for a moment, on this process of *becoming* different parts of the self. The core of this creative technique of working with internal conflict is to enable clients to become the various parts of themselves and give voice to those parts. Some people find this relatively easy from the start, others find it difficult at first, but get into it after a while. Other people just find it very difficult and get quite anxious and frustrated in the attempt. So the point of asking the client to 'give voice to' or to 'become' a particular aspect of themselves is a critical point in the process.

Becoming a different part of the self involves taking up a certain position in the world and viewing the world from that position – feeling what it might feel like and thinking the kinds of thoughts that might be thought from that viewpoint. The key is to allow yourself to be 'taken over' by that way of seeing and feeling the world. To do so you will need to let go of your 'normal' position and viewpoint.

Even if you, as a counsellor, find this a difficult technique to work with, perhaps you can see how valuable it might be in developing your empathic capacity – your ability to see and feel the world from another person's point of view. Empathy is clearly central to the capacities of the counsellor, but it's also important for the client to develop too. Social life is based around empathy – being able to see other people's points of view, especially when different from one's own.

For some people, however, the difficulty with the technique lies not so much in seeing the world from different points of view but in the whole process of seeing the world from different parts of the self. Becoming such a 'thing' proves very difficult for them. As a counsellor attempting to utilize this technique you need to be very sensitive to this issue.

Let us return to the session.

Anthony: You mentioned two other insights into yourself.

Tim: Yes – one was to do with that part of myself that I'd labelled 'Strict'. During the work I had a sense of how obstinate this part of myself can be and how powerful too – when he doesn't want to do something, or allow something, or disapproves of something, then that is very much that. He won't be budged at all. But more than that I also sensed why that might be. I feel it's because he feels very pushed into a corner by the rest of me – so he has to be very determined, very fixed – if he is going to be heard and taken notice of. For the first time in my life I could sense why that part of myself is so strict.

Anthony: That sounds like *quite* a realization for you.

Tim: Yes, it's like there's been a quite subtle, but important shift in my sense of myself – almost as if I've opened a door that I haven't noticed before, and I've seen myself in a new light. Seen the strict, obstinate part of myself in a . . . gentler way – it's like I've always been in rebellion with that part of myself but the rebellion may have just ended. Yes, it feels as though, if only I would rebel less and listen more to that part, then Strict wouldn't have to be so strict and unyielding. It feels quite odd to be saying this but, for the first time, I want to hear more from that part of myself, I want to find out more about why he is saying no and also how he sees the other aspects of myself. Normally I would either be being Strict or rebelling against him.

Anthony: How about if you become that part of yourself again then, and tell us more about how you, how Strict, sees the world and the other parts of yourself?

Tim: OK, I'd also like to move over there into that other chair.

Anthony: Go ahead.

Strict: Yes I do feel very isolated. In fact I feel quite alone with my view on things and it also feels very hard work as a result – really quite a struggle to keep the rest of you . . . *safe*. I was going to say 'in line' but it's not about keeping you in line – it's not rules for rules' sake – it's about looking after things, taking care, taking precautions, being cautious, being sensible. Yes it's about being sensible about things – and it really does feel like I'm the only person that is sensible around here.

Anthony: It sounds like you have some fairly strong views about these other parts of yourself.

Strict: Yes I bloody do – Silly in particular. He'd walk into the lions' den if he felt it would be an interesting experience. I named him 'Silly' by the way – when you asked for a name. I knew it would really wind him up and it did. He's bloody stupid about the most obvious of everyday things.

Anthony: I'm wondering what you'd say to him – directly – if you were to speak to him as if he was sitting here in this room. Do you think you could do that?

Strict: You mean imagine him sitting here?

Anthony: Yes, where would he be sitting?

Strict: Oh I don't know . . . he'd be sitting in an odd way, breaking some rule or other . . . yes he'd be sitting on the edge of the balcony over there . . . and I'd be worried all the time that he was about to fall off backwards and kill himself. He loves to do things just as *he* wants to, as if he didn't have a care in the world. That really annoys me – that really winds me up.

Anthony: So Silly is sitting over there on the balcony. What do you want to say to him, Strict?

Strict: I'm probably avoiding doing that, speaking to him directly that is, but I'd like to change my name – that's OK, isn't it? [Anthony nods.] I want to call myself . . . Sensible. Yes I have rules, but they are sensible rules and I'm only strict because I have to be with him.

Anthony: That sounds like an important change in the way you want to see yourself, and be seen by these other parts, these other internal characters. And, yes, you may also be avoiding speaking to him directly.

Note: Getting the different parts of the self to speak to each other directly can often lead to quite a release of feeling and, with it, insight and clarity with regard to the nature of the internal conflict. It's often a sticking point with a client, however – partly because it feels odd to be speaking to an imaginary character, but also because it can really open up the client's feelings and internal conflicts. This point in the process needs to be approached gently and with due regard to the need for a strong relationship, between client and counsellor, being in place and supporting the work as a whole.

Sensible: I don't like you sitting there, it makes me feel anxious. I feel you're just doing it to wind me up. In fact I don't really like talking to you – I don't really like you, there I've said it. You're always doing something stupid, something risky, something without really thinking about it at all – you don't look before you leap and you wind up in some awful situations as a result. And the worst thing of all is that I have to get you, us, out of those situations. I'm the one who always has to sort it all out – which is bloody hard work and I'd rather be doing something else. I can't trust you – if I turn my back you could be doing anything really stupid. That's why I have to be so strict with you and that's why it's me that keeps you under lock and key half the time. In fact more than half the time, most of the time. Yes, life is more boring, but at least it's not such hard work for me. I'm sick of clearing up after your messes – that's why I lock you away. You're a real pain, a selfish little creature.

Note: I now sought to facilitate an even stronger expression of emotion – a deeper release of pent-up feelings about this other part of the self.

Anthony: It feels to me as though there's a great deal of feeling here. If you were to allow yourself to express these feelings even more strongly, how would they come out?

Sensible: I'm not sure what you mean.

Anthony: Well you've just called that other part of you a 'real pain, a selfish little creature'. Try filling up those words – fill the words with the feelings associated with them, let the feelings out. It's OK here – you might even exaggerate the feelings a little.

Sensible: You're a right fucking pain you little fucking bastard. Why the fuck don't you grow up and fucking well think about things a little more.

[Silence]

Anthony: Wow! Some powerful feelings were allowed out for a moment then. Then I noticed that you seemed to dampen them down again.

Sensible: Yes . . . it's difficult.

Anthony: Just say if you want to stop?

Sensible: No, it felt good to let out some of my anger at him. Difficult, but it did feel good to express it. I'd like to try again.

Anthony: I noticed your fists were clenched when you were shouting at him. What would you do with your hands if you were free to do so?

Sensible: I'd fucking punch his head in, the little fucker. Punch some fucking sense into his stupid head.

Anthony: I don't know, but I was wondering, at that moment, whether you would actually like to knock him off the balcony.

Sensible: You're bloody right I would, I'd love to punch him right off the balcony. That would really feel . . . but I don't want to do that.

Anthony: Rather than cutting them off, what would it be like to exaggerate your feelings even more? It's OK *here* to be enraged and to have a fantasy of hurting this other part of yourself – it's a giant step between having the fantasy and actually carrying out a violent act against another person. In fact, I believe that violence is often the result of *not* allowing oneself to feel and express these kinds of feelings – they then get all pent up and finally get out of control and explode.

Note: At this point in the session I've intervened to give the client full permission to express whatever feelings he has, to have whatever thought or fantasy he has. We tend to have very powerful ways of repressing our feelings – especially our feelings of rage and hatred. It's very questionable, however, whether repressing our feelings reduces violence. It's certainly the quickest and most *obvious* solution, but as I've suggested to Tim here, repressing such strong feelings may actually increase their strength in the long run, until eventually they become uncontrollable and explode in a violent act – often targeted at someone weak and vulnerable who can't really defend themselves or retaliate.

We might also note how deep the conflict is actually becoming. At this moment we are no longer dealing with a simple argument but a self-destructive conflict. The original issue – of whether to see the friend again or not – has now receded and the content has very much become the pattern of this internal conflict. Tim and I are now working with an explicit, powerful, internal conflict in which one side of the self is enraged with another side. Rather than an argument between two sides of the self we are now looking at a war.

> Sensible: I'd punch, punch, punch his head in. I hate him, I hate him, I hate him. All I want him to do is fuck off. I'd love to chuck him off the balcony. I hate him so much.
>
> [Silence]
>
> Anthony: I don't know, but it looked like it was really good to get that off your chest. You seem more relaxed now.
>
> Sensible: I don't know about being relaxed, I still feel really angry with him. But yes I do feel . . . freer. It was certainly very good to shout at him. But I could keep on doing it.
>
> Anthony: OK.
>
> Sensible: I hate you, damn you, I hate, [screams] *hate, hate, you!*
>
> [Long silence]
>
> Sensible: I feel a bit depressed now. The problem is I've got to live with him, I can't get rid of him, I can't kill him, I can't avoid him. And that's really quite depressing. I feel so exhausted by it all, it's such a struggle and I never get any help – I only get hindrances. Right now I could give up and just let him get on with it. I feel quite down, quite despairing, quite hopeless.

Note: What is this work with Tim also saying about the nature of the self – how, for example, can we picture the self? Perhaps we each develop certain ways of organizing our subjective experience of the world. In the example we've been following, each of the client's characters is, in essence, an area of Tim's subjective experience. The aspect of himself that he called Sensible sees the world from a certain perspective – it's quite a rational part of himself whose main concern seems to be one of control and not letting things get into a mess. When Sensible is at the centre of Tim's consciousness certain perceptions and experiences are valued and included and others are devalued and excluded. This part, particularly as Strict, is very close to the Freudian concept of the super-ego but perhaps as Sensible this aspect is a little closer to Freud's concept of ego.

When Tim sees the world from Sensible's point of view he wants the world to make sense. Silly, sitting on the balcony, doesn't make sense from Sensible's point of view. Each aspect of Tim's self has certain likes and dislikes and certain aims associated with those motivations.

Through further exploration with Tim we might discover that Sensible likes to go in a straight line from A to B – to clear away anything in the way and to have things well organized and well planned out. We might also learn that Sensible likes everything to fit neatly together. Sensible wants to arrange everything so that the different elements all link together well – this leads to that, and everything functions smoothly and efficiently. Further exploration might also uncover that when Sensible manages to organize the world in this way he feels ordered, in control, clear and, most of all, *safe*. As we've just seen, Sensible is also a very angry part of Tim's self – perhaps protective of all his order and neatness. When that order becomes lost and he feels chaotic, then, as we saw in the last of his statements, he can become quite sad, hopeless and despairing. And, perhaps underneath that, *unsafe*. In the despair it's as if all he has worked and struggled for, all the order he has managed to create, has collapsed into chaos. All his efforts, therefore, are pointless.

I am describing all of this to you, but it arose through a series of counselling sessions. What we finally agreed was that once Tim can be clear about the needs of the Sensible part of himself (needs for order, control, making sense and feeling safe) he can also become clearer about asking for, and then beginning to meet, some of those needs. Tim also made sense of other personal experiences – for example, his ongoing sense of 'moving uphill' all the time, of always having to make an effort, to struggle. This is part of the subjective world of Sensible – a way of seeing and feeling and thinking and fantasizing about the world in which certain subjective experiences are included as OK and others are ignored or definitely excluded. Tim, and Sensible, finally came to see that the problem is that the world isn't organized as Sensible would like it to be and so it really is a struggle to try and organize it as he feels he needs it to be. He could see that the order he craves and seeks to create is always crumbling at the edges and sometimes at the centre too.

Much of that which is not contained in the world view of Sensible we found in the character of Silly. Sensible had excluded certain subjective experiences from his world but they couldn't be excluded from Tim's self as a whole. The self always consists of the totality of its subjective experiences – although many subjective thoughts and feelings may be kept well outside of a person's immediate consciousness by a dominant internal character such as Sensible.

Once again, let us return to the counselling.

Anthony: We've focused a lot on Sensible and that has, I believe, been very valuable but I'm wondering whether we could now hear from that part of you that's still sitting, precariously, on the balcony?

Tim: OK – do you want me to actually sit on the balcony and become him?

Anthony: How about just leaning against the balcony?

Silly: The first thing is I'm not willing to be called 'Silly' – I find that quite an offensive name and he has admitted to choosing it simply to wind me up.

Anthony: OK, what would you like to call yourself?

Silly: Extrovert, or vivacious, or life-loving or experimental or artistic or sensual or colourful or . . . I'm not sure any single name quite feels right. . . but maybe I'll give Sensual a try – yes, I like the fact that it sounds very similar to Sensible but means something very different.

Anthony: OK 'Sensual' it is – for the moment at least!

Sensual: I feel quite artistic, quite sensual, in a *gay* kind of way – you know, those gay artist types who kind of dance with their hands, sensually [moves his hands in a circle]. I feel a bit like that at the moment. I don't actually find myself attracted to Peter or to men in general. I'm probably just saying that I'm feeling gay to wind up Mr Sensible over there – he's a bit of a you know what, I forget the word . . . I enjoy life, I *need* to enjoy life, and before the great Master over there took control of everything I did enjoy life. Now I just sit around under lock and key – as he put it. I need to enjoy painting, dance, music, writing poetry, travelling without any particular goal in mind. Just enjoying. Oh it was lovely – when I had 'control' of Tim. Control isn't the right word – that's his word. When I was *free* – yes that's a much better word.

Anthony: When you were free?

Sensual: Yes, I didn't need to be kept all locked up by him over there. It all stopped about 10 to 12 years ago. Things, my life, had got into a bit of a mess, it's true, but he basically stormed in, locked me up and took over the place. I get let out occasionally, but under close supervision, you might say. I don't feel it was my fault that life had got into such a mess though. It just got into a mess – life is messy sometimes, life creates disorder with the unexpected and the unforeseen.

Anthony: Tell me more about you.

Sensual: I love life – what more is there to say? I love beautiful places, I love meals with friends and interesting people, I love sex, I love to dance. I used to dance a lot. Since he took over I must have danced about three times in the last ten years. He's absolutely terrified of me. . . I suddenly realized that – he is absolutely terrified of me. He's angry with me, but he's also terrified of me.

Anthony: It feels as though something important happened for you at that moment. You stopped quite still.

Sensual: Yes. I suddenly thought that if he is terrified of me then maybe, maybe, I can just, well, not let him lock me up. That I'm not as imprisoned as I've come to believe.

Anthony: And if you weren't in prison, if you weren't locked up, what would life be like?

Sensual: Mmmm . . . I don't know. I've changed, over the past 10 or 12 years, matured. What would life be like?

[Silence]

Anthony: Perhaps it would help if you imagined you were free right now. What would it feel like? What would you do? What would you want? What would you need? What would life look like? What would be important to you?

Sensual: If I was free right now . . . I would feel tired – it's late and I feel tired but also he's been driving things, work, life, far too hard and I feel very tired from all of that. I'd want to rest, to slow down, to recover. I feel as though I'm fading, wearing out, growing old. I wouldn't feel very vivacious. For a while I wouldn't want to do much. I'd relax, recover, rejuvenate. I'd want to do some painting, some dancing, creative things. I'd want to spend time with friends, people I enjoy being with, my girls, my partner, just enjoy life with them for a while. A lot of what he feels is important, mainly work, wouldn't seem very important to me.

Anthony: It feels to me that this is a very crucial area of work and something that we need to focus on – perhaps in our next session. It's nearly time for us to stop, however. Is there anything you need to say or do to come out of this exercise and get ready to go back into the world out there?

Tim: Yes, I would like to focus on this next time. It does feel very important. It's certainly given me a lot to think about and I don't feel particularly finished. But I'm OK to finish now – thank you.

Questions

1　How do you imagine this work might continue?
2　How would you work with Tim?
3　What might your aim be?

Working with the imagination – an extension of the technique

Extract from a session with a long-term client in which the client explores an imaginary room:

Fritz: Hi, Paresh, it's good to see you . . . How would you like to use this session?

Paresh: I want to explore the feeling that, at heart, I'm deeply unhappy. It's something that arose during the week since last session and feels really . . . at my core, at my essence.

Fritz: That your essence is one of deep unhappiness?

Paresh: Yes. It's there, if I look into myself, this deep sense of sadness and despair and it feels like my life is just a way of avoiding that feeling. It's like my life is all designed around *not* feeling that . . . feeling of being very, very miserable. Not miserable – as in sorry for myself. More like, not taken account of, yes never taken account of. It's like I live my life around myself, never actually being in touch with my core – because my core is so miserable and unhappy. Because it's so miserable and unhappy I never acknowledge it, never listen to it, never give space or expression to it. It, I, live in this room inside myself, alone in the world, alone even from myself. 'It will never end!' – that's what I believe at my core, it will always be like this, I'm trapped for ever, alone and unhappy.

Fritz: That sounds pretty awful.

Paresh: It is, although it's also difficult for me to acknowledge that. This feeling rose up, or I sank into it, but it's also quite difficult to stay with it. All the time I want to be somewhere else, doing something to distract myself from feeling who I am – a very unhappy person out of touch with myself and tossed as a result, by the winds of life from here to there.

[Long heavy silence]

Fritz: I'm not sure what to say, Paresh.

Paresh: You don't have to say anything, Fritz, I'd just like you to try and help me to get in contact with myself. It feels really important that I open that inner door and find myself, that I stop locking the door or ignoring what is, and instead . . . go there . . . go into the room – because that's where I am. Lonely, miserable, unhappy – that's very uncomfortable and it is awful, but it's me. But it's also like I'm saying these words but that's not enough – it's like the words aren't connected into me, they're not rooted in my experience. I'm in the lonely room of despair.

Fritz: I'm wondering if you'd like to take up a chair in that lonely room – as we've done before in relation to other parts of yourself. How does that sound?

Paresh: It sounds a good idea, but a difficult one . . . OK.

[He moves to another chair in the counselling room.]

Paresh: I'm the person in the lonely room. It's very difficult . . . I'm so alone, so very alone. There was a rage there for a moment, like an earthquake in the room and then it was gone. Covered over, I guess? My eyes are blank, dead. There's a voice saying 'This is stupid to be doing this.' But it's not stupid, it's the first really sane thing I've done, or that's what it also feels like.

Fritz: You're alone in the room?

Paresh: Yes, the room is utterly isolated, it's curved around – there's no point of entry or exit. It's like an oval ball, a shell. Nothing comes in and nothing goes out.

Fritz: And in the room?

Paresh: In the room . . . [puts his left hand over his eyes]. In the room I'm safe. That's the good feeling, that's why I'm here. Because I feel safe. Nothing can disturb me, nothing can interrupt me, nothing can . . . ruin everything . . . tear everything apart . . . yes, it's like without the room – or perhaps before the room – there was a moment there of a memory of destruction and pain and blood, like arms ripped off, no like . . . no I don't know . . . an image of living roots, like an arm, cut off and bleeding to death. I once wrote a poem about something like that.

Fritz: So you live in the room to avoid this horror?

Paresh: I think so. But, although I'm safe, I'm also very alone and very unhappy – and it's difficult for me to stay with that. Easier to stay with the image of destruction. Look, just then . . . I just wanted to get up and leave, go to the toilet or something.

Fritz: And if you don't leave?

Paresh: Masturbate, I thought about masturbating – I thought about how nice it would be to masturbate – later on that is, not right now.

Fritz: I'm wondering who you'd masturbate about?

Paresh: [silence] I don't know. I'm in the room, I'm feeling lonely, I'm feeling a bit churned up, a bit sick, like I'm really drunk and reeling around . . . [silence] Rina, I'd masturbate about her. Rina was the first girl I was infatuated with – when I was 12 or 13. Yes, she was completely unavailable, or so it seemed to me then . . . Suddenly I felt this deep hope and yearning, no that's not quite right. I felt she was in the room with me and that felt . . . it's very difficult, my mind keeps wandering off.

Fritz: Rina is in the room with you.

Paresh: It feels like I would just be intensely happy, it's difficult to let myself feel that feeling but that's something of what it would be like. Like this gorgeous, unbelievably beautiful, attractive girl – she was a year or so older than me – is there, and she's with me, I can touch her, worship her . . .

Fritz: Stay with it Paresh, stay with it.

Paresh: The room seems to explode, fragment and I'm with her out in the world. Walking with her, playing with her, in bed with her, on holiday with her, at the fairground with her, on the big wheel. But then it fades, turns unreal and grey and I'm back in the room alone. Alone and deathly. Miserable and safe.

Fritz: Can you stay at the fairground with her, Paresh?

Paresh: I'm sitting in the big wheel with her, she's gorgeous, everything I dream of, just to be with her is to be . . . so happy. I want to caress her, kiss her feet, hold her hand, look at her eyes. Love her. We are so happy, I feel as if I'm flying with happiness. My heart's in my mouth . . . And then, suddenly, I smack her face . . . and she turns to stone . . . and the world is all cold and grey and stormy and I hate it, the world, I hate everything and everyone. And I feel really frightened.

Fritz: It sounds like a lot more is contained in that imagery. You're flying with happiness, your heart's in your mouth and then suddenly you hit her in the face, she turns to stone and the world becomes a grey, frightening and hated place. I'm wondering if we can slow that sequence down – to try and discover whether something more is happening in that 'suddenly' moment?

Paresh: OK Fritz, I'll try . . . I'm sitting with her at the fairground – on the big wheel again. I'm so happy, then something seems to leak into the image . . . blood, like a wound, and I don't want her to see it, so I knock her out. It's like I'm really, really terrified that she'll see this . . . whatever it is.

Fritz: Try going through that sequence again, Paresh.

Paresh: OK, I'm in the big wheel, I'm so happy to be with her. . . [silence] . . . but I'm hiding who I really am, or there's another part of me that hates her. Yes, an aspect of me is utterly infatuated with her, but another part of me . . . the part that hides in the corners. . . that part of me is sitting there with her, hating everything about her [silence]. This feels really important, Fritz.

Fritz: Yes I think you are right, Paresh, and I'm also wondering whether it's because of this hating part that you are hiding in the lonely room. Perhaps you could become that part of yourself?

Paresh: You mean I'm afraid that he will appear and ruin things, ruin my happiness, so I avoid being happy in order to avoid myself destroying that happiness.

Fritz: Just a thought, that's all. Can you become that hating part?

Paresh: I'll try . . . [He takes up another chair and settles for a minute or so.] I'm sitting in the big wheel and the Idiot is just doting over her, he'd be her slave if she'd have him, I'm looking at her and thinking 'pretty little bitch' and I want to throw her out of the seat. I really hate her. He's fallen head over heels in love, and I hate her for it.

Fritz: Can you tell me more about why you hate her?

Paresh: Why do I hate her? Because of the power she has over him. Because she's a bitch – she doesn't care about him, she only cares about being pretty and being doted on, that's what she likes – being treated in the way he's treating her. She'll use him, then abuse him. She'll shit on his face. Yes, just like I'm hiding behind 'Good old Paresh', there's a part of her that's hiding behind 'Miss Beautiful' – but she's not, she's a real bitch that just loves to hang him on the end of her finger and then flick him off, like a bit of snot.

Fritz: So she's a kind of mirror of you?

Paresh: In a sense, yes. But she's got the power, she's the one being doted on.

Fritz: This is a very powerful image, Paresh, I feel it needs absorbing in some way. I've also been wondering about the wheel. Perhaps the big wheel is also an important part of the picture here – could you become the big wheel too?

Paresh: I'll give it a go [changes seats again]. You know I always find it difficult to imagine being things rather than people . . . I'm going round and round, I'm full of people, not just couples, brothers and sisters, colleagues at work, all kinds of relationships, yes, it's like in every seat there's a whole microcosm of relationships. I just go round and round. No one gets off, no one gets on. Well, only occasionally. All of them, all the people have these two sides to themselves and they're all playing this kind of hide-and-seek game – now you find me, now you don't, now I love you, now I don't. Oh look at my pretty face, here's a smash in the teeth. It's very confusing, very repetitive and very pointless. You know something, I feel like I'm the Great Wheel of Karma – I don't suppose you'd know about that – it's something from my religion.

Fritz: I think I've come across it, Paresh. Is there anything else you can discover about being this Great Wheel of Karma?

Paresh: Yes, I feel like I'm all rusty and creaking, I feel like I'm a worn-out wheel and I could just collapse into a pile of rusty metal. Either that or just screech to a halt. I can't be bothered any more – I just go round and around and nothing ever changes. They all keep on playing the same old games – I feel like I just don't want to bother with it anymore, I want to fall down.

Fritz: And if you do?

Paresh: [relaxes into the chair] That feels really . . . peaceful. I just want to be here for a long time . . . and rest. I feel so tired going round and around. . . [silence] . . . Now I have the image of a bright new wheel going faster and faster and faster until it's spinning around so fast that it makes me really, really dizzy. It's like I'm whizzing round and all of the people in the seats in their different worlds are whizzing about too. Like a speeded-up movie. And if you'd put your finger into it, to stop it spinning, it would just chop it off.

Fritz: It feels to me there's just loads here in this waking dream work but I'm wondering what you'd like to focus on for the final part of our session, Paresh?

Paresh: I think I'd like to go back to the lonely room, it feels important to keep staying with that part of myself. I'd also like to see whether this work we've been doing today has changed anything for that lonely, despairing aspect of myself.

Fritz: OK Paresh, why don't you take up that chair again and become the lonely and despairing man in the oval room?

Paresh: I'm in the room . . . I don't feel as unhappy as I did. I can remember how happy I felt in the big wheel with Rina. I can feel that and it brings a smile to my face. I can also see that there might be some truth in what that hating part of me was saying, that there is a not-so-nice side to Rina and that she could be cruel to me, she could reject me! Wow!! A door suddenly appeared in the room – not an open door but a door in the wall. It appeared just when I was thinking that . . . Just because she has this other side to her it doesn't mean she is hateful. I can see both sides to her and seeing both sides to her like that, together, she doesn't seem so bad, but neither does she seem so magnetically attractive – like some kind of goddess – and neither is she someone to despise. Yes, I'm in the room and there's a door in the room now but I don't feel any great urge to rush over and open the door. Still, it's quite nice to feel that it's there, that I'm not so alone and isolated [silence]. Now I'm sitting in the room and it seems to grow old and then new again, like the big wheel, old and faded and then rejuvenated. And now it feels like quite a 'living room'. As if the room itself is alive in some way. Humming, or even beating, like a heart. I don't mind being in this room . . . and I don't feel so alone . . . it's like I'm *with* the room. . . [silence] I think I'd like to stop now.

Fritz: It does really feel like you've been through quite an intensive piece of work today. We only have a few minutes left. I suggest that you use this time to fully come back from this visualization?

Paresh: Sure . . . shall I get back into my original chair?

How might you have worked with Juliet and Tim using the extension of this technique for working with internal conflict?

Three exercises to explore your internal conflicts

Creating a psychological dialogue

In the previous personal development exercise (at the end of the last chapter) on 'two faces' the idea was to experience a basic *division* within the self – between your 'public' and 'private' faces. The aim of this exercise is to help you experience the creation of a psychological *dialogue* between two sides of a psychological division.

Note: not all students find this very comfortable – don't push!

Freud described dreams as 'the royal road' to the unconscious. Dreams are like picture stories. If you can remember a dream then you might use it in this exercise. If not, this first part is designed to help you come up with a kind of dream-image.

Part 1 You could set about this by literally painting a picture 'without thinking about it'. Easier, perhaps, is to paint a picture with words –

again 'without thinking about it'. The 'without thinking about it' is, for most of us, the difficult bit. To help you *not* think about it, write quickly, don't stop and don't judge what comes into your mind. Simply write whatever thoughts, feeling and images arise. Write in this fashion for two minutes starting with the phrase 'In the picture I see . . .'

Part 2   Stop and read through what you've written. Ask yourself, 'What element stands out for me here?' and note it down. Now ask yourself, 'What element is least noticeable here?' and note it down.

Part 3   Put out two 'dialogue chairs'. Sit in one and, as you do so, *become* the first element (the one that stands out). Imagine the other element in the other chair (the one that was least noticeable) and 'react' to it – with words, feelings, movements. Change over and become the other element and 'react' back. Work to help yourself create a dialogue between the two elements of the picture, using these reversals. If you get stuck, or it seems to 'run out', then allow yourself to be creative, allow yourself to play around – imagine, for example, that you're the chair and ask yourself-as-the-chair what it's like to have this 'element' sitting on you.

After spending some time dialoguing in this way, put a chair in the centre, sit in this chair and feel what it might be like to be in the centre of these two elements of your picture.

Finally ask yourself, 'What quality is within me, without which I would no longer be the person I take myself to be?' Answer without thinking.

Review this exercise in your journal.

The divided self: learning to trust, and value, the 'non-verbal' side of yourself

That which we usually identify to be ourselves, that which we usually experience in our everyday habits of thought and attention – the verbal and 'real world' side of ourselves – may shadow important sides of ourselves that also need our attention.

This exercise asks you to begin a process of learning to trust the non-verbal side of yourself by shifting your everyday habit of attention away from the 'real world' verbal side of yourself towards the other, less acknowledged, non-verbal side of your self. Through giving attention and value to the non-verbal you may gain important insights or even feel more at home in yourself.

One way of thinking about the exercise is that perhaps you can allow yourself to have two ways of seeing the world and that one view doesn't have to negate the other, even when they appear to be very different. Two (brain) hemispheres are better than one! We all yearn for a sense of wholeness, often looking for that which is missing in ourselves in another person – for example in our marital partner, our children or in our heroes and heroines.

What sense do you make of the above paragraphs? What value do you give to the non-verbal side of yourself? If you do give that part of yourself value sometimes, what is that like? How does the 'everyday' verbal side of yourself view the prospect of allowing the non-verbal side of yourself the light of attention?

There is a paradox in trying to converse with your non-verbal self – you will need to focus on feelings, imagery, intuitions and bodily sensations for the next two parts of the exercise.

1   Think of a decision you need to make or a problem you currently have and need to sort out. See if you can ask your 'non-verbal' self to make that decision or sort out that problem.
2   What would your non-verbal sense of self really like to do with your life now? Give your non-verbal sense of self full permission (for a few minutes) to take control of how you perceive yourself and your life.

Review this exercise in your journal.

The divided self: exploring your non-verbal ways of knowing

Explore your non-verbal ways of knowing using the following as a guide:

•   What's it like to be a body, here and now?
•   Take hold of your right hand in your left hand, for a minute or two, and describe the experience of that right hand being held in your other hand. Reverse this and take hold of your left hand in your right hand for a minute or two and describe the experience of your left hand being held by your other hand. Explore the subjective difference between your right and your left and between physically holding the other (hand) and being physically held by the other (hand).
•   What is your intuitive sense of the atmosphere of each side of yourself?
•   Allow yourself to follow your non-verbal ways of knowing by repeatedly finishing the following phrase – 'Non-verbally I feel/ sense/intuit . . .'
•   What do you tend to not be very aware of, or not give value to, in your non-verbal ways of knowing?

Review this exercise in your journal.

4

The Repeating Past

The greatest suffering is not to know that one is suffering. (Anon)

I am growing old!

> Anthony: I'm growing old. Moving from youth to middle age. Middle age! I have studied the life stages in developmental psychology books. According to these theories each stage in a person's life has its themes and special issues, its particular challenges and problems. But the books didn't really tell me what it's like, what it's like inside, subjectively. They didn't take me into the experience but instead remained very much at a distance – an 'objective' perspective on it all. So, in all honesty, they haven't really been much use. Not much use in terms of my work with clients and their experience and not much use for me in the challenge I'm facing in growing older and leaving behind my youth – becoming a middle-aged man. A middle-aged man!

A few weeks ago I said to my therapist 'I don't want to grow old.' He replied: 'You've got a problem then.'

I felt angry with my readers for a moment then. Why? Because I have spent the last decade working too hard – working too hard for 'you'. Working to establish myself in my career – so that I can sit here writing a book about this crazy business called counselling. I have done it well, I have indeed established my career, but at what price? Then, when it hasn't been my career, it's been my family. Notice how they come second in this – not a good sign – you shouldn't be that impressed with that. Anyway, the point I want to make is that I haven't had time for me – it's been either 'you' or my family and I've been lost in the process.

What's worse is that before all this work was a decade of confusion and messing things up – I didn't really know who I was or what I wanted. Sure I wanted to travel, and I wanted a good time, and I loved music and dancing, and I loved studying, and I did a great deal of all of that. It was exciting and interesting but it wasn't how I'd do it now – if I could go back and do it all again. I ruined so much! I made such stupid choices – in terms of relationships and other areas of my life. I really didn't know who I was, so it was difficult to know what I really wanted. Then before that decade of my twenties I was basically a kid –

which doesn't quite count because I knew even less about who I was or what I wanted, and even if I had known, I wouldn't have been able to do much about it.

Now, however, I do have a much better idea of who I am and what I want – partly because I've been in years of therapy trying to work me out (I'm very grateful for that – that's been a really good bit) and partly also because I am getting older (and hopefully wiser). The problem now, however, is that, just when I'm beginning to really feel that I have some idea of who I am and what I want from my life, I'm entering middle age – which feels a bit too late! Perhaps it isn't actually too late, but it can really feel like it is. Sometimes I even catch myself feeling jealous of someone younger than me, someone who has their life before them. I kind of know they, like me, aren't going to 'get it right' until they've first got it wrong and that actually gives me a kind of comfort (which I feel guilty about – 'You shouldn't feel comfort in someone else's suffering!'). But I have still thought, 'If only I had their youth, what I could do!'

Whereas here, as I enter my middle age and the grey hairs begin to appear, I feel so tied up by responsibilities – of career and family – that it seems I hardly have an inch for me. Tied up, that's what I feel, it's like I am beginning to know who I am and what I want and I'm tied up – prevented from doing it. Then, even if I wasn't tied up, I'm getting too old to do it. That's what it feels like – entering the middle stage of the life cycle. That's what it feels like to me in my despairing mood tonight.

Time for bed, I think.

The Russian doll

> Anthony: So you can see that this second perspective, working with personal history, is based on the concepts of change and repetition. Certain psychologically important events shape a person's self and their pattern of relating which then shapes future perceptions, actions and relationships. A useful image here is a Russian doll – open up the top doll and you find a smaller copy of the original. Open that and you find a third copy, and then another and then another. In the same way a client can be helped to discover, for themselves, that their current problem has been shaped by a past experience – that it is a repetition of a past situation – which itself was shaped by an earlier situation, and so on. Does anyone have any comments or questions?
>
> Jane: It all sounds very deterministic, like we are all inevitably bound to repeat things – that we are stuck with things as they are and always will be.
>
> Henry: Yes, I don't really like this idea – that I'm just repeating things over and over. It doesn't feel real – life is different, has been very

different, has changed very dramatically for me, I don't feel I've been repeating life at all. Maybe rats or pigeons go on repeating the same things over and over, maybe they're forced by their genes to do this or that, maybe they have no choices to speak of, but human beings are different, they have free will, can make choices – that's what makes us human, isn't it?

Anthony: You're right that this working perspective does assume a kind of fate – that we are forced by the past to repeat, that there's no free will in the normal meaning of that term, that we can't really make choices. At first sight that may seem to be blatantly wrong – we all make lots of choices every day, we all feel we have a great deal of freedom to shape our lives. We are not, for example, feudal serfs tied to the land, we don't live in a society where other people decide who we shall marry or what work we'll do. We are much freer than some people living in other societies or at other periods in human history. What the theory is saying, however, is that we are shaped not by people around us making decisions for us but by the very processes by which we make our choices – that our perceptions and decision-making processes are shaped by the past. That history repeats itself – not in the sense of the same events but in terms of underlying psychological events.

Let me give you an example. I grew up with a bossy older sister and developed certain patterns of relating to her that in later life repeated themselves with any other woman who reminded me of my sister. In fact, at certain moments, I would be reminded of my sister by all the women that I knew, including my two little girls! And I still am. My partner reminds me of my sister sometimes and I react to her as if she was my sister. Nowadays, however – and this is the hopeful bit, the point of this working perspective – I can catch myself doing this. I notice that I'm reacting to her as if she was my older sister and I can then stop. I can untangle my partner from my sister – *I untangle the present from the past*. This simple activity now makes a huge difference to our relationship.

Belinda: What do you mean, a huge difference?

Anthony: Obviously you haven't lived with a bossy sister, five years older than yourself. When she wasn't being bossy she could be quite nice, but when she was bossing me about I used to get very frustrated with her, I used to feel trapped by her, almost claustrophobic, and I used to get *very* angry with her. It's like I felt I could always be invaded – it felt as if I didn't have my space because she could always come in and have a go at me. I used to get very enraged with her, very defensive and also very withdrawn – I'd storm off and barricade myself in my room. So when Josephine – my partner – would boss me about in a way that reminded me of my sister I would either blow up at her or storm out of the house. I used to do that – storm off down the road –

sometimes for a couple of hours. Or I'd start shouting and swearing at her – which was not at all pleasant for her, or us.

Jane: You say that you used to be like that but that you changed? That you're not repeating the past in the same way?

Anthony: Yes, in comparison to a number of years ago, I hardly ever get into that kind of situation with her any more. I still feel it sometimes, and sometimes I blow up a little, or even storm off for a moment. But nowadays it generally only lasts a moment or so. It's like I used to be unconsciously driven to sometimes see and react to her as my big sister but nowadays I'm almost unconsciously driven to untangle her from my sister – in other words the repeated untangling of Josephine from my sister has become a habit . . . Or perhaps even a skill and, like riding a bicycle, after a while you just don't notice that you are riding it, you do it unconsciously.

Henry: So what are you saying is that you developed certain skills in relation to your sister that helped you to deal with her and now you have learnt a kind of unlearning skill?

Anthony: That's pretty good, Henry, I'm impressed.

Henry: But I still don't see that as meaning that we are determined, that we have no free will, that life is an endless series of psychological repeats – like those awful Sunday afternoon B movies that keep appearing. I choose not to watch them, I do something I want to do.

Anthony: Unfortunately, or rather fortunately, life is not like TV – you can't switch channels if you don't like the programme. That's what we all try and do, it's true. It's painful, let's switch it off. But all we do then is make that pain unconscious – we repress it out of consciousness, but it's still playing. Actually this is the reason, in essence, why we are so determined by the past. Unconscious pain, unconscious desire and unconscious stories continue to be played again and again because they haven't been allowed to resolve themselves. I repress my grief but it doesn't go away. When I come across something that makes me sad, 'pop!' off comes the top of Pandora's box and 'What the hell?' I'm overwhelmed by this grief and it doesn't make sense because the present loss just doesn't deserve this kind of grief. So then I develop subtle and clever ways of avoiding getting into any situation where the top will come off – I try to avoid getting into any situation where I might be sad.

Amanda: Oh God! That sounds just like me . . . Whenever I get into a situation like that I can't stop, I just get really tearful. It's awful. I've always thought that it was because I was just too sensitive, that I was the kind of person who is easily rejected, easily upset, I never thought that it might be because of some unresolved sadness. My mother died when I was 17 – that just popped into my head – but it just seemed really important. Oh God, what a thought – my whole life driven by unresolved grief for my mother. I feel quite . . .

almost stunned, like this is it. Like my whole life. My God! [Silence in the group] This is really intense. I don't know if I can cope with this . . . [stumbles out of the room]

[The group sits still and silent. There is a sense of a great deal going on in the silence. Some are sunk into themselves, others fidget nervously, Anthony looks blankly at the floor.]

Jane: I hate this – when you all just sit here when someone gets upset. I'm going after Amanda. It's awful. Bloody hell, Anthony! [Jane runs out after Amanda.]

[After a few minutes]:

Anthony: Linking the present with the past can be of great therapeutic benefit . . .

Paresh: [interrupts] I'm going to see if Amanda is OK. I can't carry on with the seminar like this. [Paresh gets up, takes his briefcase, and leaves the room.]

Anthony: As I was saying, as the counsellor you can help the client to link present and past and this can be of great therapeutic benefit, although this is only the first step in this working perspective. Does anyone have any questions?

[Silence]

Henry: I'd like to hear from Amanda, but I guess we will have to wait for this afternoon.

Anthony: Yes, I look forward to hearing from Amanda, if she is willing and able to share her experience with us in the next session.

Belinda: I'm wondering what I would do if my client broke down and left the room. Maybe I'd follow her . . . but maybe that would feel quite overwhelming. Like I wasn't listening to her, like she wanted to be by herself and wanted to be left alone. I wouldn't want my counsellor to come out after me. I'd want her to wait though, at least until the end of the session.

Anthony: And we have reached the end of the session. I'll see you all after lunch.

Extract from Amanda's journal

Last Thursday was a very, very intense course day for me. We'd been listening to Anthony explaining about working with personal history and then he opened up the seminar to a general discussion. I was listening to the discussion and then Anthony was giving an example from his own life. Something about his sister and his partner. He started talking about loss and how we can put something, some terrible experience, in a kind of psychological safe deposit box only it gets opened up by similar experiences in the future. But at that time we don't know it – we don't realize that the experience in the present is linked to the one in the past. Then it suddenly struck me, I felt quite stunned, like a rabbit in the headlights of an oncoming car. It was awful seeing my life like that. I was saying 'oh God, that's just like me', I saw my life, all my decisions, all my choices dominated by my mother's death. I was 17 when she killed herself and I've realized over the last few days that I never really grieved for her. It happened so quickly. One day she was there, the next she wasn't, then the funeral was over in no time at all. Dad was in a state, I had to look after him, and my little sister, she was devastated. I never really had a chance to grieve for her at the time. I was looking after other people. Nobody was looking after me.

We looked at the process of grieving at the end of last year. I looked back through my notes on Worden's tasks of grieving: accept the reality of the loss, experience the pain of loss – I realize now that I never really did that. I put my pain in a safe deposit box somewhere inside myself and left it there, and my life has been shadowed by that pain ever since. I saw it all last Thursday sitting there in the group – how I could never cope with any kind of rejection from my friends, how breaking up with a boyfriend would absolutely devastate me. So I'd do anything to avoid that, I'd put up with so much from them – just to avoid the pain of breaking up. I also saw that, although I didn't realize it at the time, I settled on Jim mainly because I knew he wouldn't reject me – one thing I could be sure about Jim was that he wouldn't leave me. I remember talking about that to my friend Annie before Jim and I got married. How Jim was perfect – because he was so solid and reliable. That's what I wanted, or so I thought at the time.

Sitting there last Thursday I saw that I chose Jim for the wrong reason, I chose him because I couldn't deal with being rejected, because I had never had a chance to grieve for my mother. I was, how did Anthony put it, driven to make that choice by the past.

We've been married now for 13 years and he has proved to be solid and reliable. We have two beautiful (well, some of the time at least) children and life has been, well, OK. I realized quite soon after we were married that Jim wasn't quite the perfect person I had thought him to be. Yes, he was solid and reliable but along with that he was also pretty boring. There's not a great deal that we actually have in common and, in all honesty, I don't really enjoy being in bed with him. Or out of bed, for that matter. But there was no way I was going to break up. I can see that I was just too terrified to face 'loss', not loss of Jim, but the feeling of loss inside me. Then came the kids and well, I got caught up in them and Jim seemed less important then. Right now, though, I feel very sad, quite despairing – that it's been like this. That my life has turned out this way, that I didn't work through my mother's suicide, that I chose Jim, that I had my children with someone that I didn't really love. Yes I feel quite despairing. At the end of Thursday I spoke with Anthony for a minute or two. He suggested it was time for me to find a counsellor and gave me a list. I think it's time too, I think it was time when

I was 17 – but counsellors weren't so available then. It's late but I guess it's better than if I was 68, not 38.

It feels strange to have made this decision – 'I'm going to find myself a counsellor.' I knew I would have to some time – for my training – but it was always 'later', not now. What shall I say? What if I don't like her, or him? Could I reject a counsellor I didn't feel I could really work with? What, on the other hand, if I really like them, if she, yes, that's important, I feel I want a woman counsellor, what if I really like her? We looked at the client–counsellor relationship in last term's course unit on interpersonal relationships. How, in longer-term work, it's important that the counsellor becomes significant for the client, and to some extent, the other way round. How, if such a relationship is established, then the ending of the counselling can be an opportunity to work through feelings about endings in general. What a thought – it didn't make that much sense to me at the time but it does now. If she did become really important for me then ending the counselling would be really difficult. I can see that it would be a very powerful experience – evoking the loss of my mother. Pheww!! I don't know if this is going to be very easy at all – this counselling. And what of Jim? It's not true that I don't love him. There are things I love about him and things I don't. But ... you know I suddenly thought ... feeling stunned there last Thursday, feeling despairing about my marriage, perhaps these are all part of the feelings in my 'safe deposit box'?

Time to make those calls. Where is the list Anthony gave me?

Hidden stories

Extract from a later seminar

> Amanda: I have to admit to you all that I chose to present this seminar on 'stories we live by' because I thought it would be an easy one. But over the last month I wished I hadn't chosen it, because it was really hard. And that is one of the stories of my life – choosing something for the wrong reason and then regretting it later. It was the wrong reason – imagining it would be easy. A good reason would have been that I was really interested in the subject. Which isn't to say I'm not interested in it – in fact I've become very interested, having to work it all out in order to present this seminar – but that wasn't why I chose it.
>
> I've read the recommended readings and then tried to put it all together in a way that makes sense to me and my work with clients – which is how we are supposed to do these seminars. Doing it this way, however, does make it much harder – I've had to really play about with the ideas, test them out for myself, both in terms of my own personal history and through thinking about the histories of some of my clients. It's certainly made me make sense of the ideas,

but my guess is that if you're also going to make the same kind of sense you'll also have to play about with them in a similar way. I can see now that, although this is a much harder and time-consuming process, there isn't going to be a short route to it. Simply reading the readings and then being able to remember the ideas is no substitute at all. Anyway I'd better get on with my presentation.

The key concept, in all of this, is that during our development we create unconscious stories about ourselves, our lives and our relationships with others. It's actually the main way in which we learn about ourselves and our world and as such it's pretty important. These stories are usually quite simple stories – like the traditional stories and fairy tales of most societies. If we take a couple of examples – the princess has been captured by the evil knight-cum-dragon, the prince searches for her, defeats the evil knight in battle and rescues the princess, they get married and live happily ever after. Or the boy grows up to be a nice but very ugly man, the beautiful girl sees his inner beauty and kisses him, he turns into a handsome prince and they get married and live happily ever after. Quite simple stories but very attractive to the human mind – which is probably because they are similar to the personal stories that we make up about ourselves and our personal histories.

There are some things that need to be remembered, however, about our personal stories. The main problem is that we don't know we've got them unless we actively try to make them explicit. The second thing is that these stories aren't for entertainment, they are actually the way in which we organize our lives – we're not the audience but the main actor in these living stories, the stories of our lives. Thirdly we are constantly repeating them – a bit like replaying the same movie again and again, day after day, year after year. Fourthly we are repeating them because we want to change the ending of the story.

Let me give you an example from my work with clients. One of my clients – I'll call him Brian – has described how, when he was a young adolescent he became infatuated with his older sister. He would, for example, make some excuse to go into the bathroom when she was in the bath. After a while she picked up on the sexual overtones and told him where to get off – and that was that. However, a story formed in this young boy's mind around this experience. A story that we worked to uncover, to make explicit and piece together. The story is that his natural attraction is to the wrong person and that to let himself openly experience and express his desires will basically expose him as some terrible, incestuous person. The only way he can be saved, therefore, is if he doesn't allow himself to feel and express his desires until the 'princess' finds him (or he finds her) and through her 'kiss' (or whatever stands in for that kiss of acceptance) he is transformed from toad to princely man of good, clean, natural desire. Which is what he has been repeatedly waiting for, in his various relationships, ever since then – waiting for the 'princess' whose kiss will transform him. Of course she hasn't found him. What he has found is a lot of rejection in which he repeatedly ends up as the bad man in the eyes of both his former girlfriend and himself – in much the same way as he experienced his first sexual experience with his sister. We've also noted how he has tended to choose women who are nothing like his sister – either physically or psychologically – as a way of unconsciously trying to make sure that he doesn't repeat his 'wrong desire' again. In a recent session he talked about how he had often been attracted to women who were similar to her but he always and immediately stopped himself – 'shutting them out of his mind'.

At the moment we're working on Brian's initial infatuation for his sister and how that might not mean that his natural desires are essentially bad or perverted but simply that his sister was someone he loved and, because he boarded at an all-boys school, she was virtually the only girl in his social environment. We've also been exploring what it was like to be a young boy sexually awakening without either contact with other girls or any kind of framework for supporting or discussing his new sexual feelings and desires. Our aim is to continue this work, working it through in a way that he didn't have the opportunity for, there and then. I also hope to examine with him what the therapeutic work might mean in terms of the 'story he has lived by'.

John: Can I ask a question here, Amanda?

Amanda: Certainly. I'd like it to be more of a discussion than a lecture anyway.

John: I think I understood what you're saying about stories and I'd quite like to ask you how you see this story – of the toad and the princess – changing for him?

Amanda: What I feel is important is that he works out that change for himself. But what we're working on at the moment is basically that his experience with his sister doesn't mean he's a sexual pervert. I believe that if he really begins to feel and believe that, then the story he's been living by will die off. You don't need a princess to magically transform yourself if you're not a toad in the first place. As to what it will change into, I haven't really thought about that – perhaps because, as I said just now, it's important that whatever changes occur, he is the person who actually makes them. I feel that me trying to work out those changes for him would be quite wrong.

John: I agree with what you've said about him needing to work out his own new story.

Amanda: I'd like to give you a second, more personal example from my own personal history. It's something very sensitive, and a year ago I wouldn't have been able to examine it in the way that I have been doing with my counsellor Sheila, and I certainly wouldn't have been able to share it with a group of people – *even* you lot. This probably says a great deal not only about how far I've moved on a personal level, but also about how far the group has developed – how much safer I feel with you all as a result of all that we've worked through together on this course, in this group.

When I was 12 I was raped by a friend of my mother's when he came down to stay for the weekend. It's something that I kept a secret from everyone and to a great extent from myself. I've been working through it with Sheila for two to three months now and the client-work with Brian, because it concerned a sexual issue of early adolescence and an unwanted male advance, stimulated a lot of stuff for me. Without both my supervision and my personal counselling I couldn't have worked with Brian – which would have been really sad because he's nothing like the man who raped and abused me. When he first spoke about his experience with his sister, however, I got very wobbly, I got into a 'transference' where, for a week or so, I saw him as someone like the man who . . . [breaks off, her face full of pain. Breathes deeply] It's OK, I'm not going to break down again. Luckily I had supervision that week and my supervisor suggested that I take a long look at my abuse in my personal counselling. Anyway the reason why I want to share this with you is that as a result of my experience of being raped I created and repeatedly lived out a certain story. When I was raped I was playing a physical game with him. He got me to play the game and used it to trick me into a physically vulnerable position. I realize now that I told myself that it was my fault I was raped because I played the game with him and let him get very physical with me. I blamed my body for that – because my body enjoyed the game and the physical closeness – prior to him becoming sexual. So my story initially was that 'my body is not to be trusted because it will lead me into horror. If I live my life without reference to my body I won't end up there again. Only when I meet a man who is interested in me rather than my body will I be happy.' After further working through with my counsellor Sheila, however, I saw that like Brian I was also living a more classic story. When I was raped I felt invaded, I felt my body had been captured by this evil man and I realized that I had subsequently been living the story where 'I, the princess, wait to be rescued by the good prince'. Only he never turned up, so I just kept waiting, feeling all the time that I was living in the tower.

Questions to consider about working with personal history

1   What questions would you ask in the training group – if you were part of a seminar on understanding and working with personal history?

2 If you were to examine a pattern from your client's past, how would you set about that?
3 What might be the dangers in working with a client from this perspective?
4 How might you lessen those dangers?
5 If history repeats, in the way suggested here, what does that mean to you?
6 How would you go about identifying a pattern in a person's history – amongst all the events and experiences that life contains?

Three exercises to explore your personal history

Exploring what you have learnt about the world

That which we originally learnt about this world, and how to survive here, forms the foundation for how we live out the rest of our lives within it.

Sometimes, however, we learnt things that were true for our particular experience in the past but false for our lives as adults now.

An important part of our process of learning about the world is to expand one particular experience into a general 'model' by creating rules about how the world works. However, when we *inappropriately* generalize from one experience (or set of experiences) we build a model of the world that is wrong. Yet, because we only have this model to go on, we continue to see and behave as if that is how the world is. We have to have a working model of the world in order to live and interact within it and, even if it is distorted, we still have to use the model that we have.

In these cases our understanding of the world is not an accurate representation of how the world actually is – it is a *distorted* knowing about the world. In a sense we then live partly in our own 'fantasies' and these misperceptions then create numerous problems for us in our relations with others.

Changing what we have learnt about the world is not easy because our learning is very deep and involves forms of knowing about the world that are beyond words and reason.

Exercise

1 See if you can identify some important aspects of your 'internal working model of the world'.
2 See if you can identify some aspects of the 'distortions and fantasies' that you may be inappropriately carrying around with you.
3 See if you can identify some of the false rules about the world that you have created.

Stories of change and transition

Life has certain 'built-in' transitions. The demands, for example, of growing up and leaving behind earlier stages of life to take on new roles (e.g. from child to adult to parent to grandparent) and with all of this the reality of loss and change and, ultimately, bereavement and death. There are also many changes that arise out of the inherent ambivalence of social life – as a result of living and working with other people with whom we find ourselves both attached to and *also* in conflict. Life also contains many natural and human-made changes and transitions – from war to economic recession to cancer or AIDS. One way to make sense of all these changes is to tell ourselves stories – stories of self and other and how this led to this or that, and why.

Exercise

1   Take a few minutes to think of situations of change and transition in your life *that felt out of your control*. Events that 'came at' you, that other people decided upon, or that simply happened to you.
2   Focus on one situation, explore that experience in your journal, then see if you can identify a 'story'. Ask yourself if this story feels familiar.
3   Again, for a few minutes, think of situations of change and transition in your life *that felt in your control*. Change and transitions that you initiated, that you decided upon or created.
4   Focus on one situation again and explore that experience in your journal. Once again see if you can identify a story. Ask yourself if this story also feels familiar.

A theory of your own development

Part 1: Go back to Chapter 3. Consider and compare the stages of development of the clients David and Paresh – focusing on their attitudes to women, love and sex. Compare this to Belinda's attitudes in Chapter 2. Could you describe your own developmental theory of love – from adolescence to mature loving. Finally consider how men and women's attitudes and development differ.

Part 2: Examine your life in the same way – come up with a theory of your own development.

5

Working with Personal History

'Begin at the beginning', the King said, gravely, 'and go on till you come to the end: then stop.' (Lewis Carroll, *Alice in Wonderland*, 1865)

Finishing unfinished business

Chris stops blaming himself

Jennifer: Well Chris, you wanted to see me?

Chris: Yes, I've wanted to see you for so long. I can well understand why you cut yourself off from me all those years ago. I treated you very badly.

Jennifer: You did indeed, Chris, you did indeed. So why do you want to see me now?

Chris: Not to mistreat you – that's for sure. Partly I want to apologize. I was a fool and I was insensitive and I was a really mixed-up kid. Which is my excuse, I guess. Mixed up about relationships and the loss of relationships. I had to cope with too much loss in my growing up and that left me pretty mixed up.

Jennifer: I accept your apology. Anything else?

Chris: Just to say that I loved you, that I loved you so much. I had a terrible way of showing it but I have begun to understand now why that was. I also realize, *now*, that *then*, I couldn't have been much different. Loving you evoked in me the need to destroy that love. That was what always happened to me as I grew up – love was destroyed. In the end it felt like it was inevitable.

Jennifer: I don't really understand what you are saying but it sounds like you mean it – the apology, that is.

Chris: I don't know if there is anything else except perhaps to say that I had a terrible time afterwards, after we split up. A terrible time that lasted for years – seven years' bad luck in fact, very bad luck. I felt I was punished, or maybe I set out to punish myself. Maybe knowing that will help you to forgive me a little, that would be something good to come out of it all, all those years of punishment.

Jennifer: I did come to hate you, Chris, and I still do. I'm not sure your suffering relieves that. I don't know that I can forgive you, Chris. I feel like saying sorry, because I can't forgive you. But I'm not sorry – I loved you so much and I treated you well. I didn't deserve what you did. You were cruel to me, cruel to someone that loved you. Goodbye, Chris. I don't want to see you again, OK?

Chris: Goodbye Jennifer. I wish you the best of all possible lives.

[Silence]

Henry (Chris's counsellor): How are you feeling now, Chris?

Chris: Sad, very sad. [Tears come to his eyes, he breathes deeply.] At least it makes a bit more sense to me now. I have always thought, 'Oh if I hadn't treated her so badly and we had stayed together, I would have found out that she wasn't the right person for me.' But that's really just a way of trying to make it better. What if she was the right person? What if we were right for each other? What if we'd had kids? What if we'd lived a long and happy life together, with the normal marital conflicts for sure, but what if she was actually the right person?

Henry: It doesn't sound like you were the right person for her – at least *not then*.

Chris: Shit, you're fucking right – I really wasn't the right person for her and I wouldn't have been for at least seven years and even then, if we hadn't broken up, I wouldn't have gone through the kind of shit I needed to go through in those seven years of 'punishment' – to become the person that would have been right for her. Shit, I just realized what I just said then – to 'become the person that would have been right for her.' [Looks stunned] Is this what has been driving me all these years, all this seeking to find myself and all this counselling – all to become the person that would have been right for her? [Silence] Or become the person that *is* right for her – only she isn't any more. I have no idea where she is and, even if I did, I'm sure she'd be married with three kids and a dog called Joey. [Thoughtful silence] I don't know but maybe I've been a bit hard on myself all these years. I mean I didn't treat her that well, but I wasn't necessarily that different from many of my friends – men and women.

Henry: That sounds like quite a shift.

Chris: The first year was good, the second I was a bit tired of her, I guess – it's strange to say that but there is some truth in it. I was a bit tired of her, she was a very . . . 'homely girl' . . . and I wanted . . . an exciting wild, crazy, extrovert life – which is about the opposite of what I'm like now. I was, however, very emotionally attached to her and I didn't know how to end things – I mean a part of me was very much in love with her . . . The third year I was confused, we got into lots of conflict, we learnt to live without each other, then when we finally split up I guess it triggered for me the earlier losses of my life. When my father died, when my brother left and when my grandmother died too. The loss of Jennifer came to represent them all except, at the time, I didn't know that and so it seemed that it was all to do with her. I've never really seen it quite like this before. It does feel like I'm finally beginning to move on from her and all that the break-up triggered for me. Right now I don't feel bad about that earlier thought – that all of this work on myself might have been to make me into the right kind of person for her. That seems quite a good thing, actually.

Henry: We're coming up to time. How would you like to complete this? At least for today?

Chris: [Silence] I'm feeling clearer – in my heart. [Silence] I was imagining her here and whether there was anything else to say to her and then she changed – in my mind's eye she grew older. She was no longer the young woman I knew. Yes . . . if I imagine her now she seems very different – a woman entering her mid-life with all the cares and responsibilities of someone of that age. The Jennifer I knew is no more, just as the Chris I was has all but vanished. She has stretch marks on her breasts and buttocks, wrinkles appearing on her face and the odd grey hair. She's lived a life away from me, with another man and children I don't know. All of that makes her a very different person, someone I don't know, she's like a stranger – both of us with our memories of these other people, these other people that we were when we were both young and full of . . . foolish love.

Linking the present and the past

Henry realizes how experiences in his adolescence shaped his adulthood:

Extract from Henrys' journal

Friday, the end of a very difficult week but also a very important one. Just over a week ago, in my personal counselling, I realized that I had chosen to study counselling not because I wanted to help people but because I wanted to be seen as the helping person. This was really quite a stunning realization for me – one that shook me to my foundations and has led to an enormous questioning process. Not only that but by some unfortunate coincidence I also had to face a very difficult situation at work – that really couldn't have come at a worse time. As you know, I work in a school as a deputy head, and originally began counselling training in order to be more skilled in dealing with the pastoral side of my teacher's role. Anyway, the problem at work was the discovery that six of the year 9 pupils had been taking drugs on the school premises. Not only that, but the news of this blew up when the head was at a conference of head teachers – so it was left to me to deal with both distressed and angry parents and calls from a number of the governors. What made it even more difficult for me, however, was the overwhelming concern of so many people, not with the issue itself, but how it would be seen by people – if it got into the papers.

So there I was in my own crisis – having just been faced with the realization of my own overwhelming concern about how I wanted to be seen, and there I am having to deal with all these panic-stricken people obsessed with how this affair would reflect on themselves or the image of the school.

The evening after the day it all blew up in the school, I was standing by the mirror in something of a state and remembered the line of a song by a 1970s musician whose band I used to listen to:

> Don't matter what you think about me, it makes a whole lot of difference what I think about you!

I also recall how that line and that song had deeply struck me in my adolescence as something I would have liked to be able to say – knowing full well that it wasn't true for me. Then I got into a whole thing of remembering what it felt like to be a 15-year-old and how I used to be utterly obsessed with how I was seen by others. I recalled, very uncomfortably, how much of my subjective life revolved around this – especially how I was being physically perceived and, most of all, on the surface at least, on the state of my facial spots. It was really odd to remember it. My subjective perspective on the world in mid-adolescence seemed, well, it almost seemed to be that of a madman. Every moment in a mixed group I would be thinking about how I was being seen – my spots, my clothes, my walk, my hair, my words, everything was a kind of performance for this audience of others – particularly when girls were about. What was so odd was the feeling that that was actually me *then* – so different does my subjective perspective on the world feel now.

Then my mind was off all over the place thinking about how, if it was so difficult to recall adolescence, how difficult it must be to really remember childhood.

Then I was thinking about empathy as a whole and how difficult it really is to see the world from someone else's point of view. At that moment I thought about an acquaintance I made recently – a woman who wears a lot of make-up – and I was wondering whether her subjective world was still like that of an adolescent obsessed with her 'performance' to her audience. Then I thought about the pupils at school, who I don't really know very well, and was wondering how they were experiencing all of this. That triggered a whole bunch of stuff for me about my adolescence and how emotional and confusing and exciting and lovely and destructive it was. It was like a whole box of fireworks of forgotten memories had just gone off in my mind.

I continued to think about all of this and then began to wonder whether I really had much empathic ability at all – the world seemed to suddenly be peopled with so many subjective perspectives, so distant from my own. It seemed that empathy was an impossible idea. Then as I thought that, I had an amazing realization – that, at some very important level, I have never really gone beyond my 'subjective frame of reference'. I had been assuming, underneath it all, that other people were like me. I remembered too, that when I was an adolescent I automatically assumed that other people were more or less the same as me – I assumed that they too were obsessed by this moment-to-moment performance and associated audience analysis.

This insight felt really important. That I, and perhaps most of us (there I go again), assume a similar underlying subjective perspective in the other person and that is simply the wrong thing to do. Then I thought about how difficult it is to see the world from someone else's point of view – rather than *how I would see the world if I was in that person's shoes*. Real empathy, I realized, is *not* about stepping into someone else's shoes at all – because if I'm stepping in there I'm taking my subjective frame with me. No, empathy is about not being me and somehow being someone else – which feels very, very hard indeed. I don't feel I can do this if I'm concerned about what I am and how I'm being seen.

It almost feels like to become a good counsellor I have to give up wanting to be one. Certainly, if I hadn't discovered my secret motivation to be seen as a helping person, I couldn't begin to work on it. What would it mean for me to be a counsellor who wasn't interested in being seen as the helper? If I give up wanting to be a counsellor for this reason what motivation, if any, will take its place? Will I genuinely want to help people through counselling or will I lose my motivation to be a counsellor?

It was a little distressing to think of my subjective world as an adolescent but it was also good to do so and I want to continue to remember how I was at different times in my life. Perhaps I can use that as a stepping stone to a greater empathic ability as well as really discovering much more about myself. I'd like to go further back if I can – to the subjective world of my childhood. That almost seems like another planet right now.

Sunday morning. Depressing thoughts – that some of the major choices I made about my adult life were driven by my adolescent subjective perspective. I've been thinking that, perhaps, in my choice of career I was unconsciously choosing a situation where I hoped to gain the confidence I lacked. By becoming the teacher, for example, I probably hoped to become the good performer and I saw that as something I really wanted. As an adolescent, with my acne, I frequently felt in a cold spotlight and I hated the sense that I was being seen as spotty Henry. At the same time, however, I loved the feeling of being in a warm spotlight of attention – of my performance being appreciated, of my audience warming to me. Most of all I loved to feel attractive to a girl, particularly an attractive girl. That was more important than being attracted to someone – I loved for someone to be attracted to me, to enjoy my performance.

I've also been wondering whether, later on in life, in choosing to train as a counsellor I was unconsciously seeking to become the listening audience where the other person is 'on show'. To a great extent the helper is unnoticed by the talker, by the client. In this role, therefore, I can vanish – at least in the superficial sense of the person who isn't spotlighted ... although at another level I'm very much there, and very much wanted. In the counsellor role I can avoid the hard, cold spotlight while, at the same time, I'm also feeling deeply attractive to the client. I'm bathing in the sense of his or her warm spotlight – a feeling like 'It's good to see you again, Henry, I feel good here with you, I feel relaxed and myself, I feel cared for and listened to.'

Somehow all of this feels like I've just taken a big bite out of the 'deadly apple' and the world isn't going to seem the same again.

Monday evening. A difficult but growing time yesterday evening and today with more painful insights into myself and my personal history – much of it emerging from a deeper remembering of my subjective life as an adolescent. What stands out most of all is the sense of how much more up and down, and generally all over the place, my mental and emotional life was. How I would reach levels of intense, almost ecstatic excitement at certain times and, at others, intense emotional confusion, rage or melancholy. Oh, and how much in late adolescence my mind was taken up with issues of ideals – ideas about how the world should be. I remembered the endless conversations I would have about politics, or God or philosophy and most of all I remembered how much more I used to feel – how much more I would hurt when I felt hurt, how much more I would desire when I felt attracted to someone!

Towards yesterday evening it all began to get much less confusing. I've almost begun to feel that rather than all of this wobbling me, there's actually a rather nice crack in myself – a crack through which I've discovered an old room full of good as well as bad memories. Remembering who I was, as an adolescent and young adult, I actually feel richer in myself. I feel older too, but in a good way. I've also realized that I spent quite a time in my late twenties trying to forget what I used to be like: trying to forget not only the painful aspects but also the intense excitement, joy and lustiness of those earlier years. It was almost as if I was actively putting my youth behind me – partly so that I could deal with the challenges of family and career but also to avoid the feelings of saying goodbye to that stage in my life. In the process I shut out so much of myself as I 'took control' of my life. Whereas on Friday it seemed that my subjective world as an adolescent had the quality of madness, I have begun to wonder if it's actually the other way round. Wasn't it then that I was really alive? From the perspective of youth I now look old, tired and controlled. It's almost like the life has been squeezed out of me – or rather, that I've squeezed it out of me.

Just then I began to feel incredibly sad. I saw myself growing into the kind of adult I always despised as an adolescent and vowed I would never become, and the sadness is for my lost youth. It's like I keep switching perspectives – from good to bad, from adult to adolescent, from one view of myself to another.

When I think back to just over a year ago it seems so far away. There I was with myself and my world of school and family. Doing this counselling training has rocked that world to its roots, nothing is certain any more and I realize now that I spent much of my mid-adulthood trying to make things certain. On the one hand this feels a pretty painful thing to be doing to myself and on the other it feels like I am truly opening up to who I am. Opening up to the me, that in the more recent past I shut out and am beginning to let back in. That feels pretty good, I think!

Regression

Amanda recovers her body

Note of warning: THE FOLLOWING PASSAGE WILL DISTURB YOU

Amanda: It was a Saturday. I was just 12 at the time. Mum had gone shopping and I was playing in the living room and watching TV at the same time. There was a cartoon on when he came in. I remember that he had a towel over his arm. An old friend of my mum's, so she said, Harry was his name, he was staying for the weekend, down from London I think. I remember I had liked him, at first that is, the evening before. He gave me a present, a colouring book and some pens and a pencil case. When he left I threw them away. Mum asked me where they were and I said I'd lost them at school. She got angry with me for losing them – I remember feeling so alone at that moment, so very alone.

He asked me if I would like to play a game and I said yes. Afterwards, at night when I went to bed I kept saying to myself 'You shouldn't have played a game with him, you should have said no.' The game was called rabbit and the idea was that rabbit was looking for his rabbit hole. It was a funny game at first. He made his hand like a rabbit and it hopped about on the sofa and then on me. It tickled as he hopped over me 'looking for his rabbit hole'. First he found my armpit – I was giggling and rolling on the sofa. Then he put his fingers in my mouth. I was really laughing, it was a good game. Then he went under my shirt, he was hopping over my tummy and my back. I was enjoying it – this was a really funny man, I thought. Then, when I was lying on my tummy he put his hand under my trousers and down into my pants. The button of my trousers was undone – he must have undone it while I was rolling about. For a moment I still thought it was a game as he 'stuck the rabbit's nose' between my buttocks and went 'pooh what's this then?' But at that moment it all changed, it suddenly stopped feeling like a game and I felt terrified and I stopped rolling about and lay still – like a frightened rabbit. He was doing things to me that I didn't like and then I noticed three things – he had put the towel under my tummy, the tops of my legs were very sticky and there was an open jar of Vaseline on the floor. I remember thinking 'Why has he put Vaseline in between my legs?' and then he did it. I was really frightened. He was on top of me and it really, really hurt and I managed to say in my shaky voice, 'That hurts!' He said that it would only take a minute and then he'd have a present for me. But it didn't take a minute – he was crushing me and the pain in between my legs was awful and it seemed to go on and on and on. Then suddenly he stopped and got off me and as he did so it really hurt and I felt horribly sick in my stomach. I was shaking, I remember my hands shaking and his voice was all calm and 'nice' and he wiped the Vaseline off me, pulled up my pants, did up my trousers, rolled up the towel and he was going on about what a nice game we had played and he was going to give me a present. And I was nodding and saying 'yes' and all the time I wanted to cry and I wanted him to go away and in between my legs I felt really sore and I was feeling really sick and I felt like so awful that I wanted to crawl into a corner and die. And then I began to feel really weird – I looked at my hands and I felt like I was looking at something that wasn't really me. It was as if I wasn't quite in my body anymore. Thinking about it now it felt as if he had pushed himself inside me and I had been pushed out. Then I said I needed to go to the toilet – I just *had* to get away from him. I went upstairs to the toilet and sat on it shaking and staring at the top of my legs watching this horrid stuff dripping out of me and it felt like I was looking at someone else's legs, someone else's body. Again, thinking about it now, I was in a state of shock, but at the time it felt like I had been invaded, like in a horror movie, by a demon – that I had lost my body to this demon.

Sheila: I can see that talking about this has taken a lot out of you and I'm wondering whether you would like to stop for the moment?

Amanda: I'm feeling really shaky and I'm feeling sick too but I would like to continue. It's taken a long time to be able to talk about it with you and to remember all the details. But now that I have finally got here I would like to continue. If that's all right with you?

Sheila: Amanda, it's not a pain for me to hear your pain, this is what we have been working towards. I'm feeling upset sitting here listening to you but I'm also OK with that. Unlike your mother, you don't have to worry about me, I can cope – but what is clear is that it really wasn't right that you had to experience what this man did to you and it was doubly wrong that you had to cope with it all alone. You're not alone now. I want to hear whatever you need to say, as many times as you need to say it. I feel really quite upset [tears in her eyes] but I'm OK with that. You don't need to worry about me, Amanda.

Amanda: [breaks down sobbing uncontrollably. Sheila picks up Amanda's right hand in her two hands, then holds Amanda in her arms, Amanda reaches around her and clings to her torso with her head snuggled into Sheila's breasts. Amanda coughs silently, Sheila strokes her hair.] Thank you, Sheila [her lips shaking with emotion] thank you. [Silence except for Amanda's sobbing, which gradually subsides] Do you have a tissue? [Sits back up and blows her nose] I would like to continue, Sheila.

Sheila: Are you sure, Amanda? You look pretty awful.

Amanda: Yes, I feel worn out, but now I want to get as much out as I can, I want to get him out, finally.

Sheila: OK, but don't drain yourself too much – say if you want to stop, look after yourself, OK?

Amanda: OK, Sheila, I will.

Sheila: What I suggest then is that you try and enter the pain a little more deeply – perhaps from the moment that the game stopped being a game for you.

Amanda: OK. I was rolling on the sofa on my tummy and giggling then [breathes deeply] then when he put his fingers inside my trousers I suddenly felt trapped, trapped and tricked. In fact, I had forgotten this completely – his other hand was pressing down on my back at that moment – so I couldn't have moved even if I hadn't been frozen. I remember now – when I thought about it afterwards I used to beat myself up for freezing up with fright and not moving – just letting him do it, get away with it, without even saying no. It was at that same moment that I became aware of those three things – the towel under my tummy, the stickiness in between my legs and the open Vaseline jar on the floor. It was a bit like driving along in a car – playing a game of I-Spy – and then, suddenly, you see that the car is about to crash. Yes it felt something like that. Everything was funny and normal and then, suddenly, it was all about to go horribly wrong. I remember how, in that moment, I felt so tricked. [Amanda stops still, looking very thoughtful.]

Sheila: You felt so tricked?

Amanda: Yes. Suddenly just then when I was remembering that feeling of being tricked a whole lot more came back to me – yes, it's like I have been remembering it in bits and pieces and at a distance – watching myself on the sofa. Suddenly, just now I was back inside myself, remembering what it felt like inside my body.

Sheila: That sounds really important Amanda – you mean that up until now, as you remembered your experience of being raped, you have been picturing yourself lying on the sofa, as if you were somewhere else in the room. But just when you remembered that feeling of being tricked you changed perspective and saw the world from the eyes of yourself then, that terrified little girl on the sofa.

Amanda: That's right. I remember lying there with his left hand pressing down on the middle of my back and his right hand between my legs and I was feeling tricked and feeling like 'just before a car crash' and I remember thinking, 'You fool, Amanda you shouldn't have let him play the game' – as if it was because of me that he had gone further, as if it was, in some way, my fault. And, I don't really want to remember this, but I really felt it was my fault because I had liked the game at first. I had liked the feeling of him tickling me. Shit!

Sheila: So not only did you feel shocked and tricked, but you also felt guilty that you had been enjoying the feeling?

Amanda: Yes, I guess I felt guilty. Guilty and very angry with myself.

Sheila: Angry with yourself for enjoying being tickled. What about him – how did you feel about him?

Amanda: As you know, I can't seem to feel angry with him. Looking back I feel he was a sick man – as we've talked about – and that he needed help, but I don't seem to feel angry . . . Just as I said that I remembered waking up from a terrible dream last night. I was in my home, very angry, and these gangsters were after me but I stood my ground. One of them shot at me but the bullet just bounced off. Then I went outside and there was a driver in their car. They were still shooting at me and I just got into the car and ripped off the driver's head – tore it from his body and carried it out. They were so shocked they stopped shooting. I woke up with my head falling off the side of the bed and with a very powerful feeling that I was evil and that I was going to hell. I felt very frightened at that moment.

Sheila: And you say that you're not angry with him – it sounds to me as though your dream might be saying something different?

Amanda: It's true I was in a terrible rage in that dream – I don't think the man in the car was him, though. At least not directly.

Sheila: It feels to me that a lot is beginning to surface for you, Amanda and it may well be that there is quite a lot of anger, but that perhaps you are also afraid of that anger – perhaps there is even a part of you that thinks being so angry makes you an evil person who will 'go to hell'. It feels to me that you've already been to hell – on that sofa, and afterwards coping with it all alone. As we've explored before, in order to cope with it at the time, a part of you stayed on that sofa in some hidden safe deposit box in yourself – it feels like you are now beginning to recover that part of yourself.

Amanda: I'm certainly feeling better – somewhere deep under myself that is, but right now I'd like to recover for a bit. I haven't got anything else to do today – which is a bloody good job. I'm glad we talked about how I would need to have plenty of time to recover after these regression sessions.

Sheila: It also sounds like you are beginning to take care of yourself a bit. Not something you have been particularly good at in the past.

Amanda: You're certainly right there, Sheila but, as we've talked about, that probably has something to do with all of this . . . I never thought I would ever want to really remember that Saturday morning, never mind actually be able to. You know, I feel quite pleased with myself.

Sheila: You have really achieved something today. Is there anything you specifically need to do in these last few minutes?

Some questions

1 How are you feeling after reading the above passage?
2 Together with 'appropriate' feelings – such as revulsion – can you notice any 'wrong' or 'bad' thoughts and feelings (voyeuristic feelings for example). If you can notice any, do you have appropriate support to explore them, for example in your personal counselling?
3 Have you asked yourself how you would support yourself when working with a client's experience of child sexual abuse?
4 What would you see as the therapeutic benefits of this kind of in-depth regression?
5 What are the dangers?
6 If Sheila had been a male counsellor how might that have changed the situation?
7 'As a male counsellor I would hesitate about exploring a female client's experience of sexual abuse through regression – partly because of the potential misplaced transference of her feelings for her abuser onto me.' What is this counsellor saying and how do you respond to his statement?
8 Could you empathize with (see the world from the other person's point of view) the abuser? If not, have you considered how you would deal with a situation where a client disclosed present or past acts of abuse? Have you examined your legal position in this respect?
9 'It has been suggested that many sexual abusers have themselves been abused, in some way, as children. They are thus repeating their past in the present – but with other children.' How do you respond to this point of view?
10 Given the prevalence of physical, emotional and sexual abuse of children, and the difficulties of working with abusers, how might the field of counselling help to reduce the repetition of abuse through the generations?

Working with resistance to changing the patterns of the past

There is another problem that I want to introduce you to. When the client does begin to really grow and change for the better, he or she can be faced with the subjective experience of the opposite – that things are getting worse. This very tragic situation may be built into the human condition, and overcoming it can sometimes be very difficult. It requires a kind of steadfastness from both the client and the counsellor, together with understanding and skill on the part of the counsellor.

Let me give you some examples. A client who experienced consistent loss in her childhood finally manages to create a sense of solidity in her relationships, but at that very moment, intense feelings rise up of 'it all being wrong'. What has happened for her is that she has replayed the old story – when things were last right they next became all wrong. Another client learns to move closer to his wife, but as he takes that step he feels pushed out by her – he has opened up for himself the feeling that he has been feeling all along, of not being really with her, of being isolated. A third client makes a success of his career but as it comes to fruition he is overwhelmed by feelings of failure. In reaching his goal he becomes aware of the underlying feelings that have been driving him towards success – his deep sense of failure and worthlessness. Many clients, on managing to really 'get things together', can experience feelings of the opposite – that 'things are falling apart'.

This may sound an odd thing to have been 'built into' the human heart and mind but it is perhaps less odd when you consider that it is the unresolved, underlying, un-worked-through, uncomfortable feelings, desires and other memories that so often drive us towards where we are going. When we get there it's not surprising that we should discover that which drove us there all along. This may also sound a little pessimistic but a very real liberation from the past motivations and stories can occur; nevertheless, there is often this final hurdle – a remembering of the 'bad' past and confusing it with the 'good' present. A final hurdle that needs to be understood and sensitively handled by the counsellor.

In the East there is a commonly held belief that the essence of life is suffering. This was also a key theme in the Western world view until relatively recently and it is an aspect of the psychodynamic approach to counselling. There is a saying in the East that the worst suffering is not to know that one is suffering – because then there really is no way out of it. Such a person is genuinely stuck pedalling round a vicious circle (Paresh's 'Wheel of Karma') like a hamster pedalling in the wheel in its cage.

As a practising counsellor (perhaps too deeply involved in people's suffering) it seems to me that although we in the West may have relieved much of material suffering, little has improved in terms of psychological suffering and, in certain ways, psychological life may have got worse.

It is difficult to see suffering sometimes – mainly because, as is stressed throughout this book, *we don't want to see it* – if we do it resonates with our own unresolved pain. Once you begin to know your own suffering, however, it's easier to see it in the world around you. I've come to the conclusion that it's the avoidance of personal pain that drives most people most of the time. Only when we have begun to accept and work through that pain is there a possibility of free choice and with that a psychological life that is less tragic.

Four more exercises to explore your personal history

Exploring difficult past experiences

Using the issues identified in the following list as a springboard, explore a little of your difficult experiences in childhood and adolescence. Focus on one experience and explore it in more detail in your journal, asking yourself:

- what did it feel like then?
- how did you cope?
- what pictures and what stories about the world did you create as a result?
- what *patterns* has your response to your experience left you with – patterns in your personal history?

List of possible difficult experiences in childhood and adolescence: having to change schools; being bullied; living with an anxious, cruel or critical parent; feeling humiliated; having to grow up too soon; feeling rejected by the kids at school; sexual or other abuse; being separated from your parents (e.g. boarding school); a crisis in the family (in which your parents became very distressed); a sense of a change in your parents' attitude to you as you entered puberty; your parents' dis-approval of, or avoidance of, sexual issues.

The birthday cake – an exercise on linking present and past

Take a few minutes to draw a large cake, and a smaller cake inside the larger one. Divide the two cakes into four pieces. The outer cake represents the present and the inner cake the past. Label each of the pieces of the cake – 'desire', 'terror', 'grief' and 'rage'. In the inner cake note down the people and places from your past that you associate with these four feelings. Explore this in your journal.

Again, for a few minutes, note down in the outer cake the people and places that you associate with these four feelings in your present life. Some may be the same as in the inner cake. Note any links between the two cakes.

Continue your exploration in your journal – focusing on the links between your past and present emotional experiences.

Two stories of unfinished business

Think about the people you have known for a long time – in your personal, working or family life – with whom you have 'unfinished business'. Choose one person to focus on.

Tell the story of your relationship with this person – from the other person's eyes.

Return to yourself and tell the story from your own eyes.

Spend a few minutes reviewing this exercise in your journal.

Your earliest memory

Warning: this can sometimes be experienced as a very powerful exercise.

Describe your earliest memory.

Enter into the feelings contained in that memory and explore your earliest memory in more detail.

Explore what that memory says about you and your world then – how you might have seen your world and the people in it, your experience of your place in the world, what it might say about your relationships with others then.

Explore what it might tell you, more generally, about you and your life with others.

Can you find a story, about your life as a whole, within your earliest memory?

Give yourself time to come out of the exercise and review it in your journal.

6

Close Relationships

But what is it all about? People loose and at the same time caught. Caught and loose. All these people and you don't know what joins them up. There's bound to be some sort of reason and connection. Yet somehow I can't seem to name it. (Carson McCullers, *The Member of the Wedding*, 1946)

Who are you?

I have, once again, come to sit here and write for you. But who are you – my reader? It's difficult to write for you because I don't know you. You're just an empty chair, sitting opposite me. An empty chair – unlike my clients and my students. Perhaps one day I'll be the empty chair sitting opposite you and then you may wonder 'who are you, Anthony, the hand behind the pen behind the book?' Perhaps . . . if I finish this book.

There's something special that can happen between people – between us, perhaps – if you were here or I there. This is, for me, the essence of counselling – that there can be something special between people. Something that we, you and I, cannot experience without being together. This is why you can't really learn much about counselling through reading a book. You can only really learn about counselling through being with people – your fellow students, tutors, clients, supervisors and your own personal counsellor. You must have all of that – and for a long time – years, not months. If you're not prepared to enter into relation with these others then forget about being a counsellor and throw this book away.

I stopped writing for a while – I couldn't decide what to say next because I didn't know what your response was. How can I know what to say next if you don't respond! You're just an empty chair – piss off, empty chair, piss off!! See, I'm angry with you because you haven't responded.

So you haven't thrown me away? How did you respond to my anger? Or rather, how would you have responded if I had been with you? I said something important, you didn't respond and I got angry with you because you didn't respond.

I imagine you might feel hurt, or angry in return, or withdraw and be even more unresponsive. If all of that had happened 'live' then how would we be now? Distanced perhaps, resentful . . . you might be thinking . . . what might you be thinking? All I can do is imagine being you and attribute my imagined thoughts and feelings to you . . .

> You: I don't like this kind of intensity, I want to keep the relationship on an even keel while I work out my response to Anthony's anger. I feel really quite uncomfortable.
> [I smile, and feel quite out of place.]
> Anthony: I've sensed your withdrawal from me. What's that like – for you and for me? I feel quite sad, I've been trying to engage with you and you've retreated further away from me. I feel rejected, even hurt by you. Part of me would like to throw you out, withdraw from you too, push you away. I decide to get on with my writing and ignore you.

The nature of the self

Many important people have sought to define the self. Three of the most important of these definitions are those by three very important people – doctors Freud, Perls and Rogers.

> You: Hold it, Anthony, you can't just forget about me, that's not fair . . . I wasn't withdrawing from you, I *am* interested in what you're saying. I was just a bit overwhelmed, I didn't know what to say to you when you got angry with me . . . it's just that, just now, you unsettled me.
> Anthony: Well, it's really good to hear from you at last – I'm glad you're interested in what I'm saying. I'm also interested in you – that's what's so frustrating about this. I've been wondering why I want to write a book about something that can't be truly grasped through a book. In fact, I need to confess to you that before I started writing this book I didn't actually want to write it – I've realized that now. I've realized that I wanted to have a book published so that I could be an author and hopefully an *important* author. I wanted a book that would show the world how amazing I was – which is probably why I haven't been writing as much as I should have.
> I'm wondering what you're feeling about me now – once again you're not responding and I've just made this big confession to you . . . Honestly that's quite a confession – I've always wanted to be important and I've always felt very guilty about that. Some of the most uncomfortable moments of my life (particularly when I was younger) have been when I was pretending to be important and it was very obvious to everyone else that I wasn't. Very uncomfortable moments!

I feel that perhaps you have warmed to me a bit, that I haven't tried to be important with you and you appreciate my honesty . . . I ran out of words then and felt sad at that moment – I'm not sure why. It feels as though all of those times when I was pretending to be important I was really just wanting to feel important to the important people in my life – but not as some Great Person. No, beneath it all I wanted to be an important friend or an important and cared-for younger person – I basically wanted to be a special person to the people I lived with and cared for. Not to people in general but to those few people I lived my life with. Do I still want to be an important author? I'm not sure anymore, it certainly always felt like that was one of my weaknesses – wanting to be seen as an 'important person'.

Feeling important to the important people in your life – this is something of the specialness I mentioned above. The fact that between people there can be a sense of jointly lived lives in which each is important to each other – despite the everyday conflicts, disagreements and different ways of seeing the world, something special can still be there. In fact I've come to the conclusion that when it's there, then people are 'well' and when it's not, they are confused, distressed, seeking but not finding what they are seeking and sometimes not even knowing what it is they want.

You know something, I wish you were here, I wish I could get to know you. I wish I could be with you and share our common interest. But you're just an empty chair. Empty, nothing, no response . . . no response. I feel angry with you for that, angry and sad. I feel hurt and rejected when you don't respond to my reaching out. How can I open my heart to you and you don't respond?

I've another confession. For a long time Anthony-the-counsellor didn't know how to really be with the people he worked with. He thought of himself as a 'helper' – someone to whom others turned for help in becoming more aware of themselves and generally better able to live a more satisfying and happier life. What he didn't know was that he didn't really understand how to open himself to them. He was hiding behind the helper role – in a sense he was an empty chair for them. That sounds really hard, and I'm probably being too hard on myself, but there's some truth in it. What's different now is that my heart is more open – to my clients, my students and everyone else in my life and I'm better able to be present with all of these people. More than that, I enjoy being with them so much more and together, it seems to me, we sometimes create a little of this specialness that I'm talking about.

It feels to me as if I'm better able to open my heart – to trust, to reach out, to care for, to be willing to feel and respond, whether those feelings are comfortable or uncomfortable. And with that there is an unwillingness to give up, to withdraw, to disengage and lose hope. Now with my clients I sometimes truly feel things like:

- 'I want to know you – the real you that's locked somewhere inside and wants to find a way out.'
- 'I want to touch that you – gently' [psychologically speaking].
- 'I won't allow you to ignore me.'
- 'I won't give up on you – even if you give up on me for a time.'
- 'You are safe here with me, I know that now. You are special to me – I care.'

How can your client open his or her heart to you? As your client I really do need to feel that you will emotionally respond to my confessions, to my pain, to my withdrawal from you, to my liking or disliking, even love or hate for you. There are many 'tricks of the trade' and quite a few are examined in this book; there are many valuable counselling techniques, but, for me, the heart of the counselling process is the counsellor's open heart. A heart that is emotionally aware, emotionally experienced and emotionally responsive. Otherwise there's only an empty chair, a counsellor-free counselling, a coldness. Without two people emotionally engaged in the forming, developing and ending of a real relationship, *there's no counselling*.

How do you feel – close up?

We live in a world of emotional connection and disconnection, emotional perception and misperception, emotional response and expression and lack of emotional response and expression. Our emotional patterns of engagement, together with our emotional perceptions of others, form the foundation of our social existence. The way we are emotionally perceived, the manner in which we are experienced by others, what it feels like to be with us – in the various moods that we express – these are the essence of what we often call a person's character.

Cultures, communities and even families also develop a common character – recognizable patterns of emotional engagement. The English, Italian, French, German and American peoples each seem to have a common pattern of engaging emotionally. The same can be said of people in the English county of Somerset (where I live), or even of specific communities within a county – each has its own, subtly different ways of emotionally engaging with others.

People also express their 'feel' through the spaces they create around them. One home feels very different from another – this one feels warm and cosy, that one cold and sterile. All of this is worth noticing, all of this is worth becoming more aware of.

Exercise

What feel does your counselling setting express? What do the clothes you wear, your mannerisms, the way you sit or walk, express about your patterns of emotional engagement? What does it feel like to be with you as a counsellor?

Extract from a seminar

> Bridget [student]: I'm still not sure what you mean by 'patterns of emotional engagement' – are you saying that when people are with each other they use their body language to say that they like each other or they don't like each other?
>
> Anthony [tutor]: How about if we take an example of some interpersonal engagement and explore what it might mean to emotionally respond, or not respond, and how each person has their own particular patterns of emotionally being with others. Has anyone in the group got an example from their own life that they'd like us to take a look at?
>
> Mavis: I'd quite like to look at you and Bridget.
>
> Anthony: Mmmm, interesting suggestion. Anyone else have a suggestion? [Silence] Well Bridget, how do you feel about that?
>
> Bridget: OK, I suppose.
>
> Anthony: OK, but not that enthusiastic. Well, as the tutor I guess I have to put myself on the line [group laughs] but how about if we include you in this too [looking at Mavis]?
>
> Mavis: [moves back in her chair and looks a little put out for a moment, then smiles] I guess I have to too – since it's my suggestion.
>
> Anthony: OK – what are we trying to focus on here?
>
> Robert: How each of you emotionally connect together, how you are with each other, how you feel together – in the way you sit with and converse with each other.
>
> Anthony: I couldn't have put it better myself. How about if we, the three of us, imagine we are in the canteen together and are passing the time of day. The rest of the group can observe us *emotionally* – ask yourself what's going on here, beneath the content of the conversation.
>
> Mavis: OK.
>
> Bridget: [a little reluctantly] OK.

The three of them set out a 'canteen table' and act out a meeting over cups of coffee and biscuits. The rest of the group watch the threesome intently, some students making notes, others seeming to 'join in' with the three actors. After a few minutes Anthony turns to the side and asks the group for their comments and observations.

Sarah: I noticed that Bridget didn't seem to be herself – it felt like she was a bit uncomfortable with the exercise and was very conscious of all of us watching her so keenly, staring even. I wouldn't have liked that myself – I'd have felt very odd pretending to be in the canteen with all of the group staring at me.

Belinda: Mavis seemed quite dominant, quite expressive of her opinions and her views. She felt very confident and lively, she seemed to be at the centre of the three of you. I felt quite envious of her – I've never felt that confident in groups and I've always wanted to be able to state my opinions like that. Before doing this course I wouldn't even have been able to say what I've just said.

Robert: What I'm thinking is that what Anthony means by patterns of emotional engagement is perhaps to do with what I'd call the personality – how the personality expresses itself with other people.

Anthony: Again that's a very clear intellectual statement but I'm also wondering what you emotionally observed, Robert. Both Belinda and Sarah shared concrete observations together with how they felt about those observations – could you say something about your emotional observations, perhaps of me?

Robert: That's putting me on the spot and yes, once again you're picking me up on the fact that I tend to think rather than feel. I felt you were . . . emotionally distant Anthony, you seemed to be holding back from the women in some way.

Amanda: Yes you did seem a bit cut off. Not in any dramatic way, but at a subtle level. Almost as if you were quite shy. I haven't seen you in that way before, but come to think of it now, a part of you sometimes does seem a little shy. I hope you don't mind me saying that.

Anthony: It's important you feel that you can say whatever you observed. Simply because you perceive something it doesn't necessarily mean it is true – our perceptions are far from always 'right'. I'll admit, however, to sometimes being quite shy, particularly when on a stage like this was.

Jane: It felt as though emotionally Anthony was waiting, Mavis was looking for something and Bridget was trying to get out of the spotlight. That's what seemed to be going on – 'beneath the content of the conversation', as Anthony put it earlier. Anthony was waiting to see how the others were responding to him. Mavis was out there almost shaking people for a response and Bridget was . . . Bridget was acting as if other people were making her uncomfortable.

Anthony: Very good. So what do you think, or rather feel, it was like to be with each of us in that imaginary canteen conversation? What does it feel like to be with each of us and our patterns of emotional engagement?

Paresh: It felt as though Mavis was taking a more expressive position because she wasn't getting much from Anthony, whereas Anthony was holding back because Mavis was being so pushy. Bridget was feeling uncomfortable with everyone else staring at her and I think the other two tended to ignore her because of that.

Anthony: It's always nice to hear from you, Paresh – when you do say something it's very perceptive. Like me you can sometimes hold back – I wouldn't call you shy though, but rather contemplative.

Paresh: [smiles a big smile]

Anthony: I suggest that you all follow this exercise up in your everyday life and work – particularly your placements. Try looking and listening beneath the content of what's going on – at the emotional engagement. In this way you will gradually develop your emotional awareness of interpersonal situations, and the client–counsellor relationship in particular. Ask yourself what kinds of patterns of emotional expression, perception and response are going on here, what's it like to emotionally engage with this or that person, how do I emotionally perceive or misperceive this person, what expressions and responses am I giving off, what are my common patterns of emotional engagement, who do I feel safe or unsafe with, excited or loved by, what's it like to be with me, am I emotionally warm or cold, honest or secretive, do I reach out to others emotionally or hold back and wait for the other to reach out?

Amanda: Can you write all that down on the board, please – it all sounded very important and I'll never remember it?

Anthony: I will do in a few minutes but just now I'd like to hear from Bridget and Mavis – how are you feeling about what's been said?

Mavis: Helpful – I found Paresh's comments very interesting – it's really making me think about how I'm always looking for some kind of reassurance when I'm with people. Belinda described me as really self-confident and I can see how I might appear that way, but underneath I'm always needing to be reassured that other people are there, emotionally speaking.

Bridget: I'm feeling . . . I don't know. [her voice starts to shake a little then she suddenly breaks into tears, reaches down for her handbag and then rushes out of the room, hand over her face! Stunned silence in the group. People are looking around at each other, it feels very uncomfortable, a few of the group begin to look at Anthony for some kind of response. Anthony looks quite relaxed and not that uncomfortable. Sarah gets up.]

Sarah: I'd like to go and check on Bridget – I feel it may have been something I said. [Sarah leaves.]

Anthony: I'm imagining that Bridget was feeling the attention was all too much – I was also noticing how each of us, and the group, was responding to this dramatic exit. It feels as though we have hurt Bridget and I'm feeling guilty about that. I'm wondering what Bridget might be saying to us, and me in particular, through her sudden tears and exit.

[Bridget and Sarah return to the group. Bridget mumbles that she is sorry; she looks somewhat bedraggled and miserable. Sarah is looking very concerned and sits next to Bridget holding her hand.]

Anthony: It feels to me as though it would be kind to Bridget if we didn't continue to focus on her since my sense is that she finds being at the centre of group attention very difficult and uncomfortable. Being a counsellor doesn't really involve anything like that anyway, since there are usually only two or three of you in the counselling room. I would suggest that you all examine this experience in your journal, however, and we can perhaps invite Bridget to say something about it to us when she's feeling less distressed. I'd recommend that you explore this in your personal work, Bridget, but for now I'd like us to return to the seminar theme. I'll write up the suggestions I made earlier – for following up on your development of 'emotional awareness'. I'll need you all, however, to help me remember them.

Learning to come closer

The nature and importance of close relationships

Interpersonal closeness is a vital part of psychological health and a primary source of happiness for most people. Coping with the loss of close relationships is the great tragic theme of life – for many of us this loss lies at the core of our most deeply felt pain and suffering. But what exactly does it mean to be close to another person and why do some people find it difficult, if not impossible, to develop and maintain close relationships?

When we come to define the nature of close relationships one of the first things that we notice is that it's impossible to have many. Close relationships require a lot of time to be spent together and we simply don't have enough time for more than a handful. Generally speaking close relationships need to be maintained and developed – through that time spent together. This is why the couple who spend time together often experience a fading of close relationships outside of their partnership – especially when children arrive on the scene.

Exercise Examine, in your journal, as closely as you can, your experience of closeness with others.

Someone who cares – an extract from David's journal

We have been studying close relationships and last session we did an exercise on *experiences of rejection*. We were asked to explore how our feelings about rejection might get in the way of moving

towards closeness with other people. The exercise then asked us
to explore where this present difficulty might have come from – I
found this quite difficult to do. Finally, what came up for me was
the memory of an experience I had at school when I was about 12 or
13. It was my first day at a new school and my first encounter with
any of the boys at the school. I was standing in the lunch queue
and asked the boy in front of me what was for dinner. He replied in
a nasty voice 'Pice and shait!' I could hardy understand his
accent but worked out 'Piss and shit!' Somehow that experience
seemed to symbolize my sense of rejection and at that moment I was
filled with a deep sense of caring for that little boy – the boy
who had been myself and was still myself in some way. In my mind's
eye I saw him there at the new school with no one – no friends, or
anyone he knew, having lost his friends back in the place he used
to live – standing there in the dinner queue and making contact
with someone at the new school for the first time. I was filled
with sadness for him and tears came into my eyes. At that moment I
also noticed my fellow student, Sarah, who had been taking up the
role of 'listener'. She looked so sad too and I felt quite
overwhelmed with feelings. We sat together silently for a few
minutes. That was a very significant experience for me. I really
felt cared for by Sarah – in the midst of my feelings of being
uncared for. I felt I was with a friend in the midst of my feelings
of friendlessness and I felt a deep warmth and caring for her in
response.

Thinking about this experience, right now, I feel as though
something very important shifted for me in those minutes with
Sarah. I feel warmer, not only towards her, but also to other
members of the group. I actually feel a part of them in a way that I
haven't felt before and certainly didn't feel in my previous
counselling training. I've also noticed that there is some anger
there for me too – about my previous training being so poor, at
the level of the group experience.

More than anything I feel like caring for myself. Yesterday
evening, for example, when my wife was out at her aerobics class I
suddenly decided I wasn't going to make do with beans on toast and
took myself out for a meal at a fancy restaurant. I had two
appetizers – I normally avoid appetizers for cost reasons – a
main course, a fabulous dessert and a half-bottle of champagne.
It was the most expensive meal I had ever had and I loved it! 'Pice
and shait – fuck him!' I thought, 'I deserve the best.' Sitting
there, drinking the champagne, I contemplated how important this
course is to me – sometimes it's annoying and frustrating,
sometimes it's very difficult and very uncomfortable, sometimes
I feel completely lost and sometimes I feel 'wow'. Like last night
– I really felt inspired. It feels like I'm coming alive!

One last thing: I've noticed that since the exercise with Sarah
I've been feeling a little closer to other people outside the
group. I feel a little warmer towards my wife Jane, for instance –
this morning at breakfast I sat for a moment and looked at her and

tears came into my eyes (again). She asked me what was wrong. I
noticed how concerned she was for me and that made me even sadder.
It was an unusual moment for us. Then I said 'I love you'. I could
see that she was quite embarrassed. 'That bloody course again,'
she said with a smile – which is not always what she feels about
the course. I believe she was really touched by what I said –
because I really meant it. Often we say 'I love you' to each other
but usually it's just spoken like hello and goodbye. This time was
different. Which, in a way, was important in itself – we haven't
been having that brilliant a time of it recently and part of that
is this bloody course.

Not being alone with it – extract from a subsequent seminar

Jane: I'm beginning to understand more about theories of interpersonal closeness and I'm beginning to relate these ideas to myself
– that's been good. What I haven't been able to do, as yet, is apply
much of it to my work with clients. Can you say something about
how it can be applied?

Anthony: I've been doing quite a lot of talking today, and I could
continue, but perhaps it's more important if other members answer
that question. Does anyone have any 'application' they could offer
or suggest? [Silence]

Sarah: I have something that may help. It's not, however, in relation
to a client but to another member of the group – David. I need to
ask him if it's OK to talk about our personal development exercise
last time. Would that be OK, David? Please say if it isn't.

David: That's fine, Sarah, I don't mind at all.

Sarah: Thanks. As you all know, last session we did an exercise on
how feelings about rejection might get in the way of our ability to
relate with others and I took up the role of listener-cum-counsellor
with David. He linked his present issue with a past memory. At
first he didn't think the exercise was that relevant and I felt he was
even a little resentful about doing it. Then he suddenly stopped,
tears came into his eyes and he was filled with sadness for a time
when he was a new boy at a new school. I didn't say anything for a
few minutes. My mind was going around trying to think of
something to say, but at the same time – and this is what I wanted
to give as an example – I felt very sad with him. It felt like we
moved closer during those few minutes of silence. Today, when we
all arrived, it was David I was thinking about and it was David I
felt closest to. [Looks straight at David. David smiles in an embarrassed way.] In my journal I think I 'applied' this to working with
clients. I could see that not only would such an experience be really
important in building our relationship but it would also be very
'therapeutic' in its own way. In the discussion after the exercise
David said that it was important to feel he was with me at that

point of his remembering – that it was a 'healing' moment for him. Is that right, David?

David: Yes it was a very healing moment, and very important for me.

Sarah: In his description of the past experience David had contacted some very uncomfortable feelings but it seemed to me that it was the fact that originally he'd been alone in the world with those feelings that was the most difficult thing for him. I felt that being really there with him while he remembered that time may have changed things a little for him.

David: More than a little.

Sarah: There, that's my example. I don't know if I've explained it very well but I think I'm beginning to understand this more myself.

Anthony: You've explained it very well. It's a very good example. Thank you, Sarah.

Something missing – an extract from Robert's journal

I've been thinking about Anthony's feedback to me on my written work – that I need to develop more attention to the emotional and feeling level of things – that I'm very good conceptually but that's not enough and that relying on the conceptual rather than the feelings isn't what's needed as a counsellor. Something he said to me as well – about how I'm always asking him for references – how did he put it? 'Sometimes books can act as a replacement for people, sometimes we can come to rely on books for the kind of basic sense of being-in-relation-with-others, being held by and stimulated by others, and thus we manage to avoid putting the effort into people.' This really struck me – I fill my life with books and that, somehow, does give me a sense of a 'peopled life'. But it's a very sterile and non-interactive one, the people are authors, not living beings in my immediate world. Yes, it really made me think, and what I thought was, 'What about the people in my life – my family, my colleagues, my friends? If I am so reliant on books how do they figure in my world?'

I've been trying to get a sense of this – to feel my way instead of thinking about it and it feels as though I'm holding everyone at a distance. I keep myself away from my feelings and, as part of that, I keep other people away from me – psychologically speaking. Since I began to realize this I've been feeling quite sad – it's like I'm suddenly facing the fact that I'm really quite a 'cold' person and that my life is really quite an emotionally sterile one. Sterilized, numbed, cleansed of feeling. Which is quite something to realize about oneself: quite devastating, in fact. Especially because I also feel quite useless as a counsellor – an emotional illiterate trying to become an emotional expert. I feel as if I've been going on a long journey and I was thinking that the journey was getting near its end, only to suddenly find out that I've been going in the wrong direction, that I've spent all this time going the wrong way. Years, my life, going the wrong way!

Then I began to think, and feel, about my wife, Anne, and us, and how ... well, emotionally there isn't much there at all. I mean to say I'm, we're, almost as distant as everyone else in my life. Anne says she loves me and I say the same, and we've been saying that for years, but what do we really mean by those words? Something else I've just thought. When I'm away on business and I call her up, she hardly ever asks about me – except for a passing comment. She's always talking about what's been going on for her – it's almost as if my world doesn't exist for her. Perhaps I'm just much more sensitive to how other people listen or don't listen – this being my second year of counselling training – but I feel it's more than that. In fact right now I'm feeling quite annoyed and disappointed in her. It's like I'm seeing another side to her ... hmmm ... just like I'm seeing another side to myself! And just like I don't like what I'm seeing in myself I don't like what I'm seeing in her. I'd always thought of her as caring and loving but from this angle she looks cold, selfish and emotionally distant too.

When we spend time together she tends to talk about her world, or what's going on in the family – but from her perspective. I guess I've just held myself away from her and she's got used to that – me being distant. I don't know ... it definitely feels like there's something missing between us, something very important but also quite subtle. It's difficult for me to get a sense of it because I'm so used to it being missing from my life. Yes, we hardly ever connect up – what do I mean by that? We never seem to simply enjoy being with each other, for example. We hardly ever just enjoy the presence of each other. Maybe I'm being silly and romantic and expecting too much from a 15-year-old marriage but I feel it's more than that. I don't really remember us ever doing that – being together in that way. I can remember that happening very occasionally with other people but I don't remember it happening with my parents – or my brother or sister. Well, to some extent with my sister. That feels very relevant – about my family ... I'm feeling pretty sad again. Tears are welling up in my eyes. I guess I feel quite lonely – very deep down, in a very hidden kind of a way. It's bloody painful sometimes but I'm really glad that I'm doing this course even if I never really 'make it' to be a counsellor.

The question is, am I a lost case or is there any hope here? It feels like it could be quite an uphill struggle to change the way I am in my 'world of others'. Even more difficult because other people expect me to be 'Robert' – the Robert they know, or rather they *don't* really know. I suppose that's the key – to let them see more of the me that has been held at a distance from them. I've always got the excuse of the course. But how do I go about that? I can't exactly go 'Oh by the way I haven't really been that emotionally present with you before but I want to start being more so from now on'. I can't really wear a little badge: 'Robert is now more emotionally present than ever before'. Perhaps I'll just have to become more aware of how distant I am and simply practise being more present – learn to switch from books to people, from thoughts to feelings, from rational perceptions of situations to emotional perceptions. Not that I want to chuck the rational and intellectual in the bin, or the books for that matter, no, they are really important to me. But they are also pretty big in my life and, like big trees, perhaps they get in the way of smaller plants growing up because the big ones take up so much of the light/attention. I read that metaphor in a book a few years ago!

Four exercises to explore your experience of close relationships

Exploring experiences of loss and being left alone

Note of warning: This exercise can open you up to strong emotions. If the feelings threaten to overwhelm, and that doesn't feel OK for you at this time, come out of the depths of those feelings by focusing on the colours in the room. If you want to stay with the feelings and allow them some expression then give yourself permission to do so.

(a) Allow yourself to remember a person who was important to you, perhaps someone that you loved, someone that you lost but wished you hadn't.
(b) Explore your experience of the loss and the feelings it left you with. Explore whether you felt not only sadness but also, for example, anger or resentment. Were you able to say what needed to be said or even say goodbye to this person?
(c) See if you can identify and say any unsaid words. If you can, then imagine that person is with you right now and say them directly. Explore any feelings that arise for you as you speak directly these previously unsaid words.

Spend a few minutes coming out of and reviewing the exercise.

Exploring your experiences of intimacy

Part 1: How do you respond to the following paragraph?

At the core of mature relating, competent counselling, competent supervision and competent counselling training is found 'the intimate relationship'. The creation of this pattern of relating is, for me, a main goal of my work – as counsellor, tutor, verifier, supervisor, author – and a primary goal of my life as a whole.

Part 2: Closeness is closely linked with time spent together, but what kinds of things go on in that time? How does a close relationship become established and what does it require in order to be maintained? Consider the following questions in relation to your own close relationships:

(a) What does intimacy consist of? For example –
   • reciprocal trust and warmth.
   • interest in each other together with reciprocal empathy.
   • enjoyment of each other's company (including shared interests).
   • reciprocal caring and support.
   • a common 'wavelength'.
   • sharing of inner thoughts and feelings.

(b) What does it feel like to be intimate? For example –
   • I feel emotionally connected, in touch, engaged.
   • I feel affirmed, cared for, and I affirm and care for.
   • I don't feel 'boxed in' – I feel free to be what I am at that time, able to express my thoughts and feelings, my subjective experience – and I allow the other to be and express who he or she is.
   • I feel more alive in relation with the other.
   • I and the other are in a process of psychological change and growth.
   • I don't continue to collude and avoid issues that I, or the other, don't want to acknowledge – when I become aware of them.
   • Together we cope with the defensiveness that is associated with collusion.

(c) How does intimacy come about? For example –
   • I need to trust that, overall, I will not be 'crushed' by you.
   • I need to trust that, overall, I will not be abandoned by you.
   • I need to trust that, overall, I will not be misused by you.
   • I need to trust that if I feel these kinds of feelings I will be able to share them with you and, in that process, move to a deeper position of trust – I can be abandoned (crushed, or misused) for a short time because I trust I will not be abandoned by you in the long term.
   • What I therefore discover in all of this is that I am valuable and important enough to you to be 'stuck with' through difficult times.
   • I offer you the same.

(d) How do you deal with 'bad' feelings? For example –
   • feelings of dissatisfaction that I feel towards the other.
   • desire for the other that I 'shouldn't' have – the desire, for example, to kiss my friend.

- the desire to rage at him or her.
- other thoughts and feelings that I have towards friends – for example disapproval;.
- uncomfortable moments – either when or soon after they happen.
- feeling 'dropped' by the other.
- feelings of inadequacy as a friend or partner.

Patterns of relating

Part 1: Explore in your journal your experiences of relationships focusing on:

- selecting a partner
- sustaining a marriage/partnership
- adjusting to separation/divorce
- any other important issues in your couple relationships

Part 2: Consider what these experiences may say about your patterns of relating and/or the different sides of yourself.

Part 3: See if you can discover the origins of any patterns that you have identified.

Becoming aware of barriers to trust and openness

In this exercise you can begin an exploration of barriers (defences) that you put up between yourself and others – barriers that work against the development of trust and mutuality. Very often we put up these barriers as a result either of our misperception of the other or the other's misperception of us. This misperception is called 'transference' and is one of the main areas of work of in-depth psychodynamic counselling. Transference is the transferring of past experiences into the present and with those old experiences, old barriers and 'unfinished business' in relation to the other.

(a) See if you can find a person in your circle of colleagues and acquaintances, family or friends, who, perhaps a little 'irrationally', evokes uncomfortable feelings in you and with whom you feel there are quite clear interpersonal barriers.
(b) Explore your experience of that person and how you normally respond to them – describing any particular barriers between you and the other.
(c) Now explore whether the person reminds you of anyone from your past and, if so, explore your experience of relating with that original person.

(d) Ask yourself to what extent you relate to the present person as if they were that other person.

(e) Ask yourself how this present person is different from the person he or she reminds you of, then make a clear statement that untangles the two people in your perceptions and emphasizes the differences, for example:

> 'Sometimes when I am relating with my boss I am reminded of being told off by my father. I now see that then I am reacting to my boss as if he was my father. My father was, however, big and broad and my boss is thin and of average height. They are very different as persons and my relationship with each of them is very different.'

(f) Explore how you feel, now, about the present person – whether, for example, it might be a little easier for you to trust him or her, to have fewer barriers between you both, to be a little more open to him or her.

7

The Client–Counsellor Relationship

Mr Elliot was rational, discreet, polished, but he was not open. There
was never any burst of feeling, any warmth of indignation or delight,
at the evil or good of others. This, to Anne, was a decided imperfec-
tion. (Jane Austen, *Persuasion*, 1818)

The therapeutic value of the relationship

Extract from a seminar

Henry: I've prepared this seminar presentation on the theme of the
therapeutic value of the client–counsellor relationship. I wanted to
present on this topic after Barbara's seminar on the core therapeutic
elements of the counselling process – in which she described how
research had identified the relationship as so important. When I first
heard that I was really quite surprised and it's only through thinking
about it very carefully in relation to my personal and professional
experiences that it's beginning to make sense to me. I'd like to start
this seminar presentation, however, by looking at the idea of
repeated uncomfortable interpersonal moments.

   A few years ago, for example, I had a market stall at a peace
festival where I was selling some T-shirts that I'd made. The T-shirts
were selling quite well and then someone pointed out that the peace
sign painted on them wasn't quite right and that in fact they were
all painted with the logo for Mercedes Benz cars. Naturally, I felt
very embarrassed but what I've realized, partly as a result of
personal counselling, is that the uncomfortable feeling I felt then I
had felt before and have felt since. Another time, a few years ago, I
felt a very similar feeling when a woman I was very attracted to
expressed her attraction to me. More recently I felt the same kind of
feeling in a supervision session when I was describing one of my
sessions and realized I'd made a big mistake. I've talked to quite a
few people about this and they also seemed to have experienced a
similar kind of repeated uncomfortable interpersonal moment – at
different times and in different situations, though not necessarily the
same feeling as me.

A couple of weeks ago, I talked with Amanda about this, in our review time after an exercise, and she has a similar pattern of feeling 'stunned'. By the way, I've asked her if it would be OK to share this with the group and she said it would – if I hadn't I can imagine that right now I might be feeling my 'uncomfortable interpersonal moment'. [Certain members of the group break into a laugh.] It's like each person I've talked to about this has a string of bad memories – often really quite bad memories that stick out in their mind. But although they each saw their particular memory as a 'bad moment' they hadn't linked them together as actually the *same* subjective moment reappearing in different social situations.

As I thought about and discussed this and explored it in my own personal counselling it began to take on huge significance. It's as if this same subjective moment – or perhaps two or three moments – reappears in my personal history, partly creating many of the bad experiences and bad memories. Or if not actually creating them, making them worse – through the way in which it colours each of them.

John: So what you're saying is that we each have a pattern of problematic relating that keeps recurring.

Henry: That's too general a statement – yes I'm saying that, but I'm being much more detailed and precise. I'm talking about one way of applying that general idea – the idea of a pattern of problematic relating – to your own experience and that of your clients.

Jane: I think I know what Henry is trying to get at here. It's all right having an idea like 'a pattern of problematic relating' but what do you do with that idea? It's just an idea. What Henry's suggesting, if I'm understanding him, is that to make that idea work in practice you might look for a series of uncomfortable interpersonal situations and find, within them, basically the same uncomfortable subjective experience.

Henry: Or even look first for the subjective event – when did I also feel like that?

Sarah: I've been looking at my own experiences while you've been talking and there does seem to be something like what you're talking about in my memories of uncomfortable situations with other people – although I'd say that there are more than one or two for me. But probably only a small number. It's quite hard, though – it's quite a hard thing to think about.

Henry: Yes it is – that's why I believe the people I've explored this with hadn't really noticed the pattern. It's not only hard because it's a difficult idea to relate to but also because as soon as we experience anything like this we want to forget what it felt like. When I was remembering that experience with the T-shirts I could also sense another part of myself trying to forget it, to push it away from my awareness. The same goes for the time with that woman –

it sticks in my memory as a moment but it's also one that, as soon as I start to remember the feelings, I also want to forget them. In fact when I was exploring this in relation to myself I kept on wanting to stop, or else my mind just started to think about something else. I've done a lot of meditation, however, and I found I could notice my mind wandering off and bring it back – to focus again on these uncomfortable events.

Belinda: That sounds very useful – could you explain that a bit more.

Henry: I could do, Belinda, but that would feel like I was wandering off from this difficult-to-stay-with subject and I'd like to return to actual examples again.

Belinda: OK.

Henry: As I went on with my exploration I discovered, at the core of these uncomfortable moments, that there was a sense of a chasm between myself and the other person. In each of the bad memories, what seemed to be the heart of it was a feeling of being out of contact. A bit like a spaceship suddenly out of contact with the earth – a deep sense of abandonment, in fact. I could give you other examples – when I was unemployed I developed an anxiety about writing cheques in the presence of someone else. Exploring these very uncomfortable interpersonal experiences in my personal counselling I, once again, discovered this chasm.

If I hadn't been in my own personal counselling I don't believe I could have explored any of this. My meditation skills helped me to notice my mind wandering off but they weren't enough. One of the main reasons why counselling was so vital was that the relationship I'd developed with my counsellor worked in the opposite direction from my chasm. What do I mean by that? Well, in repeatedly working with my counsellor and sharing myself with her I've developed an opposite feeling to my chasm. I'm pretty sure that it's only because of that sense of non-chasm that I've felt safe enough to work on that very unsafe and uncomfortable feeling of the chasm. Right now I'd say that the sense of this chasm was *the* psychological problem in my life – around which, and out of which, my many other patterns and problems originate. So, for me, the developing sense of connection that has arisen through the development of my relationship with my counsellor is the primary therapeutic element of my counselling.

John: That's a very powerful argument, Henry, but I'm wondering if it applies to other people? You discovered this chasm in yourself and I can see how valuable it was for you to develop a client–counsellor relationship that bridged that chasm. But what about someone whose primary issue, or fundamental issue, wasn't anything like that – would the relationship be so important then?

Henry: I don't know, John – it's a good question but I haven't got any further with this at the moment.

Jane: I've always thought of the relationship between client and counsellor as important for much simpler reasons. Many clients, for example, when asked about what they found valuable in their counselling, have spoken about things like 'being able to share with someone' or 'she was there for me' or 'feeling cared for and listened to' or 'feeling that someone understood'. Henry's example from his own personal counselling has made me wonder about a much, much deeper aspect to the client–counsellor relationship. What he seems to be describing is a kind of deep healing of his existential sense of isolation and abandonment – his sense, at the root of his being, of being alone in the world seems to have subtly changed for him. That's quite something – actually something quite enormous. It's almost like a critique of, an answer to, Jean-Paul Sartre and that whole philosophical school.

Henry: I'm not really up on Jean-Paul Sartre's work but I'm glad you found it interesting.

Four questions to consider

1 How do you respond to the above passage?
2 Have you had similar repeated uncomfortable interpersonal moments? If so, what are they like?
3 How do you see the place of the client–counsellor relationship in the counselling process as a whole?
4 How might you apply any insights into the therapeutic value of relationship to your work with your clients?

The concepts of transference and containment

Learning to work as a professional counsellor involves learning to join with the client and together enter into, contain, explore, work with and work through the very uncomfortable and distressing experiences that are found within the client's past and present experiences of the world. Both the client and the novice counsellor, however, will often not want to focus on these experiences because they are so painful.

One way of avoiding distressful memories is to numb the memory and associate the uncomfortable feelings that are left over with current events. In other words, the residual feelings are explained with reference to something that is going on now – in this way the full painful memory is successfully forgotten. Let me give you an example.

Helena touches into a memory of overwhelming feelings of abandonment and rejection. In flight from those feelings she misperceives the current situation (say John arriving for their session two minutes late) in terms of John deeply rejecting her. Helena then reacts to the perceived rejection with repressed rage and withdrawal from the relationship. All of this is unspoken. In fact, Helena is not very consciously aware of what is actually going on for her that session.

The novice counsellor reacts to this very difficult emotional interaction with confusion – for example by counter-attacking or counter-withdrawing from the relationship. It's important to remember that such an emotional interaction doesn't make present-centred sense – it feels 'wrong' and 'out of tune' and interpersonally confusing. It isn't 'rational' – in terms of the present-day relationship between John and Helena. The situation will be further complicated by the fact that the counsellor, if he or she is staying with the client, will also have touched on the client's underlying feelings and, like a tuning fork, those overwhelming feelings of abandonment and rejection (in this example) will be reverberating within the counsellor. In other words, the counsellor tunes into his or her own related memories and overwhelming experiences of abandonment and rejection. The novice counsellor will therefore often take flight from these feelings – leading to thorough-going emotional confusion.

The professional practitioner, in contrast, is able to 'respond therapeutically' – both entering into, and staying with, the client's, and the counsellor's, overwhelming feelings of abandonment and rejection, together with containing the experience of attack and withdrawal by the client and not reacting with a counter-reaction. The counsellor's containment of these very difficult feelings and interpersonal experiences enables the client to feel much safer and trusting of the counsellor – and thus better able to explore and work through the real (past) pain and confusion and begin to further untangle the present from the past.

This kind of interpersonal experience is called 'transference' – transference of an unwanted emotional memory into a present interaction with another person and the associated misperceiving of an aspect of a present emotional interaction. Perhaps the best ways of learning to respond therapeutically are to explore these kinds of difficult client–counsellor experiences in supervision and to develop the capacity to stay with very uncomfortable experiences through personal counselling.

In a similar way to clients, students on courses will frequently touch into personal pain and, in flight from that pain, attach its 'cause' to some present event or 'trigger' associated with other students in the group, or the tutors, or the training organization, or elsewhere. If this is taken purely at face value, then it can easily snowball into very uncomfortable, and sometimes quite abusive situations. In contrast, if the student works at seeing that transference is operating, he or she can be encouraged to contain and explore the feelings, untangle the present from the past, and thus enhance his or her capacity for emotional awareness and therapeutic responding.

An example of therapeutic responding: extract from a seminar

Sarah: I have a question from last time: How can I know myself better? How could you, as a counsellor, help me to?

Anthony: Well, I could help you, for example, to gain a sense of the psychological shape of yourself, I could help you to understand your personal history and how you have become who you are and I could help you to know how you exist in relation to significant others, how your self is tied up with the way you perceive and respond to others and the ways they perceive and respond to you.

Sarah: How would you actually help me, though – that's what I don't understand? What would we do, what would happen? What would it be like?

Anthony: Well, you would talk and I would listen. Then I might point to something in particular – perhaps a sense I might have of some conflict within you – a sense, for example, that there are different voices in you, speaking to me. Voices that speak from different sides of yourself. Perhaps even a sense of an unspoken voice. Then I might, for example, ask you to speak the unspoken. But only ask – I would seek to offer that part of you a space to speak. What would you say now, for example, that perhaps you would not otherwise say?

Sarah: [Silence] I'm not sure what you mean.

Anthony: Perhaps I could give you an example: perhaps I could speak my unspoken thoughts and feelings, perhaps that would help.

Sarah: I'm not sure . . . That feels a little frightening . . . I wouldn't normally have said that.

Anthony: You wouldn't normally have said that to someone that you didn't know really well? Someone who is also an authority figure?

Sarah: Yes.

Anthony: Well there you are, you have spoken something of the unspoken. How does it feel?

Sarah: [Silence – breathes heavily, almost in a sigh] It feels OK. No, actually it feels quite good. I found that difficult to say.

Anthony: Another normally unspoken feeling.

Sarah: Yes, I think so.

Anthony: I don't know, but I felt you were quite sad at that moment.

Sarah: Which moment?

Anthony: Maybe I was wrong . . .

Sarah: No, you, you were right. [tears in her eyes – looks away] Sorry. [She reaches for a tissue.]

Anthony [thinks/feels: 'This feels like quite an uncomfortable moment, I'm not sure what to say, or whether to say anything. I could say that she doesn't need to feel sorry, but that feels trite. I feel quite full of sadness myself. It's to do with the sense of being honest together and that not happening very often for her (and for me?). If I look at this situation simply from my heart I feel a lot of warmth towards her. If I was her right now how would I want Anthony to respond? I don't know. It's very difficult. Mainly I'd feel vulnerable and exposed, perhaps I'd like that acknowledged in a gentle way?'] I feel as though you are quite exposed at this moment, quite vulnerable. I'm not sure what to say now.

Sarah: You don't have to say anything . . . I could feel you when we were silent. You seemed to be thinking hard [Both laugh.] . . . and I was feeling very real warmth from you [tears in her eyes].

Anthony: It also feels, right now, that you are out of that part of yourself, that the hidden voice has gone somewhere?

Sarah: Yes, I think I know what you mean. I'm back in my normal self [slight annoyance in her voice].

Anthony: You don't seem so pleased about that?

Sarah: What . . . No. OK, I did say that a little angrily . . . Is this counselling? [somewhat grumpily]

Anthony: And if it is?

Sarah: Well I thought we had agreed, in our initial contract for the group, that this relationship – between tutor and student – was not a counselling one. That as a trainer you were not allowed to counsel me. Ethically, that is.

Anthony: That's true, Sarah. We have agreed that ethically I'm not allowed to be your counsellor as well as being your trainer . . . But I think, for a moment, it was very much like counselling, I think I was being like a counsellor with you, at least for those few moments. How do you feel about that?

Sarah: Well actually I feel a bit annoyed. No, I feel quite angry with you.

Anthony: Do you want to say more about that?

Sarah: You have exposed me, and I feel tricked, and I feel I can't trust you anymore.

Seven questions to consider

1 How do you respond to this seminar extract?
2 If you were Anthony, how would you have responded to Sarah?
3 What if this was not an interaction between a student and her tutor but (in a different form) a client and her counsellor – how would you feel and respond as counsellor?
4 What are the dangers inherent in inviting the unspoken parts of ourselves to speak?
5 What might be happening for Sarah when she turns from sad to angry?

6   'It seems that Anthony and Sarah move closer together and then suddenly Sarah pushes Anthony away.' How do you respond to that statement?
7   How might Anthony respond to Sarah's last statement?

Feeling safe to feel unsafe

A key aspect of counselling is the professional framework – the professional structure within which the client can feel safer to feel unsafe. Like the skeleton inside a body, the professional framework helps to hold the counselling together.

The professional framework is founded upon certain key requirements, including:

- the requirement that the counsellor actively works to treat all clients 'equally' – in terms of ethnic orientation, sexual orientation, disability, etc.;
- the requirement that the counsellor keeps certain boundaries with clients – not having sex with clients and being very careful about mixing roles or relationships (for example, not mixing line management with counselling);
- the requirement that the counsellor keeps to certain rules concerning, for example, confidentiality and the non-exploitation of clients;
- the requirement that the counsellor makes clear agreements (a 'contract') with the client about the counselling;
- the requirement that the counsellor takes account of important issues concerning the setting in which the work takes place.
- the requirement that the counsellor monitors his or her personal and professional competence and finds appropriate support in the form of professional supervision (see Chapter 9), personal counselling and further training and development.

Because the counsellor works within a professional framework, one in which certain codes and rules of behaviour are framing the work, the client is able to feel more secure. The professional framework is therefore a critical part of the creation of that safe space in which clients can feel able to share their vulnerability and hurt. It helps clients to reduce their concerns about their immediate environment – the counselling situation – leaving them free to explore themselves, their relationships and their life.

Exercise

Spend some time remembering your experiences of being helped by others. Choose two or three examples. Ask yourself how safe you felt in each of the examples. Ask yourself whether you felt safe enough to feel unsafe. Take a look at the requirements listed above and consider how each of them might have affected your sense of safety. Explore this idea of the client being able to give up worrying about his or her immediate environment – what would that mean to you (both as client and counsellor)? If you were to identify ten 'commandments' that you'd want your counsellor to follow, what would they be?

Finally, consider the following dilemmas:

1   Your client asks you out for a drink. How do you respond and what do you do?
2   Your client tells you about a child that is being sexually abused. How do you respond and what do you do?
3   Your agency secretary tries to discuss your client with you. How do you respond and what do you do?
4   You are referred a client who is clearly beyond your competence to work with. How do you proceed?
5   How do you deal with a client who arrives but cannot get up the stairs to the room where you work?
6   Consider what other dilemmas you might come across, how you might respond and what you might do?

Coping with an 'emergency' situation

Jane: What in the world am I going to do?

Sandra: What's up, Jane? It sounds as if something terrible has happened.

Jane: It's David – he's dead. [Silence]

Sandra: You look terrible.

Jane: I feel terrible, awful. I've been up all night for the past four nights, crying . . . I know it was expected, but . . . I just can't believe it. I keep going into the kitchen, the lounge, the bedroom and expecting him to be sitting there and then it hits me, again and again. But I still can't really believe it.

Sandra: It feels like you're almost in a panic, Jane.

Jane: [sighs . . . starts to cry] That's just how I feel, Sandra – in a total state of panic. I've been [breaks into tears] rushing around and around. I can't stop still. Look at me – I'm even twitching. [Silence] What am I going to do? [Stares blindly at Sandra] I feel at a complete loss. Rushing around. My God. I even saw him sitting there . . . two nights ago – I was tidying up my drawer, I've been tidying up all the time, my things mainly, I've been leaving David's alone, just where they are – he was in our, no, my, bedroom. For a moment I saw him sitting on the edge of the bed. Smiling at me. He was really there, I know it. My heart leapt into my throat with so much joy at that moment. [Breaks down, sobbing intensely] For a moment I was so, so happy and then he was gone. Vanished. I couldn't cope with that – I fell to the floor and cried and cried and cried and cried, squeezing the bedcover where I had seen him. My jaw hurt with the terrible despair of it all. I wanted to scream but nothing came out. I was lying there in this blackness screaming but nothing, no sound, came out of my mouth. And then, God forgive me, I became so angry – in that moment I hated God, I hated him so much for taking David first. Oh God, Sandra. [Starts to breathe in and out very rapidly] I'm feeling dizzy, Sandra. Help, I'm going to faint.

Sandra: [takes hold of Jane's right hand, holds it between hers and calmly looks into her eyes] You're in shock, Jane. I'll look after you right now – here, lie back and focus on your breathing. I want you to look at the various things in the room. Take a look at the curtains, the lampshade, what colours are there in the room? That's right. Now see if you can relax a little. That's right. Let your breathing return to normal. [Silence] How are you feeling now?

Jane: Not so faint.

Some questions to consider

1   How would you cope with this kind of 'emergency' situation?
2   What other types of emergency might occur in a counselling session and how would you deal with them?
3   Are you aware of the sorts of signs that can indicate that someone is feeling suicidal? What would you do if you felt a client was exhibiting those signs? (I've asked these questions before – in Chapter 2 – but repeat them here because of their importance.)
4   How would you approach a client who began 'acting out' outside your sessions?
5   How would you approach a client with a history of 'mental illness'? How would you know whether a new client had such a history?

Boundaries and fences

Extract from a seminar

Henry: I've been thinking about our session last week on boundaries and wondering about a couple of things. My first query concerns the seeming paradox that, on the one hand, client and counsellor are in a real, living relationship (and that this is perhaps the major thera-peutic element of counselling) and on the other hand the counsellor has to maintain boundaries with the client. I can understand the need for boundaries in relation to sexual activity but I'm not so clear as to, for example, the need for counselling to be distinguished from friendship. My second concern relates to the whole notion of boundaries. Perhaps, rather than them being for the benefit of the client, they are really for the benefit of the counsellor – perhaps even some form of defence against the client.

Anthony: Does anyone have any thoughts on these two concerns of Henry's – can a counsellor enter into a living relationship while maintaining boundaries, and are boundaries for the benefit of client or counsellor?

Amanda: I would say that without those basic boundaries I wouldn't feel safe to enter into a 'living' relationship with my counsellor. For me, as a client, such boundaries are definitely for my benefit. They make the space safe. Safer for me to be unsafe, as Anthony always puts it. I don't see them as getting in the way – but rather as going *around* the space.

Anthony: A nice image that, Amanda – that the boundaries are not between client and counsellor, not put there to get in the way, but rather put around the two, so as to make the space safer for the two people to get on with the counselling. Does anyone else have any thoughts on this?

Jane: That certainly helps me, Amanda. It reminds me of children and how they need a safe space to be children. Part of that space is that parents stick to their boundaries. I would say that one of the worst effects of incest is that the child doesn't have that safe space to be a child anymore – because the parent hasn't kept the boundaries, because the parent has actually abdicated the parent role.

Anthony: That's another good example, Jane, of how boundaries actually facilitate a living relationship rather than get in the way of it. And again that boundary is of great benefit to the child.

Henry: Thanks. That's also a good example of how boundaries are really important. I hadn't thought of boundaries as actually circling the two people, but I can see that they are vital for the parent–child relationship and I can see what you're saying about the client's perspective, Amanda.

Anthony: Mixing up relationships can be very confusing and problematic and this is especially true of something like a parent–child relationship – where there's dependency on the child's side and power on the parents'. The example of incest is more dramatic than the parent simply mixing up, for example, parent and friend, but I believe that this kind of mixing up can also be very damaging for a child. Imagine what it would be like, as a young child, to have a parent who also tried to relate to you as a friend.

Amanda: My mother did something like that. It's something that's come up in my personal counselling – how she always tried to treat me like a confidante. It was something that I always used to see as making me special for her, but I began to realize in my counselling that it was also a real pain. It's like she cheated me of something very important – a proper mother. In fact I came, as a result, to partly mother her – which didn't do me any good later on in life. Particularly when she killed herself. I now really wish I'd had a proper mother and not a mixed-up mother-cum-pseudo-friend. It meant she was neither one thing nor the other and it left me with a deep unmet need for a secure parent. That really screwed up my adult life.

Mavis: That sounds really awful, Amanda, but I always wished that my father would have treated me as a person and not a little child – I felt I never really knew him. He was always so distant and impersonal – I was 'daughter', he was 'father'. We never went beyond that – he never recognized me as a person and I always felt that was such a huge waste. I don't know what that says about boundaries but I know he would have been a much better father if he'd shared himself with me – if only a little.

Anthony: That sounds important, Mavis. Does anyone have any comment or response to Mavis's description of her father as this distant man who never shared himself?

Henry: It's something like what Mavis is saying that I was trying to get at about boundaries between client and counsellor – how they might be used for the benefit of the counsellor and not for the client. It almost sounds like your father used the boundary between father and daughter as a kind of defence, as a barrier that got in the way of a living relationship.

Anthony: Yes it does sound like Mavis's father might have put up a barrier between himself and his daughter and that was very detrimental to their relationship and to Mavis's experience of being his daughter. Is this what we mean by a 'boundary', though? A boundary marks out a space as a certain kind of space – in counselling terms it marks out the space as 'counselling'. The counsellor aims to keep out of that counselling space other forms of relationship such as lover or friend – but he or she doesn't put up that boundary to keep out the client. On the contrary, the counsellor is putting it around them – I really like Amanda's image. When I put up a barrier between myself and my client I'm not holding the counselling boundary at all – I'm actually destroying that space by kicking out my client. I'm not sure that Mavis's example of her distant father is a good example of a parent holding the parental 'boundary'. You haven't really said enough about your relationship with him but I'm wondering whether what you are seeing as a boundary might have been more of a fence dividing him from you.

Mavis: I'd like to think about that, Anthony.

Seven questions to consider

1 How do you respond to this distinction between boundaries and fences?
2 What other kinds of boundaries need to be kept?
3 How important are the counselling boundaries to you – both as a client and as a counsellor?
4 How do boundaries benefit the counsellor?
5 Are there occasions when boundaries might get in the way of counselling?
6 What boundaries are you required to keep, according to your code of ethics?
7 What boundaries exist for you in your other social and working contexts?

Two perspectives on one relationship

Amanda: Good morning, Eric, my name's Amanda, I'm one of the counsellors working in this agency. There's one or two things I need to say to you about myself, and the nature of counselling, before we start, if that's all right with you?

Eric: I'm all ears.

Amanda: Well, I'm still in training, so I'm not a fully qualified counsellor. Everything you say to me is confidential to this session, with one or two exceptions – firstly I'm ethically required to have supervision on my work with a more experienced counsellor and I may talk to her about our sessions. If so I would only talk about our work in a way that would not identify you. I also reserve the right to break this confidentiality agreement if I judge you to be a danger to yourself or others.

Eric: That sounds fine with me.

Amanda: We have an hour together today and we can discuss later in the session whether you'd like to continue and, if so, what you'd like to focus on. Finally I'd just like to say that my role here, as counsellor, is to help you to find answers to your problems, not to give you advice or solutions.

Eric: I'll have to think about that one, but OK.

Amanda: So can I begin by asking you what it is you'd like to talk about?

Eric: I'm in a total state, my life is a complete mess and my whole family hates me. No, I'm only joking, you don't need to look so shocked, I'm not such a handful. [Sighs] It's just my way . . . trying to make a joke about everything. That's one of the things that Freda, my wife, is always complaining about. 'You never take anything seriously, Eric, you're always making a joke about it!' Anyway things aren't so good at the moment. Not at all. In fact she wants to leave me. Says she's going to.

Amanda: Your wife is threatening to leave you, and you're feeling? How are you feeling Eric?

Eric: Not very good, Amanda, not very good. Oh I feel really stupid coming here. Me, coming to counselling. Part of me thinks its a load of . . . [Tears well up in his eyes.] I'm sorry. [Silence].

Amanda: It feels to me as though you're in quite a state, Eric. Maybe counselling can simply be the place where you can let some of these feelings out.

Eric: Thanks, I feel stupid. [Wipes his eyes] I just never thought it would happen to me – my wife leaving me, that is. I mean it happens, sure, but to me – I thought we were happy. Of course we've had our problems but it's been good, the kids, the holidays, it's been good. Why?

Amanda: So it doesn't make sense and, I don't know, but it also sounds like this has all come as a bit of a surprise to you?

Eric: You can say that again – a right jack-in-the-box. I feel quite stunned by it. There we were – a 'happy' middle-aged couple. Then one day 'puff!' it's all gone – like a puff of smoke. Yes, it feels like my whole life's gone up in smoke.

Amanda: Sad, shocked and, perhaps angry too?

Eric: Yes I'm angry with her. Bloody angry. I mean, it doesn't make sense. I feel really betrayed by her, pushed out into the cold. Yes I feel as though its midwinter, there's a snowstorm and she's thrown me out of the house, *my* house, and I'm alone in the storm.

Amanda: That sounds pretty awful, Eric.

Eric: It is. [Silence, Eric's body flops and he stares at his hands.] Damn it! [His hands clench.] Who is she? I don't know her anymore.

Amanda: Like you've been living with this person so long and then, all of a sudden, she's different?

Eric: Yes, that's right . . . Oh well, I guess I'll get over it. I'm quite a resilient person, really. It's just come as such a shock. I'm sure I'll be OK in a month or so.

Amanda: It's not easy to stay with those feelings, is it? [Silence]

Eric: They're too much, they've always been too much.

Amanda: Always?

Eric: Well, I mean feelings in general, uncomfortable, painful feelings I mean. Just a bit much at the moment. More than I can cope with. That's why I came.

Amanda: I'm glad you did.

Eric: Thanks. [Tears well up in his eyes again but this time he lets them stay there.] Funny old thing really – me coming along here, not knowing you, that is, and telling you all about myself, spilling myself, with you in here. Strange, really.

Amanda: We still have plenty of time today but I'm wondering, at the moment, if we can look at whether you want to come back – perhaps for a few sessions, and if so, what we can work together towards?

Eric: [breathes in deeply] I want to come back, if that's all right with you?

Amanda: Good . . . I'd like to suggest that we meet for a further five sessions and that we review where we are on the fifth.

Eric: Sure, sounds all right to me.

Amanda: I'd also like to suggest, based on what you've been saying, that we focus on two things during the remaining time in this session and continue during the next five. Firstly we could explore your feelings about your wife's decision to leave you and secondly we could take a look at your relationship with your feelings in general. How does that sound? [Eric nods and his body sinks – in a way that seems to express that he has found the space he has been looking for.] Perhaps we could also agree on a clear objective for our work together – in relation to these two issues?

Eric: [thinks for a few minutes] I'd certainly like to feel I was coping with this situation – that I wasn't spilling out all over the place and I know that I'm not that good at dealing with my feelings, as I've said. Yes, it would be good to get a little bit better at it.

Amanda: Is there anything else you would like to add, anything else you would like to use this time for?

Eric: Those two you've picked out feel right. I'm sure I'll think of something else but they feel pretty important.

Amanda: OK, so we'll use the time we have left today to begin to look at your feelings about your wife and her decision to leave you. We'll also try to help you to relate a little better with your feelings as a whole. [Eric nods again.]

Extract from Eric's Diary

I've decided to keep a diary again. I used to keep one years ago, before I got married, and it seemed like it might be useful while I'm in counselling. I mentioned the idea to Amanda and she seemed to think it might help. So here I am writing my diary again, after, how long? ... About twenty years or so. Long time no see, old diary, old mate. Yesterday was my first counselling session with Amanda. It was a lot better than I thought it would be. How was I feeling – that's what I'm going to try and focus on in this diary, my feelings, that is. How was I feeling? Nervous, pretty shaky – I remember walking from the car to the door of the agency and finding it quite difficult to concentrate on what I was doing. It was rather scruffy when I got inside – I guess they're not the wealthiest of organizations. When I

spoke to the secretary I could feel my voice shaking – I
made some silly joke like I usually do. Sometimes I hate
myself and my stupid jokes. Anyway when I got into the
room I was pretty nervous and still making stupid
jokes. Didn't really listen to a lot of what Amanda was
saying at first but she did seem to know what she was
doing. I calmed down a bit and then I nearly started
crying! God, that was awful, I'd only met her a few
minutes and I was sitting there on the verge of breaking
down in tears. I really beat myself up for that – 'Pull
yourself together, you fool! Pull yourself together!'
Amanda wasn't saying that, she was saying that
counselling could be a space to let my feelings out.
Like a Laundromat for feelings – there I go again,
making a joke of it!

We were talking about how it felt, with Freda leaving
me, and I was saying it was like being shoved out in the
cold and it was all too much to cope with. Then she said
that she was glad I had come and well, I felt like crying
again when she said that. I felt very different at that
moment, like I wasn't out in the cold. It was as if she'd
put her arms around me. I kind of feel bad about this but
I really wanted her to put her arms around me – it's
terrible but I was sitting there feeling like she was a
really special woman and I was just wishing she'd put
her arms around me. I hate to admit to it but I kind of
fell in love with her.

I have fantasies about other women and have done all
through my marriage with Freda but they haven't meant
much – I never really felt anything more than lust. It's
funny but I didn't think I was capable of falling in
love, not anymore. Too old and sour – underneath all the
joviality. Bloody stupid woman to fall in love with – I
mean a no-hope situation here. Anyway we agreed to meet
for five more sessions and then review our work. Right
now I feel quite depressed – what am I doing falling in
love with my counsellor? Things are already bad enough.

Amanda's client-work notes

Session 1, Eric, aged 45. *Presenting issue*: wife, of many years, has
decided to leave him. Sudden and unexpected. Agreed on a series of six
sessions in total with a review on the sixth. Agreed on two themes and
goals for the work:

1   Exploring his feelings with regard to his wife leaving him.
2   Aiming to develop a better internal relationship with his feelings in
    general.

Discussed issues of confidentiality, boundaries, my qualifications and the nature of counselling.

First impressions: Eric came across as a slightly irritating person – wanting to make a joke about everything. He was, however, aware of this and had been consistently criticized for it by his wife. This 'joker' face soon dropped away and it was clear that he was in quite a state of emotional distress and shock as a result of his wife's sudden decision to leave him. My second impression, therefore, was of a person in a very vulnerable state – hiding behind this mask of 'the joker'. In response I found myself being a little more directive than I normally am – suggesting the focus for our work and the need for him to come for a number of sessions. I guess his vulnerable state evoked a kind of motherly response in me.

Progress of the session: He expressed some disbelief in the value of counselling but that seemed to fade out of the picture fairly quickly. He touched into his sadness on a number of occasions, together with anger and despair. We agreed on a focus to the work (see above) and spent the main portion of the session examining his shock on hearing his wife's announcement that she was going to leave him. They haven't really spoken much since – which was a little over a month ago. I got the feeling that his wife finds it difficult to talk about her feelings with him and, during the session, it was never made clear to me why she'd decided to leave him. Eric is really reeling from this however. He took to the counselling very well, despite his initial lack of belief in it.

Assessment: A case of major loss – with William Worden's theory of the Tasks of Grieving can be applied here. He seems to have partly accepted the reality of the loss but is finding it difficult to experience the pain of grieving – including his anger. This isn't helped by an underlying difficulty of relating with his feelings – he's aware of this as a problem. It's important that he has the opportunity to experience the pain more fully before he can move on to the later tasks of grieving. In order to help him on this second task we'll also need to focus on the wider issue of how he relates with his feelings.

Final thoughts and feelings: I was left feeling sorry for Eric. His world seems to have fallen down around him and he is standing in the ruins. I certainly had a lot of motherly feelings going out to him and he does feel, underneath, like a lost little boy. I'm pleased that he seemed to take to the counselling so well – especially given his early comment about it.

Six questions to consider

1   What went on in this session – in terms of the relationship and the therapeutic process?
2   How do you imagine these two experiences of the relationship might clash – at a later date?

3   What could Amanda have added in her contract that might help her later on?
4   What else might she have done in the session?
5   What might she have 'missed' – in terms of the emotional interaction?
6   How do you feel about the way *she* defines the objectives of the work?

Extracts from a long-term relationship

Sandra [thinks/feels: *'Actually I'm feeling quite panicky right now – this must be what it was like for Ronnie when he was on his way to see me last week – only worse, probably. I don't like driving anyway and going to see a new counsellor really gives me the butterflies. I do feel really nervy and edgy, in fact I feel quite sick. If I were to let the feeling take over I'd have to stop the car and be sick – right here by the side of the road! Mustn't do that.'* Sandra lets out a big burp. *'God, I hope I don't do that with Beverley – how embarrassing. That would make me feel even worse. I think I see what Marjorie means – I don't cope with anxiety at all. If I hadn't been thinking about it today, trying to stick with the feeling, I'd be doing my best to think of something, anything, else.'* The image of a mangled car passes through Sandra's mind. In that mind's eye she sees her arm broken and bloody, a piece of glass protrudes from her left breast, her left eye is closed and her right eye blurred. The thought* I'll never see properly again, I'm blinded *pops into her head. She shivers, holds the steering wheel even more tensely and focuses her mind on the road.]*

Beverley's doorbell rings. Beverley notices that her anxiety level has just risen substantially. She had been feeling quite relaxed making her notes in relation to the session with Mark, her previous client. This is the first session with Sandra and she knows that she always feels nervous at the start of the first session. She also knows that her client is likely to be feeling much more nervous than her. Once upon a time she would have steeled herself at this moment of anxiety. Steeled herself against the feeling and put on her nice Mrs Milner façade. She would have walked to the door preparing herself to be the calm and collected and controlled helper that she believed she should be. There would have been that nice Mrs Milner smile and the upbeat welcome 'Hello Sandra. Good to meet you – hope you found the place without too much trouble. Come on in and make yourself comfortable. Here, would you like me to take your coat.' Even bigger smile. She would also have spent the last ten minutes making sure that the hallway was tidy, the counselling room carpet free of any bits of fluff and the various items on the side table positioned 'correctly'. There's no way she could have sat there writing her notes, no way. And as nice Mrs Milner she would have noticed very little about her client. No time for noticing her client when all her time and attention was focused on being nice Mrs Milner. 'How hopeless I used to be,' thought Beverley. Now, as she walked to the door she felt it was OK to be nervous – an uncomfortable feeling yes, but not something to avoid, an important part of her experience of being in the world. How was she feeling about meeting Sandra? They had only spoken on the phone for a few minutes and most of the focus of that time had been on arrangements. Her colleague and friend Marjorie had recommended her to Sandra. It was interesting that she no longer even felt that she had to be 'good' to justify Marjorie's referral – something which, again in the past (and before her long-term personal counselling) would have played on her mind at this moment ('I must do well or else Sandra will tell Marjorie and I will disappoint not only Sandra but Marjorie too').

Along with the nervousness she was feeling quite excited – a new client, a new person, someone new to get to know. She had always liked people and enjoyed her work – more so now that she felt free of many of her former patterns and personal issues. *Beverley opens the door.*

As she stood there waiting for Beverley to open the door, Sandra found herself 'pulling herself together' and preparing for this moment of meeting. As always, she had been thinking about what she would say and, in the moments of waiting for the door to open, she carefully rehearsed her words. 'As I mentioned on the telephone, Marjorie suggested you as a possible counsellor. Marjorie is my supervisor and she feels that there are certain issues I need to examine if I am to develop as a counsellor. I'm not in a crisis or anything like that but there are certain things I need to look at with someone such as yourself. As we agreed on the phone, I'd like to see how we get on in this session before deciding whether to continue working with you.'

Sandra [thinks/feels: *'That sounds so in control and clear and together – which is exactly the opposite of what I'm feeling right now. God, I feel awful. I just want to get this beginning bit over with. I'll be all right after the first ten minutes or so.'* She imagines a hole opening up on the doorstep and swallowing her up. Then she wouldn't have to deal with this meeting at all. If only she could stop this bit. For a moment she feels like giving up on the whole counselling business, getting back in her car and driving off.]

The door opens: As she opened the door Beverley found herself noticing a great deal in that moment of meeting. The first thing that struck her was the sense of a really frightened little girl standing on her doorstep. The image of a young girl who has lost her mother in a big shopping centre passed through her mind. She also noticed her response to this 'young-girl Sandra' – she wanted to put her arms around her and say 'Don't worry Sandra, we'll find Mummy, it'll all be OK.' Beverley let some of that feeling come through into her first, spontaneous words.

Beverley: Hello, Sandra, it's good to meet you, please come in.

As the door opened and Beverley came into view, Sandra's decision to get back in the car vanished. It's difficult to describe exactly how she felt because there were quite a few feelings and they were all a bit mixed up. She didn't really hear Beverley's words but she did feel them – they felt very good, and as she stepped over the threshold she had a very strange feeling – as if she'd just come home.

Sandra: Thank you.

As Beverley guided her towards the counselling room Sandra felt slowed down – almost as if she was in a slow-motion film. It felt quite strange but it also felt quite OK, quite safe to be feeling strange. They both sat down in the counselling room and, for a minute or so, neither said a word. This was all very, very unexpected – the feelings, the silence, but it also felt OK. No it felt *good* just to sit there and, for that minute or so, absorb each other without words getting in the way.

As they sat silently in the chairs for that first minute or so Beverley felt 'grounded in the world' and thought how far she had travelled since her first few clients. 'How impossible it would have been to sit here like this then, how much would I have been driven to speak, how important it was to be seen as Mrs nice Milner. How good it feels to be able to sit here and not say anything – settling into each other's presence without the need for words. And how does Sandra feel to me? 'Thin' – not that she was that skinny – she just felt psychologically thin, psychologically undernourished. As if she hadn't been digesting life very well. That's how she felt to Beverley in that first minute or so in the counselling room.

TIME OUT

Reader: I've been thinking about the whole concept and experience of anxiety and it's beginning to seem pretty big. I mean, as I understand what you have just written here about Beverley and Sandra, the whole need to 'fake it', to present a certain kind of image of myself to the world of others, could be driven by an unconscious anxiety. That feels pretty enormous. I've also been thinking about the way you've been describing Sandra's (and Beverley's) reactions to the feeling of anxiety. Rehearsing her words, the desire to flee the meeting, the way Sandra seeks to defend herself, the way Beverley used to become someone else, the way in which anxiety can destroy all sense of spontaneity and real contact between people. It feels like there's an awful lot here and I'm still not at all clear how Beverley conquered – that's probably the wrong word – her anxiety and how Sandra (and Ronnie – Chapter 2) can be helped to cope better with theirs. Where are we going Anthony? I'm losing you.

Author: Where are we going? That's a pretty big question. I suppose that the most honest answer is that we are all going to die. That's where we're going. But that's not the answer you were looking for. Where are we going in the writing? You seem to be getting somewhere, getting a sense of how we tend to deal with our anxiety – by fight or flight, by defensiveness and aggression or by resistance and escape. But you want to know the answer to the question how has Beverley come to deal with her anxiety more effectively – that's the wrong word too – how has she come to the point where she is able to stay with her anxiety and not be driven into fight or flight? How has she come to the point where she doesn't have to work it out beforehand, where it's OK *not* to know where she's going? Not to know where she's going and *still to go on* – that sounds like the essence of spontaneity to me. What would it be like for you to stay with (and even exaggerate) that feeling of not knowing where we are going? What if we were to go off 'track', off the well-worn and predictable paths completely – into the unknown? 'Our mission to explore strange new worlds . . .' I forget the rest of the *Star Trek* intro. What would you need to be able to do that?

Reader: I think I get what you're saying. Being able to cope with anxiety is also being able to cope with the unknown. Life is bound to be full of the unknown because, try as we do, we simply don't know what's going to happen next and for most of us the worst thing that could be around the next corner is the Grim Reaper – or something terrible like that. For Sandra it's the car crash, for me it's . . . what? Cancer, I think – suddenly finding out that I have this death inside me. For someone else it might be AIDS or an aeroplane crash. What would I need to face the unknown? I'm reminded of Bowlby's attachment theory – I need a secure home from which to step out and explore the world. Without that sense of a secure home – originally my 'good enough' parents – I can't face exploring the unknown.

Author: You're really quite a theoretically sophisticated reader, aren't you? You know that's exactly what I would have pointed to, perhaps adding that the young child (over time) introjects that secure base – initially through the use of 'transitional objects' such as a teddy bear or a blanket but eventually developing an internal sense of psychological security without the need for external comfort objects. At this point the child feels that the 'good enough' parent is inside her and therefore, in some sense, always to hand. By the way, the concept of 'good enough' parent and 'transitional object' are Winnicott's not Bowlby's, but I'm sure, being such a sophisticated reader, that you are well aware of Winnicott's theories too.

Reader: So if Sandra and Beverley didn't have very secure parenting as children, they wouldn't have developed that sense of psychological security and they would be easily overwhelmed by anxiety. They

would also have developed ways of coping with anxiety such as I
was describing above – essentially fight or flight.

Author: Alternatively they might have had a secure base and then lost
it at some point in their lives – that's another possibility. In which
case it would be the loss of that secure base that would probably
feature as the central experience of the predicted 'doom'. In other
words, for Sandra the car crash might symbolize, for example, her
mother's death when Sandra was six. If this was the case then that
loss would always be around the corner waiting, like a sea monster,
to gobble her up.

Reader: At least until she was able to look at that experience in her
own personal counselling, to explore and work through that which
was all too much to cope with as a child. Yes, if she is helped to
work through that which was originally overwhelming, then she
would be able to move on from that trauma. Doom wouldn't be
about to happen and she would be able to explore the unknown. Or
would she? Would working through such a trauma mean that she
felt secure?

Author: If it was a case of sudden loss then it might well be sufficient
to work through the trauma because in doing so she could well
'remember' that which had existed before the loss. My feeling is
that is *not* that likely, though, and some form of present-day
internalization (of the 'counsellor-who-is-there-for her') would also
need to take place. It's also unlikely that Sandra would be able to
feel safe enough to explore her early trauma without such a secure
counselling base having been developed between her and her
counsellor. If, on the other hand, her personal history was not one
involving loss of a secure base but one in which there wasn't a good
enough parent in the first place (perhaps an insecure and anxious
mother or father, for example) then the primary aspect of the
therapeutic process would be the gradual development of a present-
day secure base, in the counselling, which Sandra could gradually
internalize. The rocky road to that, however, would probably be
fairly intense positive and negative transference – here we are in the
realm of working with special psychological needs and beyond
the boundaries of this book.

Reader: You mean the traditional process in the psychodynamic
approach – of creating a counselling relationship in which the
counsellor is experienced as holding those aspects of the client's
parents that were experienced as *not* good enough. Then gradually
enabling the client to untangle that perception (rooted in the past)
from the reality of the present – the reality of someone who is not
his or her parent.

Author: Yes, except I would add something to your description. Often
the client will begin with a positive transference – in which the
counsellor is idealized as the all-good parent figure that she never

had but always deeply wished for. This could well be what has happened (at some level) for Sandra at this meeting with Beverley. Gradually, however, as the deeper sense of the reality of a present-day secure base develops, the client begins to see that the counsellor is not this ideal being she wished she was and will switch, sometimes quite dramatically, to a very negative transference in which the counsellor is viewed as the all-bad parent figure. That, as you can imagine, can be pretty rocky! In time though, if the counsellor manages to remain herself through this process and the client remains committed to the venture, the client begins to see the counsellor for who she is – neither her negatively or positively idealized parent-figure but a person who (although having a mixture of good and bad qualities) has provided her with the sense of a secure base.

A.N. Other Reader: Hold it, you two, this is all getting very complicated. My head is beginning to swim with all this theory. I really have no idea *what* you're talking about anymore – can't you write about this in your normal way, Anthony? I understand it when you're describing Sandra or Marjorie or Amanda or John. I'm really getting lost with all this jargon. All these ideas with no illustration – it's just a bit over the top, OK? Just shut up and get on with the story! It feels like you're both trying to show off how knowledgeable and how brilliant you are.

Author: Maybe you're right – and it's fun to show off. Sometimes.

Session 52 (55 minutes into the session)

[Silence]

Sandra [thinks/feels: *'It's just over a year now since I first came to see Beverley and yes, it has been an immensely valuable experience and yes, I have worked through so much and yes, I feel different – better than I used to feel, in lots of different ways. These last five or six sessions, however, have all felt a bit flat – like we've gone as far as we're going to go and it's time to call it a day while we're still on top. I mean, what have we been doing for the last 55 minutes? I'm beginning to feel that we're wasting our time, and my money. I've always wondered about whether, in long-term work, it just gets to be a habit and well, the counsellor just gets used to the client coming along and gets used to the weekly cheque. Not that I'm saying this is what has been happening here. No, Beverley has really been quite a wonderful counsellor – I couldn't have found a better one. It's just something that I've been wondering about, sometimes.'* Sandra smiles at Beverley.]

Beverley [thinks/feels: *'It feels like we've got into a stuckness these past few sessions. Its just over a year since I first saw you, Sandra and right now we seem to have got all "clogged up". Yes, I like that image – it's as if lots of little things over the year have built up between us and the gutters need a clean-out.*

*Silted up with . . . with what? Little disappointments, annoyances, frustrations, bruises, mistakes – yes that's what it feels like. You're not really one to confront me about anything like that. I've felt, from the beginning, that you needed to see me in a very positive light – the good authority figure, the good mother. And that's been OK – it's been a good basis for a lot of very therapeutic work but perhaps it's time to move forward a little in that respect. It's not a very real way of relating together. You're still not truly seeing me, we're still far from what Rogers calls person-to-person relating.'] I'm wondering, Sandra if there's anything you'd like to say to *me* before we end today's session, anything you're feeling about me, or us, but not saying?*

[Sandra feels a bit shocked by that question – as if she's been caught out thinking what she was thinking. Caught out and reprimanded.]

Sandra [thinks/feels: *'What does she mean by that? That's not like Beverley, that's the first time she's told me off. Perhaps she's having a bad day – her period, perhaps. Nevertheless there's no call for that kind of tone with me. Yes, I think it's definitely time to call it quits – while we're still on top. Things always get stale in the end, I don't want that to happen here – it's been too good for that to happen. No, it's time to call it a day.'*] Well there is actually, Beverley. I've been thinking recently that perhaps we should wind up our counselling relationship. You know – spend a couple of sessions reviewing the year together and, well, bring it to an end. [Thinks/feels: *'There, phewwuuu, I've said it.'*]

Beverley [thinks/feels: *'So you did have something pretty important to say that you weren't saying. I wonder, however, what's behind you wanting to wind up the counselling right now? Could it be this sense of stuckness?'* Just then a feeling of great tediousness passed through Beverley's consciousness. A feeling of endless struggle, an endless swimming against the tide and with it a sense of ingrained frustration. The image of grinding teeth came to mind.] It's pretty near to the end of the session. Could we take a look at this next time? I'd quite like to take a look at the reasons behind you wanting to end the counselling as well as a review of where we've got to. I suggest that we start our next session where we're leaving off right now. OK?

Sandra [thinks/feels: *'That's a fair enough point, I guess – perhaps we do need to get clear about why now is a good time to end. I don't want to turn it into an excuse to drag out the ending, though – I couldn't bear it if this all went stale and rotten.'* In her mind's eye she saw them ending on a really nasty note and that being awful.] All right Beverley. I'll look forward to seeing you next week – same time? [Beverley nods her agreement.]

Session 104 (first few minutes of the session)

Beverley [thinks/feels: *'You're looking incredibly sad today, Sandra. I feel quite touched by your pain. I guess it's the growing realization you have been developing that your mother was never wholly there for you. That she seldom made any real contact with you on a person-to-person basis. That you are coming to mourn the loss of a mother you never had and never will have. I feel quite overwhelmed by that thought.'*] You are looking very sad today, Sandra.

[*Sandra's tears leak into her eyes. She sighs and looks down at the floor and then into Beverley's eyes. She wipes a tear from her left eye and sniffs. She feels empty, bereft, at a loss. The feeling moves through her in giant waves. She makes no effort to repress the feeling, no effort to pull herself together, no effort to cheer herself up or pretend to be anything other than what she is feeling. All of that she would have done a year ago. She remembered how, about a year ago, she had wanted to end the counselling with Beverley. 'How foolish that would have been, how stupid! God it has been a painful year this last year of counselling!' At one point she had actually puked up in the bin over there. Puked up in the middle of a regression to a time, aged five, when she had felt incredibly anxious. When she felt totally on her own in that prep school. Beverley had been there for her throughout. She'd helped her to explore and express so much – including all the bad feelings she felt towards Beverley. For a while she'd hated Beverley – or rather the Beverley that wasn't her ideal Beverley. Neither of which was the real Beverley – the Beverley she was just beginning to get to know. Silence.*] Oh . . . I wish you were my mother.

[Beverley laughs, Sandra smiles.]

Sandra: Yes I could just lie back, you could hold me in your arms and I could suckle on your breast. Oh how delightful that would be. Sailing in the blue and beautifully calm waters of the Mediterranean Sea. Sailing in your arms, Mummy. [Sandra wipes another tear from her left eye and breathes in deeply.] Peace at last. [They both smile at each other.] Peace at last . . . actually I've had quite a good week. It's just on the way here, in the car, and then as I sat down in my chair. That's interesting – it does feel like *my* chair. As I sat down I felt really sad, terribly sad – I could fall into that sadness again, it's right here on the edge of me.

Beverley [thinks/feels: *'We've worked together for quite a long time now, Sandra and it is beginning to feel like we are coming towards a person-to-person way of relating. The anxiety that you presented with has become much more manageable. In many respects you feel like you've really matured – grown up from that frightened little girl I felt you to be on the doorstep at our first meeting. We've also been through your 'adolescence' – during much of this second year of our work. Perhaps it's time that we began to think about the ending of our relationship. I remember it took me over a year to end my own counselling – perhaps it's time for us to begin thinking about it.' Beverley remembers how the ending phase of her own counselling brought up huge issues for her about loss and abandonment. The image of one session where she felt in utter despair in relation to the loss of a friend at school passed through her mind. 'Yes, I'm pretty sure that we need to allow plenty of time for the ending of our relationship.']*

Session 156 (45 minutes into the session)

[Silence]

Sandra [thinks/feels: *'Quarter of an hour left – and that's it. Part of me wants to avoid this moment at all costs – think about what's next today, how I must talk to Alan about the leaking pipe in the bathroom or how I need to rearrange an appointment with Bill because it's parents' evening next Thursday. But part of me doesn't want to avoid it at all. No, that part of me wants to stay with the feeling, although it's terribly difficult and terribly painful – because it's real, real life. Not running away, not trying to defend myself against the feeling. This is me, with Beverley, at the end of this most valuable of relationships. This is us, saying goodbye.' Tears come into her eyes but she lets them dribble down her cheeks. 'I love you Beverley, that's what I want to say, I love you. I've never said that to you before but that's what I feel and that's what I want, no that's what I* need *to say to you, right now.'*] I love you, Beverley, I love you so much.

[Before Sandra speaks, the image of Sandra, the person that is Sandra, not the physical face or body, passes through Beverley's mind – the Sandra that grew up, the Sandra that rebelled, the Sandra that is now leaving her. Beverley sighs and her eyes seem to grow a little older. She remembers her own children and their growing up, their rebellion and their leaving home.]

Beverley [thinks/feels: *'I feel like an old woman today. A little jealous of your youth, Sandra.' Sandra speaks. A ripple of sadness rolls through Beverley's heart, she breathes in deeply and tears appear on the edge of her eyes. She looks into Sandra's eyes and the two of them 'meet' – in the deepest meaning of that word. The silence returns. Both wait in that silence. The line of a Leonard Cohen song plays in Beverley's mind.*] Five minutes until the end of the session.

Sandra: As if I didn't know that. [They both laugh. Sandra's laugh turns to a smile. Beverley returns the smile.]

Beverley [thinks/feels: *'Its good to have met you, dear soul, so good to have met you.'*]

Not all good relationships are nice

The following is included as a challenge to fixed notions about the client–counsellor relationship and what is OK and what is not OK.

Extract from counselling session 999 in the prison of life

Jeremy: Morning, Martin, how are you?

Martin: Look, Jeremy, you know I'm not going to answer that question. You always ask me how am I, and we both know that you don't really want to know the answer, it's just a way of you avoiding the beginning of the session.

Jeremy: I still have to fucking ask it, though. I still want to start with . . . a chat. You know . . . like a cup of tea between friends.

Martin: Am I your friend?

Jeremy: Well, I'd like you to be, well, no I wouldn't, actually. I like you being who you fucking are, someone who listens to *me*, someone I don't really know. It's true I don't need to ask 'how are you?', and it is nice to not *have* to fucking ask that question. Yet I still need to ask it, it's like a ritual, like opening the door to the session. I ask you how you are, you don't fucking answer. I feel, well, safe. Safe to not have to fucking bother with you. It's like you don't need looking after, then I can, well, sink. Sink, that's what I feel like fucking doing, sinking down and down and down. [Sinks lower and lower in his chair]

Martin: You don't look too good today, Jeremy.

Jeremy: I feel . . . fucking shit, really shit.

Martin: I'd like to hear about that.

Jeremy: Would you. I don't fucking know why, you must be fucking loopy, Martin, if you want to hear about my shitty life.

Martin [thinks/feels: '*He's right, do I really want to hear about his shitty life? What a silly thing to say. What a silly thing to be doing, sitting here listening to pain and confusion, session after session. Maybe I am loopy, maybe I'm plain stupid.*'] You're right, I don't want to listen to your shitty life, I lied.

Jeremy: That's what I like about you, Martin – you don't try and bullshit me. Well, I'm going to just tell you anyway, since we're here, that is – you fucking tosser.

Martin: Go on then, you turd-brain.

Jeremy: Right you are, you fucking wanker.

Martin: Shitface!

Jeremy: Tosspot!

Martin: Just so long as you don't try and beat me up again. [Martin and Jeremy break down laughing.]

Jeremy: You are the weirdest fucking counsellor, Martin, you are a fucking weirdo! . . . But I fucking like you for it.

Martin: So what do you want to talk about, dogfart-breath? [Silence]

Jeremy: [laughs with a very different tone] I had a dog once. Dad kicked it to death one day. He came home from work and tripped over it. Must have been in a bad mood. He didn't half whack it. I fucking hated him for that. I hated him anyway. But I fucking hated him for that – much more. Used to work out how I would kill him – by poisoning his tea or knifing him in the back. That's not what I want to talk about today though. I want to talk about Sarah.

Martin: Sarah is your new girlfriend, right?

Jeremy: Well, not exactly. That's what I want to talk about. It's sort of on and off. On account of . . . well, you know, my problem.

Martin: Your uncontrolled anger.

Jeremy: Yes, my uncontrolled fucking anger, as you put it. It's not that I've got violent or anything, no, that's been really, well, in control I guess. But I'm still shouting and stuff.

Martin: Stuff?

Jeremy: Well, I did throw something, not at her, but it wasn't good, it frightened her. I could see that, and it's not how I want it to be. No, I understand now that I'm violent because that's what I learnt from him, the bastard, and I want to be free of him. I'm not going to let him ruin my life anymore.

Martin: And you don't want to talk about your dog?

Jeremy: Fuck you, Martin! [Silence]

Martin: That really hurt, didn't it, when he killed your dog.

Jeremy: [breathes in] You know I can't cry, Martin. Stop fucking trying to make me [tears in his eyes]. Yeah it hurt, I did cry then, up under the bedclothes, at night, quietly, so *he* couldn't hear.

Questions to consider

1   How do you respond to this extract?
2   Counsellors 'should not' insult their clients – is Martin wrong to be so 'rude'?
3   Most counsellors (and clients), are white and middle class – how do you feel about that?

Three exercises to explore your patterns of relating with others

Exploring your personal issues concerning 'being pushed away'

Note: If the feelings threaten to overwhelm, and that doesn't feel OK for you at the time, come out of the depths of those feelings by focusing on the colours in the room. If you want to stay with the feelings and allow them some expression then give yourself permission to do so.

(a) Explore in your journal your experiences, and responses to, 'being pushed away' based on the following guidelines:

Experiences of 'being pushed away' might include examples of how you may have, psychologically, reached out towards another and were responded to 'badly' or when you have found it difficult to 'take no for an answer'. Explore your underlying feelings of such experiences.

(b) Explore how your experiences of being pushed away affect how you live in your world of others now. How does it affect your choices, decisions, 'extroversion/introversion' or capacity to trust or to be intimate with others?

(c) Explore, in a similar way, how you approach pushing another person away – how you go about saying 'no' to others.

(d) Review this exercise in your journal and relate any insights to your client-work.

Exploring your difficulties with particular interpersonal feelings and emotions

In certain interpersonal situations it may be more difficult for you to be emotionally open with the other person. Through exploring our personal difficulties with certain feelings and interpersonal situations, we can expand our capacity for facilitating emotional openness and honesty in the client–counsellor relationship.

Part 1: Consider how you emotionally perceive, respond to and express yourself in different social situations.

Part 2: Read through the following two lists of phrases that describe a variety of potentially 'difficult' interpersonal emotional situations. Choose from list A those that you find *most uncomfortable to receive* – interpersonal emotional situations that you are often tempted to escape the truth of, to hide your reactions from by staying with the 'official' layer of the conversation. Repeat this for list B, which concerns your communications with others. Once again, after the exercise review your experience in your journal and apply any insights to your work with clients.

A. *Situations where the other:*	B. *Feelings you find difficult to communicate:*
feels angry with you	you feel angry with him/her
feels attracted to you	you feel attracted to him/her
feels afraid of you	you feel afraid of him/her
feels guilty towards you	you feel guilty with him/her
feels sad because of you	you feel sad because of him/her
feels shy with you	you feel shy with him/her
feels suspicious of you	you feel suspicious of him/her
feels competitive with you	you feel competitive with him/her
feels repulsed by you	you feel repulsed by him/her
feels hurt by you	you feel hurt by him/her
feels betrayed by you	you feel betrayed by him/her
feels criticized by you	you feel criticized by the other
feels defensive with you	you feel defensive with him/her
feels jealous of you	you feel jealous of him/her
feels confused by you	you feel confused by him/her

shows affection to you	you show affection to him/her
feels rejected by you	you feel rejected by him/her
feels disappointed in you	you feel disappointed in him/her
feels bored by you	you feel bored by him/her
feels love for you	you feel love for him/her
feels anxious with you	you feel anxious with him/her
yearns for you	you yearn for him/her
relates to you as special	you feel he/she is very special
feels inferior to you	you feel inferior with him/her
feels superior to you	you feel superior to him/her
feels frustrated by you	you feel frustrated by him/her
feels used by you	you feel used by him/her

Exploring my process of engaging with others

Explore your experience of engaging with others – focusing particularly on beginnings and the experience of developing trust and openness:

- What is your experience of engaging with others? Think of actual experiences of 'engagement' – particularly during first meetings and the 'getting to know each other' process.
- How have you developed commitment to particular others in the past? How have your relationships moved towards closeness and intimacy? How have they 'gone bad'? Were you able to express the 'badness' with the other person? If yes, then what was that like? If not, what was that like?

The following phrases may also help your exploration:

- My experiences of forming and engaging with others who went on to become very significant for me
- My difficulties with engaging with others, my fears, my sadness
- My motivations to engage with others
- Closeness, safety and holding
- Conflict, rejection, fear
- What I would need from him/her if I were to engage with a counsellor
- What I need from him/her if I am to engage with a client
- Levels of my closeness – to my friends, my family or my clients
- Previous experiences of beginnings and how they may shape my present experiences of beginnings
- Previous experiences of endings and how they may shape my present experiences of endings.

Review the exercise in your journal and apply any insights to your client-work.

8

Developing Your Understanding of the Therapeutic Process

The truth is rarely pure, and never simple. (Oscar Wilde, *The Importance of Being Ernest*, 1895)

Jamie makes sense of his experience as a client

Mavis's project

As part of my research project examining the process of therapeutic change I asked 12 clients with positive experiences of counselling to write a description of their experience, how they felt it had been of benefit to them and what they saw as the process of therapeutic change. I then interviewed each of these clients three times – which was a lot of interviews!! In the first interview I focused on developing a working research relationship with them, in the second I orientated the interview towards their description of their counselling experience – seeking to explore, expand, add detail to and generally clarify what they were saying. In the third interview I presented them with my summary of their counselling experience and what they had identified as therapeutic – putting it into my own language – and thus a common language for all 12 client experiences. I also needed that third session to check on the accuracy and focus of my summary and conclusions and to make changes or additions where necessary. I finally gave some time, at the end of the third interviews, to the ending of the relationship and for me to say my thank you.

I found the process with each of the client-interviewees to be a very intimate one – because it involved a focus on their intimate subjective lives. It was also an experience that they all found of value – because it provided them with an opportunity to review, assimilate and clarify what had been gained from their original counselling experience. The following description, written by someone I shall call Jamie, encapsulates many of the themes common to the description of the clients as a whole. I thus present it as a representative sample of what this particular group of clients saw as the key elements of their experience of a positive counselling process.

Jamie   I have been asked to write about my experience of counselling and why I feel it was helpful to me. I found this request quite challenging. How can I put into a few words all that has occurred in my counselling and my life over the past nine months? How can I express some of the intense, and the subtle feelings and encounters that have been the heart of my experience?

For a couple of weeks I would try and start this account, write a few words and then stop. I finally had to force myself just to write – without trying to summarize or whatever – for a fixed number of hours. When I did that I found that, once started, it just seemed to flow out and although I went back to add or change bits here and there, on the whole I felt fairly satisfied that what I had written did manage to express some of the key aspects of my experience of counselling.

I went for counselling because I needed to. I was in a right state, emotionally speaking. My mother had died a few months prior and that had really unsettled me. I found that it affected my judgement, my relationships at work and seriously lowered my self-confidence. It was much more of an event for me than I could possibly have imagined. Looking back, I should have gone for counselling after she died – I was even contacted by an agency but didn't think I really needed it. I was used to coping with crises – I was a manager, I'd be OK. If I had gone for counselling then, a lot of pain and problems could have been avoided . . . Or perhaps it would have been just as painful anyway. Worst of all would have been if it had happened when my wife and I were much older – with kids! Better sooner rather than later. Thank God!

A few weeks after my mother's death, my wife Sylvia expected me to be fully recovered and she began to show a side of herself that I hadn't seen before – well, perhaps I had glimpsed it before but had ignored it. Life since our marriage had always been pretty full. Full of executive-style parties and various other gatherings. Full of hard work too – both of us had our careers and we both had to take work home for the evenings and the weekends. We never really spent that much time alone together, simply being together. If we had, I might have seen this other side to her much earlier. But perhaps half the point of all those social occasions and hard work was to avoid spending time alone together. That way we didn't have a chance to find out much about each other – in particular our nastier sides. Not that I feel I have a particularly nasty side to myself.

So what took me to counselling was the realization, over a period of three months or so, that the person I had married two years before was not the person I had thought her to be. In fact I discovered that I was living with someone that I really didn't like, a person for whom the word 'nasty' does seem to be appropriate. That was my, what do you call it, 'presenting problem', yes, that was my reason for going into counselling. I was in very real emotional turmoil and confusion over the fact that my physically very attractive wife had turned out to be a really ugly person. And, as I realize now, I was still in the middle of grieving for my mother. The combination of the two made me feel like I was on some kind of emotional roller-coaster.

Jane, my counsellor, was someone a friend at work (who I knew had been in counselling herself) recommended to me. I wasn't sure about going to a woman, because I wasn't sure how she'd react to the nature of my problem, but now I'm glad that I did. Going to a man would have made it more difficult for me because my 'primary issue' (as Jane called it) was with women – and she is one of them. I'll try and explain that a bit more later on – when we get to the relevant bits in the counselling.

It was strange, at first, to be talking so intimately about myself, my feelings and my life to someone I didn't really know from Eve. But I was too confused at the time to be able to bother about that very much. The fact that she was there, that she listened and that she seemed to understand what I was describing all felt really good. It was really good to have someone and somewhere to go to and spill it all out and feel that it wasn't too much for her. Yes, because Jane seemed to take it all in, because she didn't seem to be shocked and confused by all my confusion, I felt more confident in her and more confident in counselling as a whole. I felt that coming to her was the right thing and it was going to work. It gave me hope – hope that this state I was in now wasn't how my life was going to continue for the rest of my days. I began to feel confident that it was a state that wouldn't last for ever – although there wasn't any light at the end of the tunnel at that time, there would be at some point. That was really important for me – the first key to my recovery process.

After about six sessions we reviewed where we were and I realized that, in fact, I wasn't as emotionally confused as I'd been when I started the counselling. I was still very confused, and things were far from rosy, but already something important had happened. When I went back to look at my description of this first part of my counselling experience I thought deeply about why this might have come about. It was very hard, however, to put into words what the experience was and why things might have changed in the way they did. The only way I could describe it was through a metaphor. Before I went into counselling it was as if my life was like a cup of tea in an aeroplane that is going through a very wobbly bit of turbulence – I was spilling out all over the place. After six or so sessions, however, it felt like the aeroplane had started to leave that turbulent airspace – coming into counselling was like gradually entering a more stable airspace.

At our review in the sixth or seventh session . . . no, it was definitely the seventh session because I remember that in the first session we agreed to meet for a further six sessions and review where we were in the last of those. Not that I took that much in during that first session, I was far too confused and also very nervous of going to a counsellor. In fact, I wasn't really in a state to make any sensible decision about any agreement. No, it was more like Jane suggested we meet for more sessions and I thought to myself, 'Do I feel better coming here today or not?' and, at that time, I think I answered myself with something like 'Not really, but what else am I going to do?' So, since I couldn't think of anything else to do, I said that I would come. That was the best decision I think I've ever made – I really believe that. Strange though – how I came to make it. Back to what I was saying, however . . . At the review session Jane and I agreed to focus on a particular theme over the next six sessions and, once again, review where we had got to on the sixth of those.

What came up for me during that second series of sessions was a deep sense of frustration – I remember coming into the session one day feeling like I was grinding my teeth over my colleagues at work, my friends, my family and, most of all, my 'bitch of a wife'. It was an intense feeling of all of them constantly irritating me and I just couldn't get them to stop it. We used that session to really go deeply into the feeling and I remember saying to Jane that I just wanted to tell them all to shut up: 'I want to be really rude to them, I want to stop being Mr Nice Guy, I want to tell them all to go to hell.'

Jane encouraged me to say whatever I wanted to say to them – as if I was speaking to them right there and then. On that invitation I imagined Sylvia doing her face at her pine dressing table and I said:

'You've turned out to be a really nasty woman, I wish I'd never laid eyes on your pretty shitty face. Look at yourself – pruning away making yourself even more bloody beautiful – yet underneath you don't know how to care for another person. Your heart is as cold as ice.'

I've just realized that I haven't really explained why I feel she is such a bitch. Well, to give you one of many examples, I was feeling pretty awful one Friday evening – about a month after my mother's death. We were scheduled to be going out to some fancy party or other and my wife was getting ready to go – at her pine dressing table, in fact. I went into our bedroom and sat on the bed and said something about how I was feeling pretty down and didn't really feel like going out that evening. She didn't even turn around and stop making herself up, but just said,

'You're really something of a misery-guts, aren't you? Before we got married you weren't like this at all. I don't want to spend the evening with a miserable bore anyway. Why don't you find someone else's shoulder to cry on tonight?'

When she said that I felt as though she had just stuck a dagger in my heart and given it a nice twist. I just sat there completely bewildered, dumbstruck. Then, as she finished off her face, she stood up to leave the room and looked at me with these new, oh so cold eyes, smiled a really nasty smile and left for the party. I continued to sit there on the bed, feeling cut up into little pieces and wondering who the hell was this person I had married. There, I hope that gives you a sense of what I mean by a 'nasty' bit of work, a right bitch in fact.

Jane felt that my description of Sylvia as having a heart of ice was something we could focus on further – which we did for the rest of the session and the next, and the next. What emerged in these sessions was how, up until now, I had always seen women in a very positive light. It was as if I hadn't looked at the bad aspects of a woman but had been wearing rose-tinted glasses. Men did all the bad things in the world – men made war, men bullied people, men raped and abused women and so on. Men were . . . imperfect, they did all these bad things. Women, however, I unconsciously viewed as almost more than human – not really capable of bad things at all. All women had warm and loving hearts, kind and caring personalities – that was their natural state of being. Writing like that, right now, it does sound pretty stupid. How could I think that? It's obviously not true.

Well the point is I didn't really think it, it's more that I just tended to assume it, unconsciously. It's difficult to explain this in words – I feel a bit frustrated, right now, trying to do so. But the fact is that realizing this came as both a real revelation to me and, at the same time, I felt an enormous sense of 'things in my self and my life are fitting together' (again words are difficult here). It was like my life suddenly made a lot more sense to me. Here was an understanding of my situation that explained things not only in relation to Sylvia, but also to many other women in my life – socially, at work and, as I thought it through and remembered, all my other relationships. It felt like 'here is the key to it all'. Of course it wasn't the key to it all but it was an important key. This was also, I would say, the second step in my counselling process.

During our third series together, Jane and I explored my life in terms of this 'key to it all' – how this rose-tinted-glasses way of seeing women ran throughout my life and how it had affected my life. It was a bit depressing to discover how it had affected so much of my relationships, my choices and my responses to the various events of my life. But it was also a liberating feeling to have actually uncovered something like this. During this series of sessions we also began to explore where this 'psychological pattern', as Jane called it, had come from. What we soon realized was that it had come from my mother. Well, not quite from my mother but rather from the way I had looked upon her. In essence, I grew up looking upon my mother with a very positive vision – I idealized her as this beautiful, caring person who could do no wrong. Then, unconsciously as an adult, I saw 'women' as 'mother' and viewed all women as essentially like her.

I had been the only child in our family and most of my close relatives were male. My cousins, for example, are all men and my two aunts were seldom seen. Few women came to the house to visit my mother and, when I went to school, I went to an all-boys one. My mother, therefore, was 'most of the female race', or so I experienced her as a young child, and as I grew up.

By the end of our third series of sessions the sense of stability that had begun to emerge at the end of the first series had deepened. We hadn't been talking about my relationship with my wife very much in those recent sessions but, as I felt myself getting more emotionally stable, I also began to feel a lot clearer about Sylvia and the fact that I didn't want to live with her any more. In our review of where we were, on the 19th session, I said that I now wanted to look at this – I wanted to tell my wife I was going to leave her and file for a divorce.

When I told Sylvia she was actually quite shocked – she didn't particularly see a life of being nasty to each other as that much of a problem. She didn't actually say that, but it was the feeling that she left me with. I think she was also quite stunned that I was going to leave her – the beautiful Sylvia, the desirable creature that all men's eyes turned towards. As a result she got even nastier, quite vengeful and vindictive. One day, for example, she smashed an antique vase that my mother had left me and tore up a section of my appointments diary. I got in a real rage with her that evening. Then the next day, while she was at work, I moved all my personal things out to a friend's house and I haven't stayed at the house since.

Not unnaturally, all of my sessions with Jane were taken up by the effects of all of this and although, once again, I became very emotionally wobbly and confused I found the sessions to be enormously supportive. Without them I might have got much more caught up than I did in a cycle of vindictiveness with Sylvia. I was also unbelievably glad that we hadn't got round to having children (or even buying a home together). In those respects I feel I got off very lightly indeed.

One session I remember as really important: soon after I had moved out of the house. I arrived feeling an incredible yearning for Sylvia – wanting to go back and ask her for forgiveness. We worked on this and what emerged was the irrational feeling that I had been thrown out by her and, associated with that, the feeling of being very alone and at a loss. I also realized then that there were still huge issues for me about my mother's death and leaving the house had somehow triggered them for me. When I could see that, I also saw that it wasn't true that I wanted Sylvia and it lifted things for me emotionally. I didn't go back to her.

If I look at all of this period of counselling in terms of my therapeutic process then I would say that exploring my 'psychological pattern' in the in-depth way we did (in the third series of sessions) gave me both a new confidence in myself and a new clarity about who I wanted to live my life with. So that would be the third key step in my therapeutic process. My fourth 'step' was to find the support I needed from Jane during the period leading up to, and after, my separation from Sylvia. As I've already said, it might well have been a very different experience if I had been without that support. I can imagine, for example, things getting really nasty – on both sides.

As I was writing that I began to think about all the people who do continue to live together – in a state of viciousness and marital war. It seems an amazing thing to put up with. Utterly amazing. And yet it's probably relatively common. There are certainly plenty of relationships where there is such a war going on – not always on the surface; sometimes it's a hidden war. Not for me!

Things calmed down a bit between Sylvia and myself about six weeks after I left the house. I got the sense that she could see there wasn't much to gain for herself any more and she decided to shut me out of her life and get on with her dinner parties and her career. Perhaps she found another man to dote on her beauty. We haven't had much contact since then and, in all honesty, I don't really care about what she's doing or who she's with!

I finished my counselling with Jane about a month ago. We explored where we were at in one of our six-weekly review sessions and I felt that there was a lot more I could work on, on a therapeutic level, but also felt that I just wanted time to recover from a very difficult year. We agreed, however, to have a final series in which we would focus on my mother's death and then I finally managed to begin to really grieve for her properly.

I got quite sad when it came to saying goodbye to Jane. She had become an important part of my life – someone I had learnt to turn to for help and support. In fact, perhaps that's the most important therapeutic aspect of the whole experience – that through my counselling with Jane I learnt how to share my thoughts and feelings with another person. I also learnt how to look for, and find, emotional help and support. I can feel that this has changed all of my relationships – subtly, but so much for the better. Last weekend I even began to think about asking a woman friend out for a date.

Questions for you to consider

1   Can you summarize Jamie's counselling process?
2   How might you have worked with him differently?
3   Could you set up a similar piece of research – to study, for example, your own clients' experiences of their counselling process with you?
4   What other kinds of things would you like to know about therapeutic change – that aren't covered in Mavis's project?

Robert develops a theory of the therapeutic process

Extract from Robert's journal

Thursday evening Anthony has asked us to do an exercise entitled 'Being a counsellor and being myself?' A lot of really important

stuff has come up for me over the last few days, however, and I'd
first like to explore that. It all started when I came across
another exercise in a book I've been reading called *Inside
Counselling* – the exercise involved remembering a time 'when you
felt very mistreated by someone and to explore that experience
both during the event (or period of mistreatment) and then
afterwards'. It then asked the reader to consider what kinds of
effect that experience of a 'horrible other person' might have
had upon 'yourself, your development and your emotional patterns
of relating'.

At first when I thought about it I found it difficult to think
of people but then I remembered a man who had it in for me for about
a year when I was in college. Remembering him I also remembered
other bullies in my life – both male and female – all of whom would
fall into this category of people who mistreated me. Then I began
to think about more subtle forms of mistreatment – how, for
example, a girlfriend, Denise, tried to use me as her 'ideal man'.
Being with her was like trying to fit in with what she wanted –
with who I was 'supposed to be' – all the time. Thinking about
that more subtle form of mistreatment I also remembered a teacher
who used to make me very uncomfortable by getting me up in front of
the class to laugh at the mistakes in my work. Then I began to
recall more and more examples of how people had made me very
uncomfortable – sometimes quite clearly enjoying my discomfort.
A couple of boys at school when I was a young teenager 'set me up'
with a girl at a forthcoming disco. I arrived at the place only to
find that she hadn't expressed any interest in me at all. They
loved it – my pain, that is. I remembered another girlfriend
whose intense jealousy of other women friends was really a form of
mistreatment. More and more incidents and relationships began to
arise in my mind until, whereas at first I could hardly think of
anyone, it began to seem that my life had actually been full of the
unkindness, the self-centredness or outright cruelty of other
people.

Then I realized that I'd always tended to see myself as one of
the most selfish and unkind persons in my life. I have never,
however, consciously enjoyed being nasty to people or enjoyed
the act of causing them suffering and pain (although I have
begun, over the last two weeks in my personal counselling, to
look at whether that is because I have repressed such nasty
feelings). At the same time I have always thought of myself as a
rather selfish person who was quite capable of being unkind to
others and felt that I had to keep a watchful eye on myself as a
result. I felt I had to monitor myself – checking out whether I
was being self-centred, unkind or simply thoughtless. Then I
asked myself something like, 'How do you, Robert, actually
compare, in terms of the mistreatment of others, with how you
have been mistreated by others? Is this view of yourself, as one
of the most selfish and thoughtless people around, actually a
fair and honest view?' In comparison I decided, I was a

relatively 'nice guy' and the fact that I really didn't feel I'd
ever enjoyed hurting others meant that I came out pretty low in
terms of being a bully or abuser. In contrast, I realized, quite a
number of people who had caused me pain and suffering had clearly
enjoyed it. Surely, I thought, there is a huge difference between
the person who enjoys causing other people pain and the person
who causes other people pain but doesn't realize it – someone
who, for example, is being selfish.

This felt like quite a shift in the way I viewed myself – from
'basically a bad person who has to constantly correct himself in
order not to be a bad person' to 'basically a good person who can
sometimes act in ways which are experienced as selfish or
unkind'.

Then I began to wonder what was the difference between 'acting
in ways that are selfish and unkind' and 'acting in ways that are
justified but are experienced by another person, or persons, as a
source of pain and suffering for them'. This seemed quite an
important, if subtle, difference. When am I acting in a fashion
that isn't 'right' and when am I acting in a 'right' way, even
though someone else might feel it was 'wrong'? In the former I
would feel that I needed to change what I'm doing and learn
something, whereas in the latter, I would feel that I needed to
support myself – and explain it to the other person. When am I
being 'selfish' and when am I being 'true to myself'? It felt as
though there was a very important key here, for I suspected that
part of my problem was that I tended towards the former rather
than the latter – towards seeing myself as 'selfish' rather than
'this being a situation where I need to be true to myself'.

Just now – as I was writing about this insight – I noticed that
I was feeling quite frustrated. I've been moving about on my chair
and my mind is finding it difficult to concentrate. I've also
begun to think about getting up and stopping writing this
journal. This is something that I have noticed with my
counsellor, Maria, on occasions – whenever we are working on the
edge of what she calls a 'no go' area. She has said to me that it's
important to notice when this might be happening because it can be
an enormous clue to important areas of personal work. She's also
pointed out, however, that it's just as important not to push
myself at those times. She believes that our defences against
difficult personal material are there for a reason – our defences
are an important part of us and they need to be respected. 'I don't
rip down a wall without first exploring what might happen if I
did. What if it turns out to be load-bearing? The whole house
would fall down. What if it turned out to be there to hold
something in – like the wall of a reservoir? If I rip down that
wall I'll flood the whole valley. I try not to do anything violent
to myself, I try to respect myself – I believe that I deserve
respect, even those parts of myself that I might not like or want.
I have learnt that perhaps they require more respect.' She once
said something like that to me and it really stuck in my mind.

Thinking about Maria's words, I've decided to take a break from this work and mull it over for a few days.

Sunday afternoon I haven't really been doing the exercise yet, but what I have been doing does feel valuable – so for the moment I shall continue to write about that. In thinking over what I'd written last Thursday it occurred to me that what I was finishing up talking about was 'self-esteem'. Knowing the difference – on a day-to-day practical basis – between being selfish and being true to myself is another way of talking about self-esteem and self-confidence. I have to be confident in myself to be true to myself. What I noticed, however, was that working on this in my journal was actually quite frightening – I seemed to be triggering the opposite feeling in myself. In exploring concepts of self-confidence I was evoking strong feelings of its lack – feelings of being very unsure, a sensation of 'butterflies' in my stomach, I even developed nervous diarrhoea. Then, when I allowed myself to enter into the feeling even more it was as if I was suddenly faced with something I couldn't cope with – my breath became very shallow and short. It felt like I was only just surviving the situation, although there wasn't any 'situation' – very strong feelings seemed to have been stimulated by my personal work, not by an external situation in which I felt insecure.

In such a state of insecurity, the notion of being true to myself seemed an impossibility. To be true to myself, I decided, I needed to feel 'grounded'. To be confident in myself I need to know and believe in my perceptions of my situation and my judgements about what kinds of actions are appropriate. I need to feel secure in myself – which, I felt, also means I need to feel secure in my family and other relationships. Given that sense of security I feel able to know who I am, what I want, what I need, what I like, what is right and what is wrong, what is selfish and what is being true to myself.

This all seemed to become very clear to me on Saturday afternoon when I was working on these things after my Friday personal counselling session. Then, unfortunately, that clarity seemed to fade, so that now I don't feel so sure about the notes that I wrote yesterday. I felt sure, now I feel unsure. I felt clear, now I feel clouded. Perhaps there is also something here that relates to the whole experience of self-esteem, self-confidence and being true to oneself – perhaps it changes, moving from confidence to lack of confidence, from security to insecurity. Perhaps self-esteem is not a fixed quality but a changing process.

That thought has reminded me of someone I know who doesn't appear to shift. He always comes over as enormously clear and confident and strong willed but he is also a pain too, and sometimes quite a big pain. It's as if other people are completely unimportant – he drives himself like a diesel train through a social gathering. It's not that he's selfish, in the normal meaning of that word, he just finds it difficult to stop being self-confident and knowing exactly what he wants. Perhaps there needs to be a kind of self-confidence rhythm that responds to how other people are. He doesn't respond to other people's needs and wants partly because he doesn't try and find out what they are. He gets his way because other people aren't generally going to have a major confrontation with him over the choice of music at a party or some other relatively minor issue. On the other hand, I wouldn't say that he had any real friends to speak of: *he* thinks he has friends but I know that many of his 'friends' don't see him like that. They put up with him, even enjoy his company for an evening, but that's about as much as they can cope with. They avoid confronting him on little things and simply avoid situations where big things might come into question. They'd go to the cinema with him, for example, but balk at the idea of a two-week holiday – 'No way!' I can hear them saying.

I don't think he'd even bother to ask me to do something like go on holiday with him – perhaps because he knows I would say no but also perhaps because there is something of him in me. Only I don't press other people into joining with me in the way he does. Thinking about it, however, I do exactly what I want, almost as much as he does – only, whereas he does it with other people and that pisses them off after a while, I do it alone.

There, that is quite a thought – it reminds me of the JOHARI window that we studied on last year's course. There are four areas in the window:

1 Things about myself that I know and other people know too.
2 Things about myself that I know and other people don't.
3 Things about myself that I don't know and other people do.
4 Things about myself that neither I nor other people know about.

The idea is to make the first area bigger by bringing things in from the other three. I was reminded of this theory of self-development because it felt like I'd just brought something from number 3 into number 1. It felt like I'd just opened up one of the blind spots in my awareness of how I relate with others – probably a very important aspect of my pattern of relating.

What should I do with that insight into myself and my way of relating? Well, I guess one of the first things would be to explore it a little more – to check out how true it is and to check out how important it is. What effect does it have on my life with others, and on myself, and how I do, or don't, get my needs met?

Then, perhaps, I could try and work out where it had come from – as a pattern of relating – and what was driving me to keep on repeating it. Finally I could explore how I might go about changing that pattern – assuming that I saw it as sufficiently important to do so. Wow – that's a pretty good theory of working towards therapeutic change:

Task 1: Identify and explore the psychological pattern to find out how valid it is and how important it is.

Task 2: Explore where the pattern has come from – what drives the person to repeat the pattern?

Task 3: Explore the pattern in terms of a 'working-through' that begins to dissolve it. This working-through process could be a combination of work on self, personal history and interpersonal relating – through, for example, internal conflict resolution, re-experiencing of past trauma or the live relationship of client and counsellor.

And I could add a fourth task:

Task 4: Follow through the changes into the person's life, supporting him or her in dealing with resistance to growth and change – resistance in both self and important others. As I understand it, resistance to growth is often in the form of a powerful memory of the opposite – with greater intimacy, for example, comes the memory of intense aloneness. It also seems to me that this fourth task is often the least attended to and the most difficult and yet any deep change in a person tends to evoke strong opposition – both from within the self and from others.

These tasks would be very roughly sequential, over a counselling series, but client and counsellor might jump from one to another and back again (in a much less sequential fashion) during a session or series of sessions.

Well, I've done the first task – identified the pattern. Rather than riding over other people and annoying them I tend to ignore other people and get on with whatever it is I want to do alone. I guess there are two immediate effects of that: firstly I get to be alone more than I would choose, and secondly other people may well feel excluded, perhaps even pushed away by me.

In terms of how valid and how important this pattern is, I do tend to choose this kind of situation quite a lot. I can think of lots of examples – both in my present life, and in my past, where I have followed what I wanted to do and excluded others in the process. It's an aspect of my character that's probably very obvious to the people around me, but it's something I've been fairly blind to. I would have described myself as independently minded and yes, I would have admitted to living my life on my own quite a lot, but I hadn't quite seen myself in the terms I'm now describing. Perhaps it's also something to do with why I've tended to see myself as basically selfish and unkind through insensitivity (rather than unkind through choice). In fact, when I think about it, perhaps it isn't being selfish or unkind at all. For me being selfish is taking 'the cake' and not leaving anything for the other person. I've lived my life 'taking the cake' – but only because I've arranged my life so as to be alone. There was no one there to 'share the cake' and so I didn't share it. If someone had been there, and I've often wished there was, I would have wanted to share it.

This isn't to say that I've lived all of my life alone, but rather that I've lived a lot more of it alone, and still do, than most people I know. I'm not a complete loner, I'm a 'half-loner'.

What about its importance? How important is this psychological pattern in terms of its effects on my life? Pretty central, I would say – it really touches some nerves inside me in terms of my sense of myself and my relationships. It leaves me feeling friendless and alone (in the depth of my being) and that has a lot of pain and unmet needs and desires associated with it. It's probably also a very important aspect of myself that other people find very difficult to take. If I was used to being fairly included by my friends and colleagues I'd probably feel quite unsure and confused by Robert's pattern of relating. And if I was actually living with Robert – as his partner – I would feel very unsure about his commitment to me and to our relationship.

So this pattern is pretty significant and one I really need to work on. On the one hand that feels a rather frightening prospect – as if I will be 'gobbled up' by other people if I stop being this 'half-loner'. On the other hand it feels like I would really be a lot happier and enjoy life a lot more – if I was living my life with other people more directly, more intimately. I can also sense how much of a change it might mean for me – since the pattern feels like such an intimate part of me.

Moving on then to my task 2 – where has this pattern come from, how has it developed during my personal history and what exactly is driving me to repeat it? How do I begin with this task?

I thought about this for a while and the only thing that has come up is something that arose in my personal counselling a few sessions ago – the feeling that I'm not in the 'right place'. We had been looking at a time when I was moved across the country and had to settle into a new school. Perhaps this leaves me with the feeling that when I'm with other people I feel in the new place and when I'm alone I feel I'm partly back in the old place. I'm not sure this really makes sense or really feels right, though. Another thought I've had is the question, 'Why might I have wanted to separate myself off from the people around me?' Yes, why should I choose to be alone rather than with people? What is it that I gain by being alone and what do I fear losing, when I'm with ... I don't know ... it's very hard, this personal work ...

Thursday evening After much feeling around myself over the past few days, I've concluded that, perhaps, I simply feel more myself when I'm alone and fear losing 'myself' when I'm with others. Being true to myself is very difficult when I'm with other people because I tend to lose my sense of who I am and what I want – or at least I fear this happening. Yes, that really feels right – this is what's driving me to repeat this pattern of relating.

So what, in my personal history, has left me with this fear of losing myself when I am with others? ... I think I shall take this to my personal counselling session tomorrow.

Saturday evening Yesterday's counselling session was pretty important and I feel I've really come up with something. When I'm with people I'm very sensitive to them – I kind of monitor them to work out what they are feeling, thinking, wanting or needing. I know about them in a way that is probably fairly unusual – at least in terms of the level of my sensitivity to others. It's almost as if when I'm with people their volume is very loud and I can only cope with that for so long. After a while I have to switch them off. I have to be alone.

Towards the end of yesterday's session Maria posed the question of why I have the volume up so high – why am I so sensitive, why is it so important, what do I believe would happen if I stopped being so sensitive, or turned the volume down. At the time I really felt, 'Wow that's a question worth exploring!'

If I reduced the 'volume of other people' I would ... a powerful image passed through me then and something painful also happened in my stomach. It was, however, very fast and it felt like another part of me quickly shut the top of that Pandora's box. I tried again and what came up was that I would trample, or something like that, on other people and that was something that ... I'm not sure, either happened to me (I got trampled on by someone) and I didn't want to be like that person, or else trampling on people would be very uncomfortable for me because of their reactions to me trampling on them.

I tried to imagine, once again, what would happen if I reduced the volume of other people, and this time I felt that a part of me would get out of control – a very 'selfish' part. I would start saying things without thinking about their effects ... shit! If I grew up with a father who was very sensitive to being trampled on then I would need to 'up the volume' in order to make ... no that's not right! If I need to be extra-sensitive to the other ... No, if my father was easily hurt by, I don't know, something I said or did or whatever, then I would need to tread carefully in order not to hurt his 'toes' and I would also need to up the volume to enable me to tread so very carefully.

So what I've learnt from my relationship with my father is to 'tread carefully'. But what this also leaves me with is this deafening volume in terms of 'what's going on in the other person', a deafening volume that feels like it drowns *me* out and which I can only really cope with by switching off the volume of the other person altogether. Shutting the door on the other person completely – at least for a time – and then doing what I want to do and being what I want to be. This feels very real and very important ...

Sunday evening I've been working on this insight that what drives me to keep the volume high is the fear that if I don't, I will be treading on the other person's toes, or something to that effect. This has certainly been feeling quite psychologically real for me, and it's also quite a self-affirming conclusion. It makes sense of the underlying feeling I've always had of being basically unkind and selfish – despite the fact that in comparison to others I come out pretty low on the scale of a 'nasty bit of work'. If I felt I had to tread so carefully, I must have also very easily seen myself as unkind and selfish.

As I wrote that, I wondered if I am also, like my father, an over-sensitive man easily hurt by the other. Yes, perhaps I also find it difficult to be with other people because I am, like my father, easily hurt and, as a defence against that prospect, remove myself. Or perhaps I never fully let myself in, in the first place – for fear of having my over-sensitive toes trodden on ... Two things have arisen for me about what I've just written – it's much easier to develop over-sensitive toes if you don't put them in the water much and I've also realized that there are many other ways in which I'm like my father. Like father like son, as the saying goes.

I feel I need to review what I've been doing and where I'm at right now in terms of this personal work. Where am I in relation to my map of the therapeutic process? It feels like I'm jumping about a bit – between tasks 1 and 2; no, I've not been jumping back to task 1. What I've been doing is exploring the history of the pattern and, in particular, what it might be that is driving me in this way. I've come up with two 'answers' that feel fairly real to me. Firstly that I have the volume too high for fear of hurting the 'sensitive' other and then, after a time, feel I have to switch it off. Secondly I am, perhaps, like my father, an over-sensitive person and keep myself at a distance as a defence against being easily hurt.

What about task 3: working through the pattern? I'm not sure how to begin.

Hmmm, it feels as though a way of beginning to work it through a little would be to imagine turning the volume down. I imagined doing that and it does feel as though I might be able to change this black and white choice between high volume or switched off. I can even imagine being a little bit different in the way that I relate with other people in my life – for example, choosing to be with people and consciously turning the volume down.

But it also feels that this is very much the beginning of task 3. If I actually began to turn down the volume with others, however, I might be in task 4 – taking the changes in my psychological pattern into my life as a whole. Hmmm ... it feels like my theory is breaking down a bit – perhaps it's not so easy to distinguish separate therapeutic tasks in this way. According to my theory, however, if I got to task 4 I'd be faced with resistance to that kind of change – both in myself and in my relationships. I wonder what such resistance might look and feel like?

I went to hang out the clothes from the washing machine. I guess the kinds of reactions I could expect in myself are those that are the opposite to what was actually happening. For example, I might actually be with the person, but my sense of aloneness might be heightened. Or, if I took less account of what I imagined the other person was thinking or feeling, I might actually feel I was actively trampling on the other person. And what about the reactions of others to this change in me? Well, what would it be like for my wife? I immediately imagined that she would react to me as an insensitive, unkind, selfish person – but that's my fantasy, not her actual response. I can't really think of anything at the moment – but then the point of task 4 is that of 'supporting the client in dealing with any *actual* resistances to growth and change', not in imagining them.

Where next with all of this? Further work on task 3, for sure – finding ways to work through and dissolve this pattern – both in my personal work in my journal, but perhaps more importantly in my personal counselling. It feels like this is going to be mixed up with task 4 too – and I will need someone there to support me in that.

Right now I feel a lot better able to be kinder to myself as a result of this personal work and some very important issues have arisen for me. I'm sure that there will also be many implications for my work with clients – the most obvious area being that of the client–counsellor relationship. I can imagine that, as my pattern of relating changes, I will become better able to be really present with my clients. It also feels like I've really begun to understand and work with my own theory of the therapeutic process, and that feels important too.

I realize I haven't done the exercise that you set for us, Anthony. Hopefully I will be able to turn to it at a later date but it does feel that it's been very important to follow through my own track of personal work. As I wrote that last sentence I suddenly realized that this is my pattern again – doing my own thing to the exclusion of the other – in this case your exercise, Anthony!

Some questions to consider

1   How do you relate to Robert's theory of the therapeutic process – personally and professionally? How do the tasks feel to you?
2   There is a sense throughout Robert's writing of a rather intellectual person working away by himself on his personal work. What might a more feeling-orientated person come up with as a theory of therapeutic growth and change?
3   How do you respond to the idea of resistance to change? (See also Chapter 5.)

4   Who has mistreated you in your life and what are the effects on your sense of yourself and your perception of others? (Complete the exercise described by Robert at the beginning of his journal extract.)

9

Three in a Room – the Experience of Counselling Supervision

All of us, from the cradle to the grave, are happiest when life is organized as a series of excursions, long or short, from the secure base provided by our attachment figures. (John Bowlby, *A Secure Base*, 1988)

Why do counsellors need supervision?

Sandra [thinks/feels: *'I really don't like driving. I wish I didn't have to drive to this supervision session. I get so tense. I really worry about crashing and I don't have safety bars in the doors, or an airbag. I'd feel safer in a big car – statistically you're much safer in a big car. But I don't believe in big cars, they use so much petrol. She's sitting down now. I'd better collect my thoughts. What was I going to say to her. Oh yes . . .'*] Today I'd like to bring a new client, Ronnie. We can leave some time to follow through on this weeks' session with Jaynie but I need some help with Ronnie first. OK?

Marjorie [thinks/feels, before Sandra speaks: *'God I'm feeling tired. These end of the day sessions are too much. I must get clearer with myself and my clients and supervisees about what I have to offer. Sandra is an enjoyable and interesting person to work with but not when I'm feeling so worn out. I should stop working at four and spend this last hour writing notes or whatever. Anyway, that's something to look at in my own supervision. Sits down and Sandra speaks. There's a certain edginess with you today, Sandra, I wonder what that's about. I better also note that my tiredness may also be more than simple tiredness – it feels as if it's almost too much to work with you today, Sandra. There might be something of importance here – some kind of counter-transference? I don't always feel as tired as this and I usually look forward to working with you.'*] That's fine with me, Sandra. Do you want to start by giving me an outline of the referral, his background, your assessment and this first session itself?

Sandra [thinks/feels: *'She always wants me to be so bloody clear and precise. I'm not like that, I don't work like that. It's hard being so precise. I just want to talk about the problem with Ronnie.'*] I can't really – not his background nor any assessment, either. I haven't had a chance to look at his background with him and I haven't come to a clear assessment either.

I'm really a bit confused about the first session too. [Thinks/feels: *'Christ that all rather spurted out. I'm not normally like that, am I?'*]

Marjorie [thinks/feels: *'You're actually looking a bit . . . confused. It almost feels like there's a hot potato under your bum and you're twitching about on that hot seat. I feel quite edgy myself sitting here with you.'*] You seem a bit . . . nervy, twitchy almost. How do you feel about this client? What's happened to you, Sandra?

Sandra [thinks/feels: *'It feels nice to be asked that question.'* She slumps back in her chair.] I feel like he's too much, too much to cope with. I don't know [silence for a minute or so] what to do with him, I guess I feel somewhat incompetent. I feel he's beyond me. There, I've said it! I don't feel I can cope with him!

[*As Sandra speaks, the image of Sandra twitching on her hot seat comes back into Marjorie's mind. She notices the image and also highlights, in her mind, Sandra's phrase 'to do with him'. Somehow these words strike her as words with special underlying feeling and energy; words that could be 'unpacked.'*] It sounds like Ronnie has had a powerful effect on you. I'm wondering what it is that you can't cope with about him and also what you mean when you say you 'don't know what to do with him'.

As Marjorie spoke Sandra felt the impact of Ronnie more intensely. She felt, for a moment, 'all at sea' but quickly her mind covered up that feeling and moved in the opposite direction.

Sandra: Perhaps I need to refer him on – to someone more experienced in panic attacks than I am.

[*Marjorie notices a feeling of being hot, she also notices that her tiredness has suddenly lifted. She thinks: 'Sandra feels different after saying that – lighter, not so twitchy. Panic attacks . . . I wonder if this is a situation of Sandra tuning in to her own anxiety? How does Sandra cope with her own anxiety?'*] Let's take a look at whether you *do* need to refer him on – either because you don't have sufficient resources to give him the attention he would need or because his issues are too far outside of your competence for you to work with him effectively. Do you want to say something about why you feel you need to refer him on?

[*For a moment in Sandra's mind's eye, Sandra is sailing on a yacht in the warm waters of the Mediterranean. Once again she collects her thoughts and once again notices a slight annoyance with Marjorie for making her be so clear and precise again. 'I don't know why I can't work with Ronnie he just feels . . . frightening. Not frightening in the sense of he might attack me. No, frightening to . . . have to work with him.'*] I'm not sure, Marjorie. I just don't feel I can help him. Actually I don't think I want to help him.

Marjorie [thinks/feels: *'It's almost as if she's pushing Ronnie away, or more probably Ronnie's panic attacks. I would guess that she doesn't deal with her own anxiety, her own panicky part of herself, very well and she is avoiding having to do so by pushing Ronnie away like this. That's only a guess though – mustn't come to any premature conclusions.'* The phrase *'premature ejaculation' pops into Marjorie's mind – which again she notices.* Silence for a minute or two] I'd like to check something out with you, Sandra – just a thought I've had in the last four minutes. I'm wondering how you deal with your own anxiety, your own panicky part of yourself. Could it be that Ronnie's problem is one that you don't feel that good at dealing with yourself?

[*Momentarily Sandra feels in a panic, as if she has been found out and is about to be really told off. Her mind quickly covers up those feelings and returns to the yacht in the Mediterranean. From there her thoughts turn to the room and how she has never really liked the colour scheme – too old-fashioned. 'Marjorie is a bit of an old fogey, really.'*] I'm sorry, Marjorie, I didn't quite catch that. I was thinking about something else for a moment.

Marjorie [thinks/feels: *'Hmmm . . . a form of confirmation, perhaps. This is something that Sandra is finding very difficult to hear. In fact it feels like she has psychologically left the room. She doesn't feel present at all. Not that present at all. How am I feeling at the moment? Tired again, like it's really quite a strain to be here with Sandra – and her client Ronnie. It actually feels like we're moving through treacle right at the moment – which probably means we're right where we need to be. We need to get more concrete – focus on an example'.*] How do *you* cope when you get anxious, Sandra? That's not quite what I said but it's a better question. Can you remember, for example, a recent situation where you felt anxious? Perhaps we can explore that. If you can keep your mind from wandering off.

[Silence]

Sandra [thinks/feels: *'That felt a bit patronizing, Marjorie. A bit over the top.' Her mind returns to the colour scheme in the room and for a moment she imagines Marjorie's life outside of counselling and supervision. An image of Marjorie in the old age pensioners' queue at the post office passes through her mind.*]

Marjorie [thinks/feels: *'What is going on with Sandra? She looks as if she's somewhere else completely. Further confirmation if ever there was one.'*]

Sandra [thinks/feels: *'A recent example of feeling anxious?' For a moment she is back sailing in the yacht in the calm blue sea of the Mediterranean. A beautiful young man – the same one she saw yesterday in the post office – at the helm, turns his head towards her and smiles. His eyes caress her, as his gentle fingers will – later that day. 'In the car – that's the most recent example I guess – in the car on the way here, anxious about crashing.'*] I don't know if this helps but I was feeling a bit nervous on the way here – driving in the car. I'm often quite tense when I'm driving – always thinking about the dangers of driving. You know, it's the most dangerous thing you can do. I don't like driving much, it *does* make me a bit anxious. Aren't we off at a bit of a tangent right now, though? I was wanting to talk about Ronnie – come to a decision about how to, well whether, and how to refer him. I'm pretty sure he's beyond me, though.

Marjorie [thinks/feels: '*You really don't want to think about your own anxiety, do you Sandra? Perhaps you're right – it would be too much to work with Ronnie right now. This is an issue, however, that's going to rise up again and again. You don't get very far in counselling without coming up against anxiety. What are we going to do with you, Sandra? You need to address this personally – in your own counselling – before you're going to get anywhere in terms of your work counselling people with anxiety as one of their issues.*'] We are exploring Ronnie and whether or not you need to refer him. It feels to me that what's getting in the way here is your own anxiety and the possibility that you have never really explored and worked through your own issues in this area. It feels like doing so is very important, not just for work with someone like Ronnie – who is presenting with panic attacks – but because most clients will have some issues associated with the way they don't cope very well with their anxieties. My guess is that you need to do some fairly intensive personal work on this – are you still seeing your own counsellor?

[*For a moment Sandra feels quite shocked and hurt by what Marjorie just said. The shock and hurt, however, is quickly covered over by anger at this old fogey, but the anger is also just as rapidly covered up. In the twinkling of an eye Sandra is left feeling . . . nothing. Empty and a little hot.*] What about Ronnie, do you think I should refer him?

[*Marjorie notices that the feel of Sandra has quite substantially shifted in response to what she has just said. It's almost as if she has turned into a little girl asking Mummy what to do. She sighs but her heart feels lighter and warmer towards Sandra. She notices that she isn't feeling so tired and worn out. An observer might have noticed, however, another tone in Sandra's voice – a resentful one.*] I need to know if you've heard what I've said about your own personal work. I'd like you to respond to that before helping you to decide what to do about this client.

Sandra [thinks/feels: '*She's certainly got a bee in her bonnet about this. Hmmm . . . Old fogey or not Marjorie has certainly been very helpful to me in the past and despite the driving I do find it valuable coming here.*' Silence for a moment in which Sandra and Marjorie look into each other's eyes. Sandra recovers the warm feeling that she often feels with Marjorie and her eyes respond to the warmth she feels. Marjorie has a questioning expression tinged with a certain uncertainty about Sandra.] I only saw Jim for 10 sessions. I was running out of money and we both felt that the original issue I had brought to counselling had been dealt with. We finished working together nearly two months ago now. I don't know that I felt it was that useful – he certainly helped me with the unfinished business I had with Ben but it seemed like a lot of money to pay out for him to sit there listening to me.

[Marjorie laughs.]

Marjorie: [humorously] Not a ringing endorsement of the profession you are seeking to enter? [*Marjorie feels an even deeper warmth towards Sandra – for her capacity for openness and honesty. The image of a young piglet, from the film* Babe, *passes through her mind. She notices the strong sense of a mother-daughter transference and smiles with old and care-worn eyes at Sandra.*]

Sandra [thinks/feels: *'I guess she's right there.' Smiles.*] So you're saying I need to explore how I deal with my anxieties in my personal counselling because if I'm not dealing with them very well then I'm not going to be much good at helping clients with their anxieties.

Marjorie [thinks/feels: *'Well done Sandra!'*] That took a while, but yes, that is what I'm saying. How do you feel about that?

Sandra [thinks/feels: *'How do I feel? I've been feeling pretty mixed up this session. Maybe Marjorie's right, though. How do I deal with my anxieties? Thinking about it right now I do have a tendency to ignore them as much as I can.' The image of the man in the post office and the blue Mediterranean waters once again pass for an instant through her mind.*] Perhaps I should give personal counselling another go. You're right that my experience isn't much of an endorsement. Maybe I'd get more out of it a second time. Maybe I need to try someone else, a woman perhaps. Yes, perhaps Jim wasn't really the right counsellor for me. And I could start by looking at the way I cope with feeling anxious.

Marjorie [thinks/feels: *'That really was like struggling through treacle but we do seem to have got there in the end although I guess you'll need reminding about this. We do need to look at Ronnie and how to go about referring him. I wonder how Ronnie felt on this first session with you, Sandra. Very anxious, I would guess.'*] So what about your client, Ronnie? What do you feel is the best for him?

Sandra [thinks/feels: *'Well there's a question. How would I feel if I was Ronnie? I'd probably take it as quite a rejection if Sandra was to refer me on. I'm not sure I'd go to another counsellor. It took a hell of a lot for me to work myself up to make that phone call to Sandra, never mind actually turn up at the Complementary Health Centre. The last thing I need is for Sandra to tell me I'm too much for her and I've got to go through this all over again.'*] I feel that the best thing for Ronnie would be for me to continue seeing him. I know that's not what I've been saying up until now but I was imagining his reaction to my referral and I'm not sure he'd go to someone else. My guess is he'd give up on the idea of having counselling.

[*Marjorie notices that she's feeling a little off-centre in response to Sandra's remarks. She focuses on the feeling and the image of being thrown into a rubbish tip runs through her mind's eye. She wonders what happens to Sandra's anxious part of her self and whether the rubbish tip is a good metaphor for where that part of herself tends to be found.*]

Marjorie [thinks/feels: '*What you're saying might well be true, Sandra but I'm not at all confident that you can offer Ronnie a therapeutic counselling experience. Perhaps we could check out how Ronnie seemed to be at the end of his first counselling session. Perhaps we need to leave this decision up to him and make sure you have as much support as you can in working with him, if Ronnie decides to continue. On the other hand this could just be a fantasy on your part that Ronnie won't continue with counselling if you were to refer him. What's been missing from this supervision session up until now is any real sense of the session.*'] I feel we're in a bit of a quandary right at the moment. I'd quite like to get some sense of the actual session with Ronnie – perhaps in doing that we can get clearer about whether or not you should continue with him or seek to refer him on.

TIME OUT

Tutor: Marjorie is clearly psychodynamic in her orientation. What do you think makes her so?

Student: She uses the concepts of transference and counter-transference.

Tutor: Yes, that's a bit of a giveaway but what does she mean by them when she uses them?

Student: Her use of the concept of transference is a fairly straight-forward one. I think the transference is there throughout the session with Sandra's angry and rebellious feelings towards her 'old fogey' supervisor followed by strong dependency feelings when, feeling empty and lost, she asks Marjorie to tell her what to do about Ronnie. In fact it's almost as if Sandra starts as an adolescent and then regresses to a younger child. Marjorie doesn't seem to particularly pick up on the former but quickly notices the latter – feeling Sandra shift to 'a little girl' and her image of the piglet in *Babe*. I'm not so sure what she means by the phrase 'some kind of counter-transference' – perhaps you could say something about that?

Tutor: OK. This is right at the beginning of the session and she's referring to the fact that although it's the end of the day she doesn't always feel the way she's feeling with Sandra. In fact the feeling that 'it's almost too much to work with you today, Sandra' is actually an unusual feeling for Marjorie to feel about her supervisee. Usually she feels quite enthusiastic about her work with Sandra. She's noticing this and asking herself if there is something important here for her work with Sandra today. In other words she's noticing that Sandra is having a certain kind of effect on her that is unusual. She is spontaneously responding to Sandra in a way in which she doesn't usually respond. The word 'counter-transference' is a bit of a confusing word because it's used to refer to different kinds of experience. Some psychodynamic writers use it to refer to all of the thoughts and feelings that the counsellor has towards his/her client. Others use it to refer to the counsellor's transference onto the client. I prefer a third definition – the response of the counsellor to the client's transference. Marjorie doesn't particularly follow through on her self-observation but if she had done, I think the most interesting thing she might have noted is the parallel between how Sandra is feeling about her client – too much to cope with – and how Marjorie is (at the beginning of the session) feeling about Sandra. She might then have gone further and linked this with the central issue of the supervision session – that Sandra's anxiety, triggered by her session with Ronnie, is too much for Sandra to cope with. This is called 'parallel process' and can often be observed during supervision. I have another question for you, however – how does Sandra actually cope with her anxiety?

Student: She censors it and thinks about something nice – the handsome man in the post office and the yacht in the Mediterranean. She makes it unconscious and thinks comforting thoughts. She quickly covers up the feeling of being 'all at sea' when she thinks about Ronnie. That's interesting – because her comforting thoughts are also about being 'at sea'. I might guess, though, that the anxious feeling is one of a cold and stormy Atlantic sea *without* a strong man at the helm. When Marjorie directly asks her how she deals with her own anxiety she actually panics for a moment before censoring the feeling and covering it up with the comforting Mediterranean daydream. She then gets a bit angry with Marjorie: 'shoot the messenger' would be an apt description of her response to Marjorie's query. Basically she's defending herself at that moment from the threat of being overwhelmed by something that she can't deal with – her own panic.

Tutor: So how does she actually come round to hearing Marjorie? What happens so that her defences against hearing her supervisor drop?

Student: Well, Marjorie is pretty challenging. She comes at it four times – each time getting more direct until she pokes Sandra on the nose. There would have to be a good working relationship between the two of them before that could work. Even then she doesn't give up because she still wants to check out Sandra's response to her challenge and finally makes a mental note that she'll probably have to remind her about it. Sandra seems to respond to the fourth challenge by shifting from her rebellious adolescent transference to a younger-child transference. It's at that moment that her defences drop and she is able to hear Marjorie. Again I would guess that this is only possible because, underneath, she feels safe with Marjorie – that there is a certain level of trust invested in Marjorie. What do you feel about Marjorie? She quickly picks up on this transference but not on the rebellious adolescent one.

Tutor: Well I also wonder about the mother–child transference – it's almost as if the supervision relationship is reliant on that mother–child transference. If I was *Marjorie's* supervisor I'd be asking her about that – how would it be to work with the more rebellious adolescent supervisee? Perhaps that's something that Marjorie would find very challenging – if she has children, how did she deal with their adolescence? How does she deal with the adolescent part of herself? There may be some important personal work for Marjorie here.

Student: What about Sandra and Ronnie? Sandra certainly needs to take a look at how she *isn't* really dealing with the anxious part of herself. Do you think she is able to work with Ronnie – would her own resistance to her own anxieties get in the way of that work to the point of making it worthless or even damaging? She's certainly very good at resisting Marjorie's attempts to focus her on her own anxiety and the fact that she doesn't deal with it very well.

Tutor: It's a difficult one, really. I don't think there can be a clear-cut answer here. If I were Sandra I'd come clean with Ronnie – tell him that panic attacks aren't my strong point. See how he responds to the idea of referral but give him the choice – which is also what Marjorie's concluding too. If he chose to continue – and I'd need to make it very clear to him that I was very willing to continue with him (but that I'd be learning too) – then at least Sandra and Ronnie would now be aware of the situation. What could be hurtful would be either to simply reject him without acknowledging my own sense of incompetence or to continue working with him while remaining unconscious of my own inability to cope with anxiety. There are things that Marjorie is missing – to do with Sandra's adolescent transference and Marjorie's possible reliance (as supervisor) on the mother–child transference – but I believe she has helped Sandra to where she probably needs to be. In that respect the supervision has certainly worked well and we can well imagine that Sandra could have been hurtful to Ronnie if she hadn't had the benefit of that supervision session.

Extract from Sandra's supervision notes

Sandra [thinks/feels: *'I'm not sure what to write about today's supervision session with Marjorie.'* Once again Sandra is in the yacht in the calm blue sea. It's dark and the sun has just set. The man from the post office whispers in her left ear. She feels his soft breath on her neck; his arms envelop her shoulders.

Then suddenly a sea monster leaps out of the darkening waters, its mouth wide open and about to engulf her. She jolts out of her daydream. The rain is thumping against the window beyond her little writing desk. Jennie and Dave are fighting about the TV channels down in the living room. She ought to go and sort it out. 'What if they wreck the place?' The image of a war-torn living room, smashed TV set and two dead children passes through her mind's eye. The phrase 'monster in the closet' pops up. Sandra straightens out the paper in her journal and draws a stick man with a big smile. Which is not how she's feeling at that moment. 'Oh dear, bloody supervision notes again.'] Marjorie and I agreed that I needed to begin my personal counselling again – this time with a woman. We had been looking at the first session with a new client Ronnie and Marjorie felt that his presenting problem – panic attacks – was triggering stuff for me that I needed to look at. I'm still not sure what to do with Ronnie – Marjorie suggested that I start up my counselling before the next session with Ronnie – which luckily is in a fortnight – and we will look at the issue again in our supervision session next week.

To tell you the truth, it all feels a bit of a drag at the moment. Yes, a bit of a drag.

Sandra [thinks/feels: *'Do I really want to pay out more money for someone to sit there and listen to me? I'm just not so sure about this whole counselling business right at the moment. It's turning out to be something very different from what I was expecting.'* Her shoulders feel tense – she notices the tension as she sits at the desk listening to the rain and the shouts of her children. She *relaxes* once again – imagining her dream-man softly massaging them and whispering in her ear. The image reminds her of a coffee advert. *'I could make a coffee. No, I'm going to sit here until I've finished two pages. That's what I've decided and that's what I am going to do.'* The rain continues to rattle against the window. The children's shouting reaches a crescendo. Jennie starts crying *'Mummy, Mummy, David hit me with the TV thingy, Mummy, Mummy.'* 'Where is Alan – he's supposed to be back by now – we agreed that I would have some time to do my work this evening. Bloody men!!! Useless, selfish creatures.' She throws down her pen on the table and rushes downstairs to find out what has been happening with her two little monsters.]

The Pen: *I want to write how angry and frustrated I feel with all of this. I want to scrape a hole in the paper with the word 'Arrgghh'. I want to grind down my tip so that I can't write anymore. I want to spill my ink all over the desk and ruin this journal. I want to spray myself on Marjorie's horrible furniture: get some proper furniture and change the bloody curtains! I want to go on strike until I get a proper deal in this household. I want to smash the TV up so the monsters can't argue over it anymore. I want to give it all up and run off with the man in the post office. I want a life!*

[Sandra returns to the room with the little writing desk and the rain splashing up against the window.]

Sandra: Right I'm going to finish these two pages if it is the last thing I do.

Author's note: The pen talking might seem like a rather strange and surreal little addition to this passage on Sandra's experience of writing her supervision notes. From a Gestalt perspective, however, it is quite an acceptable thing to do. A Gestalt practitioner might well ask his client to become the pen that Sandra threw down and, as the pen, Sandra might well be able to express some of the frustration she's feeling, but finding so difficult to express. Of course the Gestalt counsellor won't suddenly spring this on the unsuspecting client. If I was working in this way I would want to be certain that the client was open to this type of technique and would probably already have worked with more 'normal' dialoguing (for example between the client and her husband, or in this case, between Sandra and her supervisor) before suggesting that he/she become an object like a pen and speak as that object.

A useful little exercise for you to experiment with is to become an object in the room – the first object that comes to mind: for example the chair you are sitting on, the heater, the ceiling or the doorknob. Imagine what it would be like to be this object and speak as that object. It's sometimes quite surprising what can come out – the key to this is to censor as little as possible. I would recommend that you do this exercise with someone else if you can – giving yourself plenty of time to come out of it and review the experience.

If you do find it an interesting exercise then I'd suggest a second part to it – ask yourself what object would be the opposite of the object you just imagined being. Try not to 'work this out' but rather let it rise up into your mind. The opposite of a chair, for example, might not be (for you) a table but could be anything at all – a portable computer, perhaps. Become this other object and speak as that object. Set out two chairs and dialogue between these two objects. (See Chapters 2 and 3 for more details of this approach.)

You can also do this exercise in relation to the various elements and objects in a dream or a daydream. Sandra, for example, could become the calm Mediterranean Sea and the open-mouthed monster that shatters that calm. She could even become her dream-man and speak as if she was he.

If you (and your client) find this way of working OK then some very important and interesting things can come out of the mouths of these imaginary beings. I also like this way of working because it can sometimes lighten up very difficult and painful issues.

Enabling the client to express some of the surface feeling – anger and frustration, in this case – can lead to a deeper layer of feeling. Whether or not I am using this Gestalt technique of becoming an object, or simply providing the space and permission for the expression of such powerful feelings, the client often discovers that these first feelings are covering over a deeper layer of feeling. It may well be, therefore, that Sandra's feelings of anger and frustration are covering up deeper feelings that for her are more difficult to cope with – her anxiety.

All of this could only really be examined in her personal counselling. There is very little chance, as we saw in the supervision session itself, that Sandra will 'get there' by herself. In fact I'd go so far as to say that there is *no chance* of that happening.

So what happens next? Does Sandra get to work on her anger and frustration and, beneath that, her anxiety? Does she continue to work with Ronnie and if so well, or badly, or both? And what of Marjorie and her difficulty with Sandra's adolescent transference? I've given some answers to some of these questions in earlier chapters in the book but they are not the only possibilities. How would you go about these things? How would you work, for example, with Sandra? What would she need to feel safe enough to explore her anxiety? Is this part of herself – her panicky part – one that she metaphorically chucks into the rubbish tip? If so, how might she begin to see that, and beyond that how might she begin to treat that aspect, that part of herself, differently? How would you cope with, and work with, her resistance and defensiveness to this kind of therapeutic work on herself? What if some of her anger and frustration was directed at you – 'the messenger'?

There's a lot involved here, just as there's a lot involved in working with any client. As we see with Marjorie and her supervisee, there are also important things that even a very experienced counsellor misses, or simply isn't able to see. How does Marjorie 'get there' with Sandra? I'm not sure but I think it's to do with how she keeps an eye on both herself, her supervisee, the content and the process of the session – deciding what's most important and then focusing on that. If a counsellor can do something similar to this then perhaps the blind spots and mistakes won't matter, quite as much.

Helping the counsellor to stay with the focus for the work

> Govinda (Supervisor): Good morning, Belinda, would you like to start, once again, with David and then we can leave some time at the end of the supervision session for any other issues that are current for you with your other clients?
>
> Belinda: OK, although I do need to spend a bit of time in relation to another client – Geoffrey and the session with him this last Tuesday.
>
> Govinda: Is 20 minutes going to be enough for Geoffrey?
>
> Belinda: Oh yes, that would be plenty of time.
>
> Govinda: OK, so let's finish with David at twenty to.
>
> Belinda: OK [Belinda collects her thoughts and examines her notes on this week's session with David.] He arrived five minutes or so late,

which is not that unusual, apologizing for being late. I asked him to summarize his experience of the last session and inquired as to whether he wanted to tell me anything about his week. He highlighted something that I hadn't really picked up – the experience of his first girlfriend's rejection, when he was 17. It was something that he mentioned, in passing, last session, but not something that we particularly focused on then. David had found himself thinking about her again, in between sessions, he had even dreamt about her.

Govinda: Can I just check with you on the initial sequence at the start of this session: he arrived late, apologized, you responded with . . .?

Belinda: Oh . . . I can't remember, something like 'that's OK'.

Govinda: And what were your underlying thoughts and feelings about him being late?

Belinda: I don't know. As I said, it wasn't that unusual, in fact he's usually late. I guess I was feeling . . . well actually I was hoping he would be a bit late, I was feeling a bit, well, unsettled before he arrived, and I remember thinking at a quarter past – when we were supposed to start the session – 'I hope he's late, I need the time to settle myself', yes that's the kind of thing I was thinking: doesn't sound too good, does it?

Govinda: It's also interesting to note that although this is the fourth time we've looked at David it's the first time you've mentioned him being late. So this session actually began with you feeling unsettled and pleased that David was late – so that you had a few minutes of peace and quiet?

Belinda: Well, yes, I suppose so.

Govinda: And if he had arrived on time, when you were feeling unsettled – what would that have been like?

Belinda: I don't know . . . uncomfortable. I'd have felt quite rushed, quite . . . unready. I wouldn't have felt ready for him.

Govinda: Hmmm. So if he had arrived on time, you wouldn't have felt ready for him?

Belinda: Yes.

Govinda: Can you imagine being David, arriving on time and you not feeling ready for him?

Belinda: I'm feeling quite criticized about this now. Like I wasn't doing my job, like I wasn't ready to see him.

Govinda: I'm also wondering a number of things at the moment, so I'd like us to agree on a focus for the rest of this part of the session on David.

Belinda: Well it feels like you are making me be more concrete again – forcing me to take you into the session, as you put it. Which I do find useful, and you have certainly raised some questions in my mind about the beginning and what was going on for me.

Govinda: As a person *in relation with* David.

Belinda: Right, I see what you mean, that maybe I was the way I was as part of what it is to be in relation to David. Hmmm. That's very interesting. I haven't really seen it quite like that before. You mean, for example, that my wanting David to be late and my having to get ready for him might tell me something about David?

Govinda: Perhaps: that's something to start thinking about. What would you see, however, as the important focus for us right now?

Belinda: [thinks] I think I'd like to take you through more of the session. There was a moment in it that feels significant and I would like to explore that with you.

Govinda: OK.

Belinda: So he had been thinking, and dreaming about his first girlfriend – her name was Betina – and how she had rejected him. I asked him if he would like to explore that experience, what it felt like, and he said he would. He described how they had got together at a friend's party. He had been sitting on the sofa and Betina had come and sat next to him and started talking. She wasn't that attractive, apparently, but David had felt very pleased that she had chosen to talk to him. He was very shy of girls and so it was quite something for him to be approached. Anyway they both had a common interest in swimming and agreed to go swimming together later that week. He said that they went out for about four months after that, then Betina had told him that she didn't feel their relationship was going anywhere and broke up with him. I felt really sad for him at that moment.

Govinda: As I remember it, your last session with David was a continuation of your work with him on the roots of his presenting problem – the difficulties he has been experiencing with his boss at work. Last session you both seemed to have uncovered a pattern in David of him being unable to voice his point of view with authority figures – stemming from his relationship with his father. Now, this experience of rejection sounds significant but I'm wondering whether you have drifted off focus with him – considering that you only have, from what I remember, a further four sessions of work agreed. Right now I'm wondering whether you are taking up too many paths of exploration.

Belinda: [thinks] You're probably right again, Govinda – we did drift away from the work we had agreed and I guess that's my responsibility. It's just that he seemed so caught up in this memory of Betina and her rejection that I felt it was important to stay with him on this issue.

Govinda: I have two questions at this moment. Firstly, what would you have been looking at if you had stayed with his issue of authority? When I said that, a third question just popped into my mind – what would it have been like for you to 'authoritatively' focus David back on your agreed focus? My second question, however, is about the important moment that you spoke of earlier – the one you said you wanted to explore in this supervision.

Belinda: Just then, I felt quite irritated with you, Govinda – I felt like, I don't know . . .

Govinda: What do you need to say, Belinda?

Belinda: I feel a bit like you're interrupting me, not really listening to me, I feel like you're getting in the way, knocking me off track!

Govinda: I'm wondering if you have really heard what I've said.

Belinda: That I was wandering off in this session with David, that I should have been staying with the focus that David and I had agreed.

Govinda: Not exactly, Belinda, not exactly.

Belinda: Oh, what did you say, then?

Govinda: I did point out that you might be taking up too many strands, given the limited time you have left with David, but I also said something else *after that* – which you seem not to have heard.

Belinda: Something about questions, two, no, three questions, I'm sorry, my mind wandered off when you were saying that, in fact that's when I was feeling irritated by you – I was thinking about how the session with David had seemed to go really well and I was feeling that you were criticizing me, that you were getting in the way of our work and, well, that this supervision wasn't helping. In fact I even thought that perhaps you weren't quite the right supervisor for me.

Govinda: Well, Belinda, there certainly was a lot going on for you then. I ask you about David's issues with authority figures and what it would be like for you to be an authority figure with him. At that very moment, while you are 'not hearing' me, you perceive me as this questionable, interrupting and non-listening authority figure who is getting in the way of your work.

Belinda: Oh.

Govinda: Oh?

Belinda: Right now I'm feeling confused and rather vulnerable. Almost like you just slapped me across the face.

Govinda: It feels to me as though your work with David, and his issues with authority figures, is tuning you into your own unresolved issues with authority figures and right now these issues are getting in the way of our work in supervision.

Belinda: So I should be looking at this in my personal counselling?

Govinda: Yes, I would say so. Who have I become for you? What are you avoiding in the work with David – what don't you want to get into in relation to the authority figures in your present and past life? Those sorts of things could be explored in your personal counselling. But I'm also wondering about what we need to focus on right now in relation to your work with David and whether we can do that effectively while you are feeling so attacked by me?

Belinda: [Silence] I feel slapped in the face by you and, at the same time, I also don't feel slapped in the face – it's like I'm feeling both things at the same time. What should I be doing with David, then?

Govinda: You tell me, Belinda, you tell me.

Belinda: Well, I can see what you're saying about the fact that we have only agreed on four more sessions at the moment. We certainly were getting on quite well with his issues about his boss and he was beginning to see that the problem had its roots in his relationship with his parents – that he was unconsciously expecting his boss to be like his parents and that some of what he saw in his boss was probably exaggerated. I guess we should continue with that untangling process – untangling his boss from his parents and, perhaps, taking a look at what it would be like for him to voice his perspective on things to his boss.

Govinda: Sounds good enough to me – so what's your next step, and how are you going to keep him on focus when he, and you, probably want to avoid looking at this?

Belinda: [thinks] I think the next step would be to examine a concrete example, one that really sticks in his mind – where he felt he wasn't being asked for his view on things, where he wanted to speak but couldn't. We can then see if we can link that experience to what it felt like with his parents. We could also try it out in the counselling space. I could ask him if he would like to practise speaking out to his boss and, perhaps, responding to himself speaking out, as his boss – how he imagines his boss might react. We could use the chair technique, perhaps?

Govinda: If you are going to use that kind of technique you will need to check it out with him first in some way, to see whether he finds that too difficult a prospect – perhaps by demonstrating it to him and asking him how he feels about it.

Belinda: Sure, I wouldn't just spring it on him – I'm not *that* bad a counsellor.

Challenging an intervention

Sheila (counsellor): Hello Amanda, it's good to see you again. Perhaps I could start by summarizing where we got to last session and then I'd like to ask you how you'd like to use your hour here today?

Amanda: OK.

Sheila: Last session, as you know, was the third in a series where we've been focusing on how you developed a pattern of denying your own feelings and needs in preference to the needs of others.

An important insight emerged for you – the realization that you often took on the role of mother in your family prior to your mother's suicide. That seemed a pretty important insight. So when your mother died you easily stepped into the mothering role for your dad and your kid sister – once again denying your own feelings and needs. How does that sound?

Amanda: That sounds about right – although there was something else that I took away from last session and have been thinking about over the week. I think it's also what I'd like to talk to you about today. At the time it didn't seem very important, but it stuck in my mind and led to quite a lot of thought. It was when we were talking about how my mother always used to tell me all her problems. I remembered one day, I must have been 16 or so, it was just an image that passed through my mind during the last session: my mother was in the bedroom, she didn't think anyone else was in the home, I had come home early from somewhere, my friend Joan's I think, I was walking past her room to my bedroom and my mother was standing by the mirror staring at herself. But it was as if she hated the person in that mirror, as if she hated her life, everything, including me. I stood there for a moment, stunned, like when I was in the training group before I first came to see you, and like when I was first told about her death. Then I became terrified that she would notice me and I slipped on past the door. I remembered that experience for a long time afterwards. In fact I used to lie in bed at night and think about her standing before the mirror hating herself, hating her life, hating me. Then I forgot all about it. [Heavy silence]

Sheila: So, let me just check this out with you, Amanda – you'd like to use this session to focus on this image of your mother looking at herself in the mirror and hating herself?

Amanda: What, oh well, I don't know . . . it was just something I was thinking about.

[Hilde presses the stop button on the tape recorder.]

Hilde [supervisor]: I'd like you to listen to your last intervention again – particularly the tone of your voice – and tell me about what is going on for you at that moment. [Rewinds the tape and replays the last two minutes.]

Sheila: Well I was listening to Amanda . . .

Hilde: [interrupts] Were you?

Sheila: Yes, I was . . .

Hilde: [interrupting again] What did you hear?

Sheila: Amanda was talking about this time when she saw her mother in her bedroom . . .

Hilde: [interrupting again] And would you say she was at the end of her explanation of that memory?

Sheila: Well, yes, I . . .

Hilde: [interrupting again] What are you feeling now?

Sheila: [stops to examine how she is feeling.]

Hilde: Come on, get on with it.

Sheila: Annoyed.

Hilde: Annoyed?

Sheila: Yes, annoyed and frustrated because you keep on butting in and stopping me . . . [Silence] So you're saying I butted in on Amanda at that point.

Hilde: Yes I am.

Sheila: But I was asking her if she wanted to focus on that image.

Hilde: Imagine being Amanda – before your intervention.

Sheila: OK, I'm Amanda, I'm remembering my mother in her . . . bedroom. Wow!!! It's almost like this other mother butts in. There, I'm walking up the stairs, I look in the room and . . . it's like there's someone else in my mother, like this is not my mother, I feel quite . . . odd . . . shocked . . . pushed. [Sheila moves over a little to the side of her chair.] Yes, it's like this other mother pushes me off my centre.

Hilde: And what does Sheila do?

Sheila: She pushes me too. I'm sitting there absorbed in telling her about this experience age 16, I'm really there and then she asks me if I want to focus on this image. But it actually makes me . . . move away from it, yes, she pushes me off my centre, psychologically speaking that is. I did push her, didn't I?

Hilde: Well . . . yes, I believe you did.

Sheila: So what can I do now, what can I do next time? How can I recover things?

Hilde: I'm wondering how Amanda is feeling about you now, not necessarily on the surface, but underneath. How is she feeling about you, in her undergrowth, in the mud, in the underside of the nice little girl that Amanda was always brought up, by her nice-little-girl mother, to be. Amanda? Amanda, Amanda, Amanda – and what, dear Sheila, do you feel about Amanda?

Sheila: She's a . . . nice woman. Someone I look forward to seeing. Someone who seems to move forward with the counselling very quickly, someone who appreciates the work we are doing, someone who . . .

Hilde: Cares about you?

Sheila: Well, I don't know about that. [Thinks] Yes, I suppose she is someone who I feel cares about me. [Shakes her head] How come I always miss all of this, how come I always get caught by it? Will I ever not get lost?

Hilde: No, and I do the same, all the time, and I sometimes ask the same kind of question as you've just done – in my own supervision. Which is one huge reason why we, as practising counsellors, have ongoing supervision.

Containing the container

Note of warning: THE FOLLOWING CASE STUDY CONTAINS DISTURBING MATERIAL

John's case study

I've chosen to present a client, from my placement situation in Hoxley Prison, that I found very disturbing. Before I begin this case study I have to say that, in order to comply with the Official Secrets Act (which I had to sign before starting my work in the prison) I've made some quite substantial changes – not only to name and other identifiers such as age but also to certain minor details of the case. The issue of my professional need, and ethical requirement for supervision, was quite a concern amongst the prison authorities prior to me beginning my placement. If I hadn't had a background that included experience of tutoring prisoners I don't think I would have been able to arrange this placement. In many ways I wish that I hadn't and perhaps I shouldn't have been allowed to. I've actually been thinking that the course should have taken more responsibility and monitored my choice of placement more closely – some feedback to my tutors here. Anyway we managed to get over the supervision problem by spelling out exactly how I would have to change the details of both the prisoner and the case before I could speak about such work in supervision or write about it in a case study.

There are many other issues arising from this setting which really impact upon the counselling. Perhaps one of the most important is the general 'atmosphere' of the relationship between the prisoners and anyone associated with the prison staff – which, of course, includes me. I can only describe that general atmosphere as one of intense deceit and superficial subservience. It's like a large group of very naughty school-boys, all superficially saying 'yes sir' and 'no sir' but none of whom can be trusted one millimetre. This atmosphere pervades all aspects of all encounters – it's like prisoners and staff are playing a strange game of psychological hide-and-seek. (I begin to think that all of this is somehow designed to pass the time a little less tediously.) Clearly, therefore, the atmosphere that pervades all the relationships between prisoners and staff members, is, to say the least, not the best context in which to start up a counselling relationship. I might even say it makes effective counselling virtually impossible. You just don't really know why this person is sitting there with you – is he wanting a change from daily routine, or is he there to escape more mundane tasks, does he believe that he will gain some kind of brownie points with the parole system or is he simply being the 'helpful' prisoner volunteering for counselling because a certain member of staff has asked him to turn up?

After a while of having to deal with this I finally decided to ask my clients why they were sitting there. At first they tended to make up stuff about how they wanted to change for the better but usually, when I confronted them on that, they would admit their main reason. When that first happened with Michael I felt we'd actually begun to do some counselling. It was as if he'd been sitting there for four sessions talking off the top of his head – whatever he thought I'd like to hear. Only when he admitted to one of the reasons that I identified above did I feel as if he had entered the room – psychologically speaking. For the first time I felt there was someone sitting there with me; prior to that moment there was a thick wall between us.

I examined that moment with my supervisor, Sarah. We looked at how I felt when Michael emerged from behind the wall and I discovered that my primary feeling was fear. It was frightening to be with Michael, not on the surface of the actual physical reality of being in that room with him, but at a psychological level of being present with him. He wasn't someone I felt was going to leap up and attack me; rather he was simply someone who I would find it very hard to relax with. After the supervision session I spent some time examining that sense of what it was like to be with Michael – when he finally showed himself. In the end I concluded that it was frightening because I felt I was in the presence of someone who hated me. That may sound a little odd, since I had done nothing to this person to make him hate me. I wondered, however, whether he simply hated me because I was another person and that he hated everybody. I also wondered whether I had extrapolated far too much from this brief psychological 'meeting' and thus decided to forget about it – not to really consider it prior to our next session as anything other than a somewhat wild notion.

As we went on with the counselling, and on those occasions when I felt we were meeting in the room in the way I have described, I did come to feel that this was the case. That Michael hated the world of others and he hated me as a representative of it. I feel that very little of our work together during the first 12 sessions, other than what I have described, had any value at all. It was mainly, as with the first four sessions, a case of Michael telling me what he thought I wanted to hear – although occasionally he would pop his head from behind the wall and psychologically snarl at me. Then, on the 13th session he said that he was in this 'shit-hole' for 'fucking a right bitch' and that she deserved it – that she was a right tart and that he shouldn't have been put away for doing her. I had a very strong sense, the moment after he said that, that I was under the spotlight – that my reaction to what he'd just said was being very closely observed. I really didn't know what else to say so I just said what I was feeling:

'I feel as though I'm under the spotlight, Michael – like it's really important to you how I react to what you've just said.'

That seemed to quite shock him – I could feel him wobbling and then, slam, he was back behind, not just a brick wall, but a steel one. I thought, 'Shit, I've really done something wrong here.' Anyway, he asked to finish the counselling session early and I agreed. I mumbled something about seeing him next week.

As you can imagine, I felt a considerable need for supervision and managed to arrange an extra session that week, over and above my fortnightly meeting with my supervisor. We discussed the work with Michael in depth and agreed that he was probably requiring a level of work that was beyond my competence at this stage – that his basic hatred of the world of others indicated that he was probably in the category of having special psychological needs and that working with him in any therapeutic way at that level would be beyond my understanding and skills and probably beyond what the setting – of the prison – could sensibly accommodate. He was in a prison, not a psychiatric unit or a therapeutic community. We also felt that this issue needed to be communicated to the tutors on my course, who needed to take more responsibility for the monitoring of placements.

We also examined why I hadn't kept to the normal process of agreeing, with the client, a focus for the work and then following through on that focus. Finally we considered the question of referral but decided that that was, given the setting, really out of the question. Sarah could see how the difficulties of forming a meaningful counselling relationship within the context of the prison had got in the way of the normal counselling process but felt that, if he returned to counselling the next week, I should agree a contract to complete the work. We also agreed that we would meet on a weekly basis for the next four weeks – specifically to support my work with Michael, should he return. There was a sense of crisis in this supervision session and I felt, afterwards, that Sarah had felt that I had bitten off far more than I could chew and I was in danger of creating a right mess. I thought about this a lot in the days before my next appointment with Michael and didn't feel *quite* right about this supervision session. It felt as if Sarah had, herself, got a bit frightened of this case and had overly worried me in the process.

I was surprised to find Michael sitting in the allotted 'counselling room' when I arrived a few minutes earlier than our appointment time. He was in quite a jovial mood and joked with me about how I must be a 'right wanker' to actually want to come into the prison when most people in it, including the prison officers, wanted to get out as soon as they possibly could. In fact, as the session progressed, it felt as though I was with a very different side to this man – he was almost a different person.

Nearly two thirds of the way through our session I pointed out to him how different the session seemed to be this time. He laughed and said that he'd thought I was a right middle-class 'tosser' when he first met me but that, as time had gone on, I'd turned out to be more honest than most of those 'toss-heads'. He then went on at length about the middle class and their pretentious manners – how you could never get an honest, down to earth word out of them, how his mother had always looked up to them as some kind of better species and how that had always really pissed him off. 'She was always going on about what Mrs So-and-So did, or had just bought, or had said to her when she was cleaning her fucking middle-class shit-hole.'

It became clear to me that Michael didn't hate all other people, just the middle class, and that our earlier sessions had been caught up in this dynamic with me as a representative of the middle class. Then, about two minutes before the end of our session, he let slip that the woman that 'got him slammed up in here was a right fucking toffee-nosed bitch'. I didn't really know what to say then – at the end of the session. I felt quite wobbly and off balance. As if my whole perspective on the world had just been shaken. Michael said that I didn't look too good and I admitted that I was feeling a bit odd. He said, 'See you next week then' but there was a certain tone to the way he said it that made me feel that he didn't believe I would be back. I got the sense that he felt that he'd been too much for me and I fantasized that he would be thinking something about how those middle-class bastards were all useless 'toss-heads'. After the session I realized that I hadn't said anything about the contract – but then things felt very different this session. I was confused.

Things got quite sticky in my next – specially arranged – supervision session. At first Sarah seemed to not really want to hear about how things had shifted so dramatically, and that her assessment had probably been based upon Michael's working-class/middle-class dynamic being playing out over the first 13 sessions. I had to be fairly firm in my description of the session before she was willing to accept that her assessment had perhaps been wrong. I felt quite confused about the whole thing and felt a mixture of feelings for Sarah – part of me wanted to be angry with her for not being the perfect supervisor, another part felt disappointed for the same reason, another aspect of myself felt sorry for her because I could see that she (much like me at the end of the last session with Michael) seemed off balance. I guessed that she too may have been wobbled by this shift, combined with the realization of its implications for our joint middle-class perspective.

Then she confessed that perhaps she had been a bit over the top in the previous supervision session and that she herself had been raped about 15 years ago. Although she thought she'd worked through that experience in her own personal counselling, perhaps it wasn't as worked through as she'd thought. Something shifted for both of us then – I looked into her eyes and saw her pain but I also saw her strength despite that pain. It was a very special moment for me – I had a sense of a beautiful, mature woman and in that moment I feel I developed a new kind of respect for her.

Then she made a joke about how there's always another surprise around the corner when you work in this field and she asked me how I thought I should proceed with the work with Michael. I thought about it for a while and then said I didn't think it was right to end my work with him in the way we had agreed at our previous supervision session. Sarah and I then spent the rest of the session re-evaluating the work. We both felt he needed to work through his hatred of middle-class women and that, in doing so, something might also come up about his mother. If he were able to see middle-class people as different, perhaps irritating in their pretentiousness, but basically human, just like him, then that would be of benefit. I also felt that it would be good if he could explore the rape itself – my aim in doing that with him would be to enable him to see and feel his victim's experience. We agreed, however, that working on that would be more difficult – since her experience would probably be something that he really didn't want to consider. I did think, however, that the Gestalt chair technique would be an excellent way of enabling him to see the world from his victim's perspective.

I arrived early for our next session, whereas Michael arrived a little late. He said that he hadn't expected to see me this week. I spoke to him about how it might be good to agree on a focus for a number of sessions – so as to give us an opportunity to work on something in depth – and asked him whether he would like to work on the middle-class issue. He asked me in what way and I pointed to his anger and how that had got in the way between us for so long and that actually I wasn't quite the toss-head he had imagined. He said he could see the point of what I was saying but that he couldn't see what was the point of working on it. Then I took a risk and asked him whether he thought this issue might also have a bearing on the crime he had committed and thus, in some sense, might even be the cause of him sitting in this 'shit-hole'. That seemed to make him stop and think. Finally he said something like, 'So you're saying that if I didn't hate you middle-class tossers so much, I wouldn't have done her? I don't know about that, John – haven't you got a pecker or something?' To which I responded by saying that I liked it as much as any man but that I didn't force myself on women. To that he quickly replied that he didn't either.

'Not even in the case of the woman in question?'

'Well, apart from her – I don't know what happened. I felt she was really wanting it, then when we got back to her place she wasn't having any of it, so I done her anyway.'

'And what if she hadn't been a "middle-class bitch", as you put it?'

'Well, if I'd been asked back by anyone else it would have been for one thing and one thing only – and we'd both have known it.' When Michael said that I felt a little stunned.

We were coming to the end of our session – I asked him about what he would like to focus on over the next few sessions. He said he'd like to talk about that evening some more and also about the experience of being arrested, tried and sent down. We agreed to focus on these issues, and ended the session.

Afterwards, in writing up my notes, I felt that my image of Michael had substantially shifted. My mind had, over the past week, been seeing him as 'the rapist', an ugly creature with his uncontrollable sexual desire who had exchanged his freedom for a few minutes of cruel physical pleasure. That evening I began to see him as Michael, a fairly ordinary young man – a very angry young man, to be sure. A man who, partly through differences in class conventions, had one evening lost control of himself and hurt someone very badly. He ceased to be the monster-man who, at any moment, might leap out from behind some dark corner and attack his terrified victim on some lonely city street at night. That's what my fantasy of 'the rapist' had been, and Michael no longer felt like that.

In our next session, Michael talked about what he refused to call the 'rape'. He had been out drinking with his mates at a central London pub. Two 'juicy bits' had caught their attention and he and one of his friends had tried to chat them up. They were both members of his hated middle class but, as Michael put it, that was a real 'turn-on' in itself. After buying them a few drinks and much joking around they wormed their way through the young women's initial defences and, when the pub closed, it emerged that one young woman had to go and get a train whereas Michael's 'bit' had a flat a few streets away in the other direction. Anyway, when they were all ejected from the pub Michael's friend went off with the other woman to the tube and he walked Angela home. This was the first time he had mentioned her name.

Michael invited himself up for a coffee, to which Angela, I suspect in a rather drunken state, hesitantly agreed – but that's not quite how Michael put it. Upstairs in the flat Michael was wanting a fuck, Angela definitely wasn't, and as she began to sober up she asked him to leave. At which point Michael raped her, forced her to perform fellatio and then tied her up and buggered her. I felt shocked during the description of what he had done to Angela, and any queries about the nature of his crime that had arisen in my mind over the week before, vanished. Here was Michael, the rapist: not the 'monster' waiting in the dark alley but a 'monster' nevertheless. Once again, as we came to the end of our session, I felt very confused and off balance and looking forward to my supervision.

In making my notes on this session I couldn't take my mind off Michael's description of his rape of Angela. This wasn't a momentary loss of control – which in itself would have been awful for the young woman – but a sustained physical abuse of her that must have gone on for ages. I imagined myself as this young woman – out for the evening with a friend, somewhat rudely advanced upon by this man but enjoying the attention and the jokes. Then, under the influence of alcohol, allowing myself to get into the situation of being alone in my flat with a man I didn't know. Then, in rejecting his advances, my worst nightmare coming true. Then I imagined this happening to my own daughter and began to really hate Michael. I imagined the initial shock of him turning on me when I asked him to leave. Of being told to shut up, perhaps with his hand on my mouth or around my neck. Then being thrown on the sofa and my clothes ripped off. How would I be feeling by then? Shaky, sick, terrified. It was difficult to imagine it because I don't have breasts or a vagina and it was difficult to imagine a woman doing this to me. Then I thought, 'What would it feel like to be alone in my flat with a man attacking me like this, forcing himself on me and buggering me?'

That was something I couldn't bear to think about at first. Then I imagined him sitting on the sofa next to me and trying to kiss me and then when I told him to get out I imagined him getting violent and grabbing me, telling me to shut up and do what he said. I imagined him forcing me to kiss him, forcing his tongue in my mouth: what would it be like to feel his bristly face on mine? How would I feel as he ripped open my trousers and stuck his hand down my pants, as he forced me onto my front and fucked my backside?

At that moment I felt, not only sick to my stomach, but guilty. I realized that I hadn't quite understood, before today, quite what it must feel like to be raped. I also realized that I hadn't, in my approach to Michael over the past two weeks, fully appreciated that any rape was so awful – that all rape is a monstrous act and it doesn't matter whether it was in a dark street, in a flat with a man you have just met or with a 'friend' who suddenly turns on you. Nor was there a real difference between an 'ordinary' rape and sustained physical abuse – one might be worse than the other, but both are horrific.

After all of this I felt quite drained and quite 'wobbly'. I felt I couldn't work with Michael anymore and then I began to wonder whether I wanted to continue as a counsellor at all. It felt like there was so much suffering, so much pain and so much of it created by human beings – particularly by men – that I just didn't want to deal with it. I felt like I was in a rubbish tip, that the whole activity of counselling was spent in this psychological rubbish tip and I just didn't want to be a dustbin man. That there were better things to do with my life and that this was a mad choice to make – being a counsellor.

At this point I stumbled to the telephone and called up Govinda, my former counsellor, to make an appointment to re-start counselling as soon as possible. Unfortunately she was out, but there was an answer-phone on the other end of the line and I left a message asking her to call me back with a time. I'd been in counselling with her for three months, earlier in the year, but had stopped at what seemed like a natural watershed. We had agreed, at the time, that there was more work I needed to do but I'd wanted a break, and I was also finding it financially difficult at that time. Fuck the finance, I thought.

As I sat down a shiver ran up my spine, and I felt like I'd just gone down with the flu as the thought of that imaginary man's penis being shoved up my backside washed over me again. This must also be what it's like, I thought – although obviously a hell of a lot worse if it had actually happened to me. It must happen all the time, after a rape, that the woman keeps remembering – as she's sitting down or washing up. God, what a sexist thought, I thought. Why should I think of the woman as washing up rather than making a telephone call or driving into work? I felt really angry with myself at that moment – for being so unconsciously sexist. Then I heard, in my mind's eye, Govinda interjecting with something like, 'and if you weren't angry with yourself who would you be angry with?' That made me think about two things – how I was very angry with Michael for raping Angela and how this was also probably the kind of thing that happened after being raped.

I thought of Angela in her flat in the days and weeks (and months, and years) after her rape by Michael. I thought of her feeling so hurt and confused and perhaps angry with herself too, for letting him walk her home. I imagined her changing the furniture and then, because that wasn't enough, changing the flat completely – just to get away from the things and the place where it had happened. Could you imagine having to sleep on the bed where you were attacked? His presence in the flat would live on, and even if she moved he would still, at moments, invade her – even years later. Then I realized how difficult it must be to make love after being raped – especially if your partner doesn't really understand what it was like. I didn't really understand, and had only just begun to, through this imaginary homosexual rape. How easy it would be not only to distrust *all* men but to hate them too.

Then I thought about all the women who are raped by men and all the little girls who are sexually abused by men and I felt ... like I wanted to puke up. Then I thought of my own cock and how I have had certain sexual fantasies about women in which they were simply the source of my pleasure and I saw that there wasn't an unbridgeable distance between those sexual fantasies and, dare I say it, Michael! Add in some real rage and hatred towards women, add in some real insensitivity to the other person's feelings, add in some alcohol and I could see that I too could be 'the rapist'. We were both men – Michael and I – with 'our cocks hanging out'. I was left with that particularly ugly image.

That evening I felt completely unsexy when I went to bed and my wife cuddled up to me and fondled my penis. I felt quite odd – like I'd become both the victim and the abuser.

At that moment I decided to give up training to be a counsellor.

The next day I spoke to Govinda and explained that I wanted to re-start counselling, that I'd decided to give up training to be a counsellor and that I wanted to focus on that decision when we met. Later that week I also met with Sarah and explained to her something of what I had been going through, that I wanted to agree a contract to complete the sessions with Michael (and the same with the other two clients that I was working with), but that after that I would not be taking on any further placement work and would also be ending our supervision relationship.

She seemed quite sad when I told her about this decision and responded by saying that I had the makings of an excellent counsellor. She could appreciate, however, why I had made this decision. In fact she agreed that, once you really began to understand what the work was all about, it did seem an odd choice of profession. She also said that, for her, there was so much professional and personal satisfaction in seeing people move forward, grow and change that, together with her own continual process of personal and professional development, it made it the right profession for her.

Sarah also wondered whether I might be giving up the profession when really I could just give up this particular client. That I might be being a bit dramatic and that the feelings stirred up by my work with Michael were perhaps unusually difficult and confusing. I replied by agreeing that there probably was some truth in that but even so, it really felt like I had discovered that this work was not for me. Having discovered that, my motivation to continue beyond the next few weeks, and finishing the work with these clients, was zero. We then explored what it was going to be like to be completing these various sessions, having made this decision – focusing especially on Michael. We decided that it would be OK to continue with him partly along the lines he had wanted – by exploring the experience of his arrest, trial and imprisonment.

When I went in for my next appointment with Michael I felt quite lifeless. I arrived early and sat there waiting for him, wondering how I would feel when he came in. I imagined one of the prison officers coming in and informing me that Michael was ill today and unable to make his appointment and I thought that that would sort things out quite well. But that didn't happen – at 11 a.m. precisely he knocked on the door and I said 'come in'.

There was a very different feeling for me in that session. Surprisingly I didn't feel repelled by Michael – in fact I found myself listening in a way that I hadn't done before. It was as if everything seemed much clearer. I felt empty and I didn't feel like a counsellor at all – because I'd just given that up. I was just sitting there, listening – to this other person in the room with me. That was it.

Gradually however, as the session progressed, I found myself thinking certain thoughts, noticing a certain tone of voice with a particular word and being interested in this rather than that. It was like sitting by the side of a river with the only purpose being sitting by the side of that river and, gradually, noticing this turbulence over there, or that rock in the middle, or the bubbles from a fish swimming by. I was nothing other than someone 'sitting by the river'. I wasn't fishing, I wasn't studying the river for pollution levels, I hadn't come there to paint the scene or examine the wildlife. I was just sitting by the river doing nothing – and as I sat there I began to get to know the river or, rather, the river became known to me. As I completed that session with Michael I felt that I had begun to know Michael, that Michael had become a little better known to me. And there was something, somewhere far away inside me that quite liked that.

I know I'm supposed to bring this case study to an end with some kind of overall evaluation of my work with Michael. One of the difficulties in evaluating the case properly, however, is that we haven't finished our work together yet. We finished the series we'd agreed but I didn't stop seeing him. Instead I agreed a further six sessions and we are now on the second of those. I'm still in supervision, too, with Sarah – although now we are back to a once-a-fortnight session, which isn't enough, but is all that is realistic financially at the moment.

I realize now that this case was too much for me to take on, but in the real world of placements perhaps it's not that easy to either assess or choose who to work with. I do feel, however, that I should have had more support on this from the course tutors – and from Sarah, for that matter. That said, I've learnt an enormous amount through working with Michael and being in supervision with Sarah over this case. I also believe that the work has been of benefit to Michael. Over the last four sessions we talked through his experience of being arrested, tried and imprisoned and in this current series we have agreed to focus on his anger and hatred towards the middle class. Perhaps we will move on from this to the rape situation again, and perhaps, at some point, Michael will see it as a rape and even begin to appreciate a little of Angela's experience. I don't know – I'm not really that hopeful about that.

I believe I used support well – in the form of supervision – and, latterly, in drawing upon my counsellor, and I believe I managed the case to the best of my abilities at the time. There are many things about the case that I would do differently now – both as a result of hindsight and as a result of developing my competence. In particular, I would have been much firmer from the beginning about agreeing a focus – despite the general sense of him actually just saying what he thought I wanted to hear. But I've also realized that the first 12 sessions were more important than I realized at the time – they were part of the development of a working relationship and I don't know how else that might have been achieved. We certainly did manage to develop quite a good working relationship – mainly as a result of those early sessions.

I would also have called up my counsellor earlier – in fact I would have been in counselling from the start. Perhaps, if that had been the case, I wouldn't have swung so up and down during the middle part of the work. I realize now that a lot of my difficulties during that period in the case – when I was wobbling around in confusion – were partly down to my implicit values and beliefs. These have been radically chal-lenged in my work with Michael and that has been a difficult experience but also a vital one for my own development as, dare I say it, a 'counsellor'.

On that note I still feel like I've given up being a 'Counsellor' but that doing so has actually released me into being a 'counsellor' – with a small 'c'. Finally, I'm beginning to understand some of the things about transference, containment and therapeutic responding that my tutor has been going on about.

Thirteen questions to consider

1 What are the effects of the interventions that the supervisors make – in each of the above supervision extracts?
2 How might the first three counsellors approach their next session with their clients?
3 How might these counsellors work with their clients over the longer term?
4 How do you negotiate, and keep to, a focus for your work? How do you get back to focus when lost?
5 What role does John's supervisor play?
6 Consider whether John should have been working with this particular client in the first place. If you were John's tutor or supervisor how would you have assessed the prospect of him starting to work with Michael?
7 In the above short extract from a supervision session, Hilde points to an 'unconscious' process in the relationship between Sheila and Amanda. How do you understand what Hilde is saying?
8 What are the implications of Amanda caring for Sheila?
9 What is important about Amanda's image of her mother?
10 What is Hilde saying about the 'nice little girl'?
11 What do you feel about the idea of taping your client? How might your clients feel about it?
12 How is supervision being used in the above extracts? What do you feel is most important and valuable about supervision? How do you utilize your own supervision and how might you use it better?
13 'Sometimes supervisors are wrong, sometimes they can suggest things that are destructive to the work, sometimes both the counsellor and the client would have been much better off if the counsellor hadn't had supervision.' How do you respond to that sentence? Can you think of examples when a supervisor got in the way of your client-work?

10

Conclusions: Know Thyself – Especially the Bad Bits

What a piece of work is a man! How noble in reason! how infinite in faculty! in form, in moving, how express and admirable! in action how like an angel! in apprehension how like a god! the beauty of the world! the paragon of animals! (William Shakespeare, *Hamlet*, II, ii, 324–5, c. 1603)

Man, proud man,
Drest in a little brief authority,
Most ignorant of what he's most assur'd,
His glassy essence, like an angry ape,
Plays such fantastic tricks before high heaven,
As make the angels weep.
(William Shakespeare, *Measure for Measure*, II, ii, 117–22, c. 1604)

Putting it all together

How do therapeutic change, growth and development actually occur? This is a key question in the field of counselling, and each counsellor needs to develop his or her own understanding of this question, along with answers that make sense to them and their work. This book has suggested that there are three broad ways in which change and growth occur. More than anything, they are different ways of listening to clients, different perspectives:

Listening to the self and its internal conflicts

Chapters 2 and 3 focused on how the client's subjective world can be explored in a way that uncovers and helps to resolve, or at least make more bearable, internal divisions within the self. In essence this boils down to the conflict between areas of subjective experience that are accepted and identified with and areas of subjective experience that are rejected and not identified with. From this perspective the therapeutic process aims to dissolve this basic division and widen a person's sense of their self.

Listening to the client's personal history

Chapters 4 and 5 explored personal history and how, in working with patterns from the past, the counsellor can help the client to make insightful links between the present and the past, support the client in working through painful past experiences and help the client to rewrite stories and scripts that were created in response to those past experiences.

Listening to the client's ways of relating – particularly the emotional interaction involved in actually relating with this person

Chapters 6 and 7 focused on close relationships and the client–counsellor relationship. Both through exploration of the client's relationships and through the live relationship of client and counsellor, the client can be helped to make real changes in patterns of relating: emotional patterns, for example, of forming attachments with others, of coping with inter-personal conflict and difficulty and of dealing with separation and loss. From this perspective the counsellor listens to a world of emotional interaction.

A case example

When Helena first came for counselling she was in something of a crisis – with difficulties at work, a dependent relationship with a very lazy partner, and aggressive outbursts with her children. During the first few counselling sessions, John identified Helena's presenting issues as directly related to her past experience of her mother. Her mother was, for Helena, both loving and, on occasions, overly critical to the point of cruelty. Because of these experiences she tended towards perceiving and responding to many authority figures in her adult world as if they were harsh and uncaring – even when they clearly weren't. Helena also found it difficult to be an authority figure with other people – including her children. As a result she often felt powerless and downtrodden.

Prior to taking on Helena as a client, John made an assessment of what level of work she would probably require. He did this using the 'CPCAB (Counselling and Psychotherapy Central Awarding Body) model' of four levels of work:

1   The objective of level 1 is to work with current problems. The counsellor helps the client to explore, clarify and work through her thoughts and feelings with regard to present problems – problems that are associated with particular situations in contrast to more general problems associated with various situations. (This book hasn't been much to do with working at this level.)
2   The objective of level 2 is to work with recurrent difficulties. Here the key focus is on patterns that are a source of repeated life problems – problems that relate to the person rather than to a particular situation. (The book has focused mainly on working at this level.)

3   The objective of level 3 is in-depth therapeutic work. At this level the counselling focuses on the more deep-seated roots of recurrent difficulties and involves work on 'no-go' areas that the client will experience as overwhelming and fundamentally unsafe. (The book has included examples of working at this level.)

4   The objective of level 4 is to work with psychological fragility. At this level clients generally need help and support with chronic debilitating psychological issues that have been a consistent source of difficulty throughout life. (The book hasn't examined working at this level.)

During their initial session John assessed Helena as requiring work at level 2 and perhaps at level 3. He felt that Helena wasn't in the category of level 4 – if she had been he would have felt she was beyond his skills and understandings and he would have referred her to a counsellor better able to work at that level.

As the counselling progressed Helena discovered that she had a harsh authority figure within herself who would speak with lots of very heavy 'shoulds' and 'oughts', together with a criticized child part of herself. When she worked with these aspects of herself over time, the authority part became less harsh and the child part became better able to stand up for her feelings and needs.

John and Helena also worked together on Helena's experience of her critical mother. Through the counselling she was able to untangle some important aspects of her present relationships from this past relationship and, most importantly, to work through much of the unfinished pain of the past. In this process she also began to see how she had created certain stories about how to survive with a critical mother. As she did so she realized that they were important stories to live by then but, to be free of her mother, she would have to create some new stories to live by today.

Once the relationship between Helena and John was well established, Helena occasionally began to experience John as harsh and uncaring – for example over the way he held the time boundaries, or sometimes the tone of his voice when he spoke to her. Helena was repeating her pattern of interpersonal difficulty over 'authority' figures – this time with her counsellor John. She was able by this time, with John's help, to share her experience of John as harsh and uncaring. Over a period of time she was able to untangle John from her mother and begin to relate to John in a very different way. As she developed these new patterns of relating with John she found her other relationships changed for the better too. During much of this time John felt they were working at level 3 – in-depth therapeutic work.

As a result of this counselling relationship, Helena's experience of being-in-the-world subtly changed – from 'many authority figures are harsh and uncaring' towards a richer and more caring sense of authority.

She also began to be able to be more of an authority – at work, with her children, and with her partner.

Together with his understanding of the three ways of working, the three listening perspectives described in this book, John couldn't have worked with Helena effectively if he hadn't developed a certain set of professional skills and understandings. These were evident in his continuous moment-to-moment awareness:

1   Awareness of the professional framework: 'This is quite a difficult boundary issue – what's the best way of maintaining the boundary without damaging our sense of a trusting relationship?'
2   Awareness of the client–counsellor relationship: 'What's happening to me? Oh, I am feeling attacked and rejected by Helena – I can sense my own defensiveness.' Because John was very aware of what was going on emotionally, he was able to use his awareness of the emotional interaction to help Helena disentangle the present coun-selling relationship from her past relationships. Without this emo-tional awareness he could have re-enacted Helena's past experiences – perhaps becoming defensive, aggressive and rejecting and thus, for Helena, yet another harsh authority figure. John was able to do this as a result not only of his experience of supervision, but also because of his extensive personal work (see no. 5 below).
3   Awareness of human diversity: 'How can I imagine what it was like for Helena then? It's difficult because I am a man and from a different culture.'
4   Awareness of the counselling space: 'What does the counselling space feel like at the moment? It's almost as if, right now, it's being crowded out – by both of us. Yes, it's almost as if we are afraid of what we might find here today – if we were to stop, look and listen.'
5   Personal awareness: 'Have I felt something like this? Oh yes, I can also sense that I don't want to feel it – it feels very painful to be Helena right now.' John had worked through many personal issues over the period of his counselling training – most thoroughly in his four years of weekly personal therapeutic counselling. Over time he had come to accept and value more and more of himself – including, for example, the angry, frustrated, despairing, disapprov-ing and even hateful aspects of himself. Without that work on himself he would have found it very difficult, if not impossible, to stay with the diversity of Helena's feelings and the difficult moments in their relationship. Nor would many of her difficulties have made quite the sense that they did to him – if he hadn't worked through similar difficulties in himself.
6   Awareness of professional issues: 'How can I understand what's going on here – maybe this concept helps explain it?' 'Oh, I remember what I learnt when I practised that skill, and the feedback

I got – how am I doing here?' 'We examined this kind of issue in my supervision group about a year ago. I wonder if it relates here?' Without being able to draw upon his theoretical understandings, his various skills and his practitioner experience (and supervision), John wouldn't have been able to work with Helena in the way he did.

7   Awareness of the organization of the counselling: 'I'm wondering if we are drifting off focus at the moment. How is what we are working on right now related to what we were working on earlier in the session, and how does the work today fit with the focus we have agreed for the work as a whole?'

Your own theory of counselling

Exercise: being a counsellor and being myself?

In a recent supervision session I focused on the issue of being in contact with, and valuing, my personal experience and contrasted that with the constraints I experienced in the professional role of the counsellor.

What emerged for me was a clearer sense of certain implicit processes related to the professional role of the counsellor. These processes, as I experience them, close down aspects of myself – especially my more creative side and the me that would be there if I was simply meeting with this other person as another adult person (including the 'bad' me). Associated with this there is, for me, an internal conflict and frustration related to that closing-down feeling.

To be free of these implicit constraints would mean that we, the 'client' and I, would meet to 'see what happened between us'. I wouldn't be concerned with doing 'it' right – in the professional sense of that phrase. Counselling would be a space for each, and both, of us to be who we are – including the bad bits.

What emerged for me, during the session, was a deep tension between:

* doing it right – as in doing it safely and skilfully (being in a professional role)
  and
* doing it right – as in doing it creatively (being the whole of myself).

In the session I also clarified that my strongest motivation for doing it at all has always been my personal experience as a participant in personal counselling, supervision, professional support, consultancy, trainings and workshops:

This has been great for me, and it still is. It's something really important and worthwhile and I'd like to give you the opportunity to experience it.

Finally I considered what it is that has been so valuable for me and concluded there were four central things:

1   Discovering, accepting and becoming who I am – especially all those aspects of myself that I didn't want to accept. In other words, living my subjective experience,
    which I associate with
2   Feeling better able to be the whole of myself with other people – being able to express, and respond from, my personal experience of the world – in ways that generally enhance, rather than hinder or destroy, my relationships (open and honest communication)
    and as a result
3   Being better able to meet my personal and interpersonal needs for intimacy, affection, love, sexual excitement, creativity, working my way (etc.)
    and that all of this has also arisen in the context of
4   Learning to manage, cope with and, over time, 'heal' very difficult subjective experiences – feelings such as rejection, shame, guilt, jealousy, hatred, resentful anger, terror and, of course, the void of loss and abandonment

Five questions to explore

1   What aspects of yourself do you still not accept?
2   What shape would you be, as a counsellor, if unconstrained by the professional cocoon called a counsellor?
3   If you were to do 'it' simply for itself, how would you do 'it'?
4   Why are you doing 'it'?
5   What is 'it'?

Cruelty and kindness, love and hate

People are capable of acts of enormous kindness and enormous cruelty, enormous love and enormous hatred. They are even capable of cruelty in the name of kindness, hatred in the name of love – in other words, people are capable of mind-boggling insensitivity and self-deceit about the reality of their actions. Murder, torture, rape, physical and sexual abuse of young children, wife and husband battering, war, terrorism, ethnic cleansing – these are the dramatic examples of hatred and cruelty, yet they are all relatively common. As individuals we may not commit such dramatic actions yet there is a multitude of other more everyday ways to express our hatred and be cruel to each other. Some people are quite able to enjoy hurting other people, many people hurt others and deceive themselves that they are innocent of anything, many people are cruel and unaware that they are being so (or perhaps simply refuse to be aware of it).

There is a sense in which the world itself can be experienced as cruel – natural disasters, problems that result from human neglect or error, illness and disease, the normal process of growing old and frail, and then death itself. All of these inevitable difficulties would seem to be plenty enough to cope with and many people go into counselling as a result of these experiences. The source of just as much suffering, however, is a much less inevitable human cruelty. For some this cruelty is dramatic, for others it is less dramatic but its effects can be equally damaging.

Over the past year or two, in my own personal work, I have frequently returned to the theme of my own capacity for hatred, nastiness and cruelty. In the process I have come to a kind of acceptance of my 'evil' side – that there are aspects, or parts of myself, that are enraged, that hate with a sustained vehemence, that could commit acts of great cruelty – and enjoy it!

Cruelty, however, breeds enormous pain and confusion that runs, like a bloodstained knife, through the whole of a victim's life. Many of the therapeutic issues I have worked on – both with my clients and myself – have had their origin in acts of human hatred and cruelty. When I was young I was moved from one place to another. This was not done as an act of cruelty (although it felt like a natural disaster). What made it a much worse disaster, however, was the reactions of some of the children in the places that I moved to. For some of the children in my new street or my new school I provided an opportunity for them to be cruel. I was an outsider – to be ridiculed, bullied, mistreated, spat upon. Children, like their parents, are capable of acts of great viciousness and cruelty. For me the effects of that cruelty seem to be just as deep as that of an adult's cruelty, if not more so.

If this was the whole story, then it would be a miserable world indeed. Our salvation, our liberation from such a miserable existence lies in the fact that we are also capable of acts of love and kindness. This capacity for altruistic actions, actions that benefit others rather than simply benefit ourselves, is the glue that binds us together – in our families and our social and working communities.

Perhaps the simplest, and yet also the most important, of our acts of kindness is the act of sustained love and caring for our children. We might feel this to be a natural activity, not really worthy of such a label – yet because we naturally tend to care for our own child doesn't make it a lesser act. In my own view, in altruistically devoting so much of our energy and attention to the welfare of another human being, we commit a huge act of kindness that dwarfs the charitable donation or even the acts of the Great Woman or the Great Man who, for example, selflessly devote themselves to caring for the sick or needy. Few such Great Persons are on call 24 hours a day, day after day, month after month, year after year.

Counselling comes out as a poor substitute for the more basic acts of human kindness – the everyday sustained love and caring for our family and friends. This is what the world needs much more of – everyday kindness, everyday love and caring, everyday good-enough human relationships.

Unfortunately there are plenty of people who weren't cared for as children, there are plenty of people whose everyday family life as adults is more vicious than loving, and there are plenty of people who live out much of their lives in the fairly miserable world I spoke about above. It feels to me that both kindness and cruelty seem pretty natural – but what is clear is that kindness usually breeds further kindness, and cruelty usually breeds further cruelty. In this sense, we do have a choice about how we live as human beings – we are not determined by nature.

I have emphasized that kindness or cruelty usually breed more of the same. Sometimes, however, this is not the case. I have seen clients who have overcome the cruelty of their childhood to go on to become good-enough parents and, equally, when children are not forced to face some of the basic realities – for example, that their wants cannot always be met or that mummy and daddy are persons too – this can lead to selfishness and cruelty. Such a child may not develop enough awareness of other people's needs and lack the capacity to cope with the frustration of their own. In most cases, however, cruelty breeds cruelty and kindness breeds kindness.

The cruelty I experienced from some of my new peers – when I was moved to a new place – was probably the result of their own experiences of cruelty. If we are cruel to our children, not only do they learn that this is the way of the world, but they are also left with strong emotional feelings of resentment, anger and confusion. Who better to express these feelings with than someone who is perceived as weak and vulnerable, someone who is unlikely to retaliate, someone who is 'different from us'. Who better than the outsider, the new boy – anxious and unsure in this strange and unknown place?

When emotional pain and confusion are experienced but not 'worked through', when a child or an adult experiences a crisis or human cruelty that has to be coped with more or less by themselves, then those psychological wounds are left to fester and go bad. The wounds 'live' on inside us, unhealed, and occasionally exposed. In those moments of exposure we are left even more confused, hurt and wounded and the sores grow worse. The wounds may contain unresolved grief, despair, terror, rage and overwhelming anxiety but the mere fact of their existence within us often leads to a deep sense of repressed resentment. A hidden part of us yearns for the opportunity to express some of our anger and frustration and we find the opportunities when others are weak and vulnerable. At such moments, often without much self-awareness, we are as cruel as an assassin's knife, as vicious as a wounded animal. Moments for viciousness – during a gossip in the office. Moments for cruelty – at a family gathering. Moments for nastiness – at a meeting at work. Our lives are filled with such moments.

Equally, kindness usually leads to kindness. A loving parent usually leads to the loved child growing up to be a loving parent. Kindness towards a friend usually leads to kindness in return. There are just as many opportunities – at home and at work – for the expression of kindness as the expression of our cruelty. And kindness doesn't always mean 'being nice' to someone – it can be kind to confront someone, as all counsellors are taught with their basic skills of challenge and confrontation. Perhaps this is what is meant by the statement: 'sometimes you need to be cruel to be kind'.

In my personal and professional experience, counselling can transform the vicious circle of cruelty breeding cruelty, conflict breeding conflict, and it can help create new and virtuous circles of kindness breeding kindness, caring breeding caring. If there is any magic to the counselling process it is simply this catalytic role of enabling the roots of cruelty to be deadened, and the roots of kindness to flourish.

Sometimes, however, when counselling is practised by the incompetent or simply the wrong person, it can hurt rather than heal, damage rather than develop, confuse rather than clarify. And, in a way, this is one of the cruellest of things to do – for not only does it mean that this particular client is hurt or confused by their experience and never returns, but it's also likely that other people will also be put off from finding the help they need. Anyone who has a bad experience of counselling is very likely to tell a lot of other people about how awful counselling is.

This may seem a rather heavy burden to carry – the responsibility to make sure, as far as possible, that you do no harm. A heavy burden that all counsellors, including myself, sometimes *fail* to carry: sometimes, perhaps even unknown to ourselves, we do harm our clients. In my experience we are most likely to do this while we remain unaware of our capacity for hatred and cruelty, while we remain unaccepting of the 'devil within us', while we continue to cast out the bad parts of ourselves from that which we call ourselves. Once accepted, the little devil usually turns out to be a very hurt and long-lost part of ourselves who naturally feels angry and resentful about being hurt and cast out into the cold. Once accepted, the feelings may remain but their potential for unconscious acting out is substantially reduced.

If there's one thing to remember, that you'll keep wanting to forget, it's to work very hard on 'knowing thyself' – especially the bad bits, and most especially all those bits that you really don't want to know about, at all.

The ends

I'm coming towards the end of writing this book. Six months ago I was about to give up, write to my editor and confess that I couldn't do it.

That I would sit here but nothing would come out right and if it did, it did so at such a slow pace that it would take me a hundred years to complete the book.

Today I feel concerned that I haven't written it in the usual way – that I have 'talked from the inside' rather than 'talked about' and that that isn't OK. But a part of me also feels confident in what I have written and the way I have written it. If I imagine the book being used by my students, it is a book that they would have found quite useful. A part of me also feels really frightened – I've written this intimate book and I'm about to expose myself to the whole world out there. Aaaaahhhhh!

I like my students but they've worn me out – after years of intensive work with them. I like my clients and they can wear me out too. When you start to go below the surface, when you begin to work towards deep therapeutic change, then it's hard on the client and it's hard on the counsellor too. But if you've got quite a few clients it becomes very, very hard for the counsellor indeed.

I probably believe that everyone could benefit from therapeutic counselling. I probably believe that the world would be a better place if that was even slightly the case – if only enough people could work through their key psychological patterns, or even just learn to accept and share themselves. I probably believe that, but it might not be true. It just looks like it from where I stand right now.

A bad note to end on

It's late at night. I have been trying to write a certain number of words each day – I have written a little more today than I planned, which is good. But I'm not feeling good about it.

I need to tell you – I've been thinking of giving up being a counsellor and a counsellor trainer. I've almost finished writing this book on counselling and I'm thinking of giving up this profession.

It feels too hard. It feels too tiring. It just feels too much. I want to live an ordinary life. I don't want to be thinking about internal conflict, personal history or patterns of relating. I don't want the horizons of knowledge and understanding to be endlessly moving on: I understand 'this', but . . . 'what about this' – which then opens up a whole new set of questions. Some guy called this the 'impossible profession'. Well, maybe it is . . .

. . . or maybe (as a result of my own personal counselling) I'm just no longer so unconsciously driven to be a counsellor.

What is it I want to give up? What is so tiring? What is 'too much'? I feel really weighed down by something – in this role of counsellor, the 'counsellor as professional', perhaps. No . . . I just don't know . . . I just don't know . . . in fact I don't want to know! I want to be free of trying to know. I want to be free of having to try to know.

In Chapter 1 I began by asking what the book was about if it wasn't about answers. Maybe it's simply about not knowing, and that's bloody difficult and that's it. I don't know, I really don't know!!!!

So tonight I have lost faith and I am wondering if counselling is really that good a thing. That, in some way, we counsellors are fooling ourselves. Yes, I have found my own counselling to be of value, it's true, but might I have got something of equal or greater value by spending all that time, energy and money with friends and family? Making really good friends. I did wonder this morning if in fact my whole attraction to this profession was actually to avoid doing that – spending real effort and energy and commitment with friends and family. That in some way it was safer to relate in this less committed, one-way kind of way – as counsellor with client.

I know that some of my motivations to be a counsellor are pretty suspect – and the same is true of many other people who join this profession. It's as if I'm finally beginning to see that I was driven to make this choice and what was driving me isn't about being nice to people and helping them out. But now I also realize that the good counsellor is the one who knows that she isn't. Isn't 'nice and good', that is.

There's a line in a code of ethics and practice for counsellors which says something about the counsellor not getting his or her needs met through the counselling. As if! Of course we are doing it to get our needs met; the real problem is when the counsellor denies this or doesn't even know it, when he or she doesn't realize what their needs are, and how they are actually driving them to be counsellors.

A lot of counsellors, I'm afraid, are either not that well trained (including some who have done lots of training) or are simply not very suited to being counsellors. In fact, in my really disillusioned moments I see 'Counselling' as a rather sorry looking profession – a mixed bunch of survivors of who-knows-what psychological disasters, trying to help a mixed bunch of clients survive their psychological disasters.

Counselling is indeed a strange profession to choose. Sometimes I think that just as Groucho Marx wouldn't join any club that would have him as a member, I wouldn't go to a counsellor who had actually chosen to be one.

I also feel it's healthy to feel disillusioned. To deeply question what I'm doing, and this profession as a whole. It's as if there's a thin line between doing counselling and doing harm, and that thin line is something to do with both believing in what I'm doing and not believing in it too. It's not that easy to explain but it's as if the also-not-believing keeps me . . . balanced.

Right now, at the end of the book, I feel the urge to conclude on some kind of upbeat note – like it's the best we've got and it's a really important thing to be doing. But is it?

You know something? I really don't care, and *that* feels really good.

And a good note to end on, too

Suddenly it all felt like a big joke – all the twisting and turning, all the stupid things, all the confusion, all the pain, all the seriousness about myself, my life and my relationships. And I thought, 'If anyone's responsible for all of this, he (or she) ought to be bloody depressed.' Love and hate, kindness and cruelty – what a confused, mixed-up world. But in all of it, somehow, my heart was lighter, the heaviness of yesterday had vanished from today and I could laugh about it all. I was happy, happy in my heart – that deep-down and all-around happiness of innocence and youth. I was old and I was young and I had found myself again. Most of all I was alive and I could . . . play . . . and once more, enjoy the day!

Doop de doop de doop . . .

Index